# With Santa Anna in Texas
## A PERSONAL NARRATIVE OF THE REVOLUTION

# With Santa Anna in Texas

## A PERSONAL NARRATIVE OF THE REVOLUTION

### BY

## José Enrique de la Peña

*Translated and edited by*
### CARMEN PERRY

*Introduction by*
### LLERENA FRIEND

**Texas A&M University Press**
COLLEGE STATION

Library of Congress Cataloging in Publication Data

Peña, José Enrique de la, 1807–1841 or 2.
  With Santa Anna in Texas.

    Translation of Reseña y diario de la campaña
  de Texas. Includes index.
    1. Texas—History—Revolution, 1835–1836—
  Personal narratives. 2. Peña, José Enrique de la,
  1807–1841 or 2. 1. Title.
  F390.P3313        976.4′03′0924        75-16269
  ISBN 0-89096-001-1

*Manufactured in the United States of America*
FIRST EDITION

*To the memory of*
JOHN PEACE
*who brought the de la Peña*
*diary to Texas and*
*made possible its publication*

# Contents

# List of Illustrations

(Pages reproduced from the holograph manuscript)

*Following page 66*

# Translator's Preface

THE sacred function of the researcher is to keep constant vigil for the verification of facts. Much has been written about the Texas campaign and its participants by both sides. Many of the military reports of Santa Anna, Filisola, Caro, Tornel, and others have been translated into English, but as Walter Lord remarks, "folklore has always flowed through the saga of the Alamo. . . ."[1] He goes on to say that there was also reality, but some of this reality has remained in obscurity, such as José Enrique de la Peña's diary of the Texas campaign.

Enrique de la Peña's contribution is significant because he was an active participant, an eyewitness and a trained officer, who had advantages in observation and evaluation coupled with an honest objectivity. His rank of lieutenant colonel did not require that he send reports or issue orders during the campaign that later had to be explained or justified, although he frequently was present at closed meetings of his superior officers where important decisions were made.

He was unusually observant and extremely sensitive to his surroundings, interrupting the chain of events to describe in his diary the beauty of the flowers in a prairie, a house, or individual trees. He was also very objective in describing the enemy, pointing out his good qualities with the same detachment with which he deplored the weaknesses in his compatriots. Fortunately his diary has survived in spite of Santa Anna, Filisola, and others who were determined that it be destroyed so that he could not publish it as he had planned.

---

[1] Walter Lord, "Myths and Realities of the Alamo," in *The Republic of Texas*, ed. Stephen B. Oates (Palo Alto, Calif: *American West Magazine* and the Texas State Historical Association, 1968), p. 20.

De la Peña recorded the events of the campaign on the march, making his entries hurriedly when he could take time from his duties, often writing on horseback. For the most part, the diary itself is simply a record of what happened, though the author made notes to himself of things he wished to discuss at greater length when time allowed. The narrative translated here is de la Peña's own presentation of his diary. Though it incorporates observations on the conduct and particulars of the campaign which he made later on, he took great care to distinguish these from the diary itself, which he presents just as it was written in the field.

According to the records available in the Military Archives in Mexico and from his own statements, José Enrique de la Peña was born in Jalisco in 1807. The exact place and specific date are unknown, as is the name of his parents. He completed his professional education as a mining engineer and joined the navy in 1825. In 1828 he published some well-documented articles in *El Sol* under the pseudonym "El Amante de la Marina" ("Lover of the Navy") concerning the nefarious anti-Mexican activities of David Porter, a native of Boston and former U.S. Navy commodore, who in 1826 was named admiral of the Mexican Navy at the recommendation of Joel Roberts Poinsett, United States minister plenipotentiary in Mexico.

The Mexican government ignored de la Peña's accusations, and consequently he resigned, in spite of his great love for the navy. Although he was only nineteen years old when he published these accusations, his literary talent was already evident, as was his perceptive and analytical ability; in time his accusations of Admiral Porter's anti-Mexican injustices were corroborated.

In July of 1829 he was present at the attack on Tampico against the Spanish Brigadier General Isidro Barradas, where he distinguished himself.

From the records in his military file we learn that he was "a young man of good breeding, strong, of medium height, intelligent, of outstanding nobility of character, observant, tireless, and eager to hold important positions and to enrich his already wide and profound knowledge."

In none of the numerous folios in his military file is mention made of his participation in the Texas campaign or of his army career in 1836. It seems obvious that because of his critical articles concerning Santa Anna's and Filisola's participation in the campaign, all his military records covering that period were destroyed. We do know that in spite of his commission to be sent as an attaché to a European legation he was granted permission to participate in the Texas campaign and that he was promoted to lieutenant colonel in the Sapper Battalion.

His military file skips to April 11, 1837, and in folio 17 states: "Captain José Enrique de la Peña, classified as Lieutenant Colonel, having presented himself, was advised by order of the Supreme Government to report to the state of Sonora under orders of General José Urrea." General Urrea supported a plan on December 26, 1837, upholding the Constitution of 1824. Lieutenant Colonel de la Peña issued a patriotic and enthusiastic proclamation to the garrison. This uprising, headed by General Urrea, whom de la Peña greatly esteemed, caused the latter an interminable series of humiliations, imprisonment, disillusionment, and ultimately a premature death. He died in 1842, poor, ill, and forgotten. But he left a collection of manuscripts of incalculable value, as they rectify much false historical data.

In 1955 José Sánchez Garza, since deceased, published *La Rebelión de Texas,* vol. 1: *Manuscrito inédito de 1836 por un oficial de Santa Anna.* He included the diary of José Enrique de la Peña and thirty appendixes, but he deleted, added, and corrected words and sentences, which he felt made the narrative easier to read and to understand.

In this translation we have, with only a few minor exceptions, followed the original manuscript exactly as it was written by José Enrique de la Peña. Where he uses a shortened form of a name (for example, "Sesma" for the more familiar "Ramírez y Sesma") or omits a well-known first name, we have silently amended the text rather than burden the reader with brackets. Likewise, since pronouns cannot perform the same tasks in English as in Spanish, substantives have been introduced where necessary to spare the reader troublesome searches for antecedents. De la Peña spelled phonetically many names and terms that were unfamiliar to him (for example, "Fanning," "stimbot," "Hol Fort"); these have been silently regularized. The many documents de la Peña collected to support his own record, which Sánchez Garza included as appendixes to his edition, have been omitted here but are cited in the footnotes. Many of these documents are held in the Military Archives in Mexico City or in the State Archives in Austin, and copies of some of them are available in the John Peace Memorial Library of the University of Texas at San Antonio. Unless otherwise indicated, the footnotes are the author's own. The text itself has not been edited. If the author sometimes seems to be repetitious, it is because he was so determined that the truth be known and that some action be taken to correct it.

The Sánchez Garza book contains a title page which purports to be from an edition of the de la Peña diary printed in September, 1836, in Matamoros, Tamps., Mexico. However, no copy of this edition could be located either in Mexico or the United States. If indeed this edition ever appeared, it is possible that most or all copies of it were destroyed because of the highly critical nature of its contents.

The de la Peña diary, in the hands of the Sánchez Garza family for many years, was eventually acquired by the late John Peace of San Antonio. Mr. Peace, chairman of the Board of Regents of the University of Texas and an avid collector of Texana, was the moving spirit behind the establishment of the University of Texas at San Antonio.

Shortly before his death in August, 1974, Mr. Peace made the de la Peña diary and related material available to me for the preparation of this book. This valuable collection of documents will be given to the University of Texas at San Antonio, where it will reside in the John Peace Memorial Library. It includes all the field notes and the original holograph diary of José Enrique de la Peña, letters, copies of numerous articles he published, and copies of his military records obtained from the Military Archives in Mexico.

CARMEN PERRY

# Introduction

IF the mills of the gods grind slowly, so also the tapestry of history may be long in the weaving. This translation of the José Enrique de la Peña diary is a new thread in the story of the Mexican side of the Texas Revolution, a decorative thread that stands out in its revelation of the impress of the events of February-August 1836 on a sensitive and intelligent young Mexican officer. In 1962, when Charles Ramsdell reviewed Walter Lord's *A Time to Stand*, he affirmed that one could no longer lament that "the evidence about what happened at the Alamo is still scattered." In what Ramsdell called a "cool and sagacious evaluation of the evidence," Lord, citing his sources and propounding the riddles of the Alamo, enumerated the various accounts of the Alamo siege by both Anglo and Mexican participants and observed that the Mexican tendency after San Jacinto was "to say absolutely anything that might please a Texan—until they got back south of the border."

De la Peña, as a subordinate official, had no dealings with the Texan spokesmen and was not trying to placate anyone. For Travis and Fannin he had high praise as individuals, if not as military strategists; for American "pirates" trespassing covetously on foreign soil he had no sympathy; for the responsible Mexican officials, Santa Anna, Ramírez y Sesma, Filisola, and Tornel, for all save Urrea, he had the harshest of criticism. In their accounts of the fateful incursion into Texas, the Mexican officers sought to justify their own actions or to prove that others than themselves were responsible for their failures. These writers appear as the military *dramatis personae* in de la Peña's account, in which the author declares that what he actually saw he narrated and that when he was not an actual witness, he verified his facts with the most circumspect testimony.

"War," wrote de la Peña, "was the thing that could least frighten Mexicans, who seemed to have sworn not to live without it," but in

xv

this case a largely conscript army came a long distance to a part of their country that had a different climate, different institutions, a different topography, and a different language. The conflict was so brief and was terminated so abruptly by a victory over so many by so few that it was not surprising that the leaders of the retreating forces took to print almost immediately with their excuses and explanations. For the actual progress of the invading Mexican forces some news items had been supplied the Mexican newspapers, but probably the first continuous account of the war's events was read by North Americans rather than by Mexicans. Juan Nepomuceno Almonte accompanied Santa Anna to San Antonio de Béjar and on across Texas to San Jacinto, where he surrendered. The Almonte private journal, picked up by Anson Jones on the San Jacinto battlefield, was sent to the *New York Herald*, which printed it in six installments beginning on June 22, 1836. That account, later published in *The Southwestern Historical Quarterly* in July, 1944, covered movements of Santa Anna's troops from February 21 to April 16, 1836—Béjar to Lynchburg.

On May 31, 1836, Vicente Filisola, who succeeded Santa Anna in general command, was replaced by José Urrea; after word of the public treaty agreed to at Velasco had been received in Mexico, Filisola was ordered to return to Mexico and stand trial for his conduct in acquiescing to the terms of the treaty and conducting the retreat of the Mexican forces. Filisola retired to Saltillo, where, on July 12, he issued his *Manifesto [and Documents Published by General Filisola in Justification of His Conduct in the Texas Campaign]*. Later, in Mexico City just before his court martial hearing, he issued a pamphlet with the wrapper title *Representación dirigida al Supremo Gobierno por el General Vicente Filisola, sobre la campaña de Tejas*. An English translation of the *Representación* was printed by George L. Hammeken at Columbia, Texas, in 1837, and again by C. E. Castañeda in *The Mexican Side of the Texas Revolution* in 1928. Thomas W. Streeter in Part II of his *Bibliography of Texas, 1795–1845*, "Mexican Imprints Relating to Texas," describes the *Representación* as the "classic account of the retreat of the Mexicans through Texas after the battle of San Jacinto and a masterly defense by Filisola of his acts ordering and conducting the retreat." In de la Peña's opinion, the pamphlet was a distortion of facts, full of contradiction, a "poisonous masterpiece in which a dictionary of insults has been exhausted." In any case, Filisola was exonerated at the trial and was designated to prepare for a new invasion of Texas. He would write again later of his Texas campaign. Doubtless he did not forget what de la Peña had said of him.

Meantime, on July 26, 1836, Juan José Andrade signed a twenty-three page pamphlet that was printed at Monterey as a collection of *Documentos* concerning his evacuation of San Antonio de Béjar. Andrade, left by Santa Anna in command at Béjar, had been ordered to evacuate the post by Filisola on May 24, but José Urrea counter-manded Filisola's order. On June 14, Andrade wrote Urrea that be-cause of the tragic condition of his troops he would continue his re-treat. That Andrade pamphlet, containing information corroborative of complaints voiced by de la Peña, describes the deficiencies of food and clothing and the inadequacies of medical and hospital facilities for the Mexican army.

Filisola's *Representación* elicited a printed response from Agustín Alcérrica in the form of a fifteen-page imprint from San Luis Potosí, a *Manifiesto* to justify his abrupt departure from Texas. Alcérrica had carried out the massacre of Fannin's men at Goliad under orders from José Nicolás de la Portilla and was later appointed to occupy and defend Matagorda. When, on April 28, 1836, he heard of the reported death of Santa Anna and others of his staff, he left his post so hastily that part of his force was left undefended. Streeter attributes the flight to Alcérrica's fear that he and his men might be captured and executed in retaliation for the executions at Goliad.

By 1837 all the Mexican commanders had crossed the Rio Grande and more reports were printed. Santa Anna's justification for his 1836 campaign was dated at Manga de Clavo, May 10, 1837, and was printed at Vera Cruz as *Manifiesto de sus operaciones en la campaña de Tejas*. In his *Manifiesto* Santa Anna characterized his secretary, Ramón Martínez Caro, as an "infamous betrayer." Caro, "supported by perfect justice," was impelled to answer and prepared his *Verdadera idea de la primera campaña de Tejas*, or *True Account*. The manuscript was dated May 30, 1837, and postscripts added before publication were dated June 20 and August 31, 1837. While Martínez Caro was still adding up his *True Account*, José Urrea was busy at Durango laboring over the manuscript for his

*Diario de las operaciones militares de la división que al mando del General José Urrea hizo la campaña de Tejas,* which was not published until 1838, after he had read Caro's *True Account,* which he quoted generously in his postscript. Furthermore, he quoted directly and at length from de la Peña, citing his source as the "Diary of an Unknown Officer," as he reported the misfortunes of April 29, 1836. In his chapter 14, de la Peña casually footnotes his manuscript with a statement that in the Urrea publication he found a quotation from his diary with the tense changed from present to past, "perhaps because it was not copied from the original." In his struggle with Filisola, Urrea had no more ardent defender than de la Peña, and it would be interesting to locate that copy that was not "original" or to know how much exchange of manuscript material took place.

No sooner was the Urrea pamphlet in print than Filisola made answer from Matamoros with *Análisis del diario militar del General D. José Urrea durante la primera campaña de Tejas.* He added another bibliographic item in 1848–1849 with his *Memorias para la historia de la guerra de Texas,* the second volume covering the period from January, 1834, to shortly after San Jacinto. By 1849 Mexico had fought another war with North Americans, and the first Texas campaign received little more notice for almost a century. Meantime other manuscript records came to light. Captain José Juan Sánchez Navarro, a classmate of Santa Anna's in military school, was adjutant inspector of Nuevo León and Tamaulipas between 1831 and 1839. He was sent to Béjar to inspect invoices for military clothing in 1835 and was there when Martín Perfecto de Cos surrendered at Béjar in December and returned as adjutant to Cos during the siege of the Alamo in March, 1836. In 1845 the Sánchez Navarro records were collected in two volumes as "Ayudantía de inspección de Nuevo León y Tamaulipas." Carlos Sánchez Navarro, in 1938, published the first volume of the José Juan Sánchez Navarro records as *La Guerra de Texas.* Subsequently the two-volume manuscript index of the records became the property of the Archives Collection of the University of Texas. Written on the blank pages between its divisions was a detailed account of the siege of Béjar and the fall of the Alamo and a map of the Alamo area. This "Mexican View of the Texas War: Memoirs of a Veteran of the Two Battles of the Alamo" was translated and described by Helen Hunnicutt in *The Library Chronicle of the University of Texas* in 1951.

Apparently neither the Genaro García *Indice de documentos para la historia de México* nor the 1952 edition of *Documentos para la historia de la guerra de Tejas* gave any clues concerning the de la Peña work, but in 1955 J. Sánchez Garza printed the de la Peña manuscript as *La Rebelión de Texas: Manuscrito inédito de 1836 por un oficial de Santa Anna*. Walter Lord cited the Garza book in 1961 in *A Time to Stand*, describing the lieutenant colonel of the *Zapadores* as one of Santa Anna's fine officers. Now, at last, there is available in English the detailed story by a participant observer who had military training and who also was well read, observant of the natural scene and of human character, and passionately devoted to his country. It should help dispel some of the myths or answer some of the questions that challenge the research historian.

De la Peña actually participated in only one military engagement, the assault on the Alamo, but he suffered the freezing weather on the way north from Mexico, the lack of food and equipment in the advance from San Antonio to the Brazos, and the Mexican heartbreak of the retreat from Old Fort to the Rio Grande. He visited Goliad when the ashes from the bodies burned after the massacre were still visible, and no contemporary on either side was more bitter in his condemnation of that massacre, as much for its unnecessary cruelty as for the stupidity of the act that aroused the fury of the Texans and especially of the people of the United States. His depiction of the Mexican return to the border, with the army morale destroyed, the officers divided in plan, and the manifestations of official ineptitude and greed become commonplace, is fresh in revelation. If only there were available for comparison the contemporary recollections of Ben Fort Smith and Henry Teal concerning their conversation with de la Peña when they were checking on the progress of the Mexican retreat in mid-May of 1836.

For different readers there will be different reactions as to high spots in the reading. For some the interest will center on the account of the assault at the Alamo, with its point-counterpoint in reproducing in both fact and imagination the rallying proclamations issued by both sides. One wonders just when de la Peña learned the content of the Travis letter of February 24—Travis who "chose to die with honor and selected the Alamo for his grave." He reports the rumor that Travis considered surrender or an effort to escape. That rumor, he felt, caused Santa Anna to precipitate the assault in order that the Alamo would not be secured without clamor or bloodshed, "for some believed that without these there would be no glory." After the bloody end of the assault, Santa Anna's praise of his troops was received coolly because of a "base murder" that had taken place after success was assured. This was the execution of seven men who had survived the assault and were ordered killed by Santa Anna when they were brought before him. Among them de la Peña identified "the naturalist David Crockett." When the sappers were reluctant to carry out the execution, officers who wished to curry favor with the president-general fell upon the unfortunates, "who died without complaining and without humiliating themselves before their torturers."

The introspective de la Peña and others of his ilk pondered the "whys" of the Alamo: "Why was a breach not opened? . . . why should we have been forced to leap over a fortified place as if we were flying birds?" The same questioners considered the taking of the Alamo as "a defeat that saddened us all," but, interestingly, they placed the final onus, not on Santa Anna, but on General Ramírez y Sesma. Had he but surprised the town early, while the Texas soldiers were dancing before taking up their defense posts, the Alamo could not have been occupied, there would have been no assault, and the catastrophe would have been avoided.

Some readers may view de la Peña as a Mexican patriot. He dated his prologue on the day before the anniversary of Hidalgo's *grito* of Mexican independence. In describing this war fought on Mexican soil that seemed to be foreign land, he always distinguished between the "colonists" and the "pirates" from the United States. He recalled that Mexican army leaders ever since independence had been a series of foreign commanders. Among those who determined on the retreat after San Jacinto only two were Mexican by birth. The commander in chief was Italian; the major general, French; the commander of the First Brigade, Cuban; and the commander of artillery either Cuban or Spanish. Among the ranking officials who decided policy, Urrea and Ampudia, both Mexican, were the ones who wanted to regroup forces and redeem the national honor. In January, 1836, starting out on the campaign, Santa Anna had exhorted his troops to act with brilliance, reach the Sabine River, and plant the Mexican eagles on its banks. With benefit of hindsight, de la Peña later commented ironically that "doubtless our armies would have been reflected by its waters had there been no further imprudence or if the mournful song of a bird that appeared from Italy had not held back the flight of those that were marching to the right and to the rear of those who had been hunted down in a moment of surprise."And again, concerning the "cruel and irritating countermarch," de la Peña opined that Filisola "in his status as a foreigner is not interested in the fate of Mexicans."

From the time of the conquest by Cortés down through the exploits of Pancho Villa, there have been accounts of the women followers of Mexican troops. De la Peña adds some glimpses of their experiences in this campaign. He felt that the troops should not have marched overland to Texas but should have been transported by sea, not only to save time and expense but also to have "fewer mouths to feed," for many squadrons of women and boys followed the army by land. The women shared in the bitter weather of the February snows, but the rear guard of the army found itself short of provisions because more than half the force ahead of them under Ramírez y Sesma was composed of women, muledrivers, boys, and exploiters, "a family similar to the locusts that destroy everything in their path." Near the Navidad River, de la Peña could not prevent the women from destroying fine furniture left in the colonists' homes as the settlers had fled in the "Runaway Scrape." When they reached the Brazos River, cotton bales were destroyed for the soldiers to make their beds, and the women spread the cotton out on the banks of the river in order not to get their feet dirty as they emerged from their bath. On April 18, only two days before the first shot at San Jacinto, the women were ordered separated from the troops, a harsh measure, de la Peña remarked, but one necessary for the success and speed of the military operation. And it was the women who gossiped that Ramírez y Sesma made no effort to capture the steamboat *Yellow Stone*, although there would have been ample time to do so while the vessel was at anchor for several hours to take on wood.

Furniture, cotton bales, spinning wheels, coffee grinders, and other household goods, the swine and the cattle and the poultry were testimonials to de la Peña of the industry of those who had fled before the Mexican advance. Gaona's brigade had appropriated so much in the way of furniture and goods that they had no further space for loot, and one commander's quarters was dubbed the "Custom House." By the time they reached the Old Fort crossing, so much wine had been looted and consumed that the soldiers were too drunk to carry out their detail of inspection of the dwellings there.

This account of the Texas Revolution gives some new glimpses of landscape and events of the spring of 1836. It is not the report of an officer who had to justify his military orders and actions but that of an able and introspective soldier who could evaluate mistakes made by the other side and suffer mental anguish because of the mistakes made on his side. It further buttresses the observation of Carlos Castañeda in the Foreword to his translation of five accounts of the Texas campaign in *The Mexican Side of the Texas Revolution*: "They show that the traditional sins of Mexico, dissension and personal envy, were more deadly to the Mexican army than the Texan bullets."

Perhaps this book will provoke further writing: a character analysis of Santa Anna based on descriptions of him by de la Peña, an essay on the potential of Texas as seen by a man sensitive alike to pain and beauty and possessed also of a sense of history, or an essay on de la Peña as a writer. For he is so often quotable, even if his account is not entirely chronological and does become repetitious in spots. But he was striving for accuracy, although it meant going back to elaborate his reaction to a particular event.

I wish I were a literary sleuth with a command of Spanish and a mañana temperament. Then I'd dedicate myself to a search for information on the de la Peña family members and the girl who threw him over. I'd search Urrea's traces for his use of the de la Peña diary; I'd try to check some of the anonymously published contemporary accounts attributed to "Various Soldiers" or "An Unknown Officer" to see if they were de la Peña's writing.

For now, we are greatly indebted to Carmen Perry for her long and persistent pursuit of the de la Peña manuscript and to the late John Peace for acquiring the manuscript and depositing it in the library of the University of Texas at San Antonio, a library that now bears his name.

LLERENA FRIEND

# Prologue

THE diversity of opinions expressed concerning the Texas campaign; the accumulation of lies told to falsify the events, published in national as well as international newspapers, but especially in the latter, and the cheap adulation the former have rendered to the men least deserving of it; the ignorance, stupidity, and cruelty displayed by the ministry and the commander in chief in this war; the honor of the army, unjustly censured even by its own members, who without adequate knowledge have superficially or inaccurately passed judgment; the honor and self-esteem of every military man who participated, so deeply hurt by the great inaccuracies in the official records as to dates, deeds, and places; and above all the honor of the country, deeply compromised by its leaders and no less by the truth and the atrocity of its crimes—these are the principal causes which compelled me to publish the diary I kept during the time I served in this unfortunate campaign, and at the same time to make a brief review of what is written there.

Although this may not be the best method, it is the most practical for someone like me who lacks the necessary aptitude and practice in this type of work; besides, it has the advantage of not letting events precede dates. I shall pour out the diary just as I have written it, and whenever I see the need I shall make those observations which could not be made on the march, for at times I had to write on horseback, at other times exhausted from the journey, and always uncomfortable and unsheltered.

Thus, it cannot be said that I reach my conclusions based on the little I have foreseen, or that I belong to that group of despicable

EDITOR'S NOTE: In the holograph diary, the prologue is a letter addressed to Sr. Lic. D. Mariano Mando from Matamoros, September 15, 1836. De la Peña's signature has been authenticated by the Military Archives in Mexico City.

men who censure only when others are in misfortune; my notes will leave no doubts whatsoever to those who wish to examine them, as they were written on the dates stated.

I would like to conceal my name to avoid the criticism it will draw toward me and so that nothing will distract from the reasons I give and the thoughts I explain, for I do not pretend to be a historian; but no one in the army of operations in Texas would not know who I am, and it could be interpreted that I did this out of weakness.

As concerns General Santa Anna, one would have to write nothing at all to avoid censuring his conduct. He created the sad situation in which he now finds himself, and he would be less vulnerable if, in his misfortune, he had not dragged with him so many worthy of a better fate.

Convinced of my limitations, which I am not ashamed to admit, I would desist from my goal were I not so aware that events are being distorted to the point that we who actually witnessed them will soon fail to recognize them. This has been furthered by some documents which have been published making accusations and at the same time trying to justify them.[1] I have written as an eyewitness to these same events. I have described them with accuracy and have recorded them not from memory, but as they took place. I should be judged as an impartial observer because I have had no ulterior interest in distorting the facts, as has been done and will continue to be done by those who have written and who persist in writing to justify their mistakes. I do not have to answer any charges; I am free to be candid and I wish to be so.

Having once decided to write, I shall narrate just as if the campaign had been successful, being careful not to speak from the results. Whoever takes the trouble of writing about the next campaign will have to relate the same mistakes, for almost the same ones are being committed again, and no one seems to have derived any

---

[1] The author refers to articles published in the local newspapers in which General Urrea was viciously attacked, and to the signers of another article, published under the pseudonym, "Various Army Chiefs, Friends of the Truth," complaining of the poor medical service extended during the Texas expedition and of the irregularities committed with respect to the food supplies.—*J. S. G.*

profit from the lessons of experience; whichever general is appointed to carry it out will meet disaster anew. The nation will suffer a new rebuff, and the consequences will be not only lamentable, but difficult to correct.

In undertaking this modest, but for me arduous, effort, I find myself far from any pretensions of imitating the artistic style with which the French military men have portrayed their admirable feats, for I do not have the talents nor can I recount anything but errors, which is very sad for a Mexican soldier. Let no one expect to find in my narrative flowery rhetoric or a sublime and lofty style or ornate descriptions, even though the material is appropriate and abundant enough to fill volumes; what I would like to do, were I given the chance to speak with the passion I feel, is to write a historical novel, depicting scenes that could make the dead weep. But since this is not possible, I offer instead accuracy in describing events, as I have previously said; nearly all the army will serve as my witness, and I think that even the guilty will not dare deny them.

The infamies that have occurred in this campaign, infamies that must have horrified the civilized world and whose memory will continue to provoke pain for many years hence, should not remain hidden. In referring to them, I shall thrust aside my personal feelings, and my friends will cease to be friends from the moment that I publish the evils committed against my country and the deeds perpetrated against humanity.

Persons and events are closely knit together, but since my pen is guided by neither animosity nor ignoble sentiment, I shall when possible conceal all names. Those who in their inner conscience recognize that I am speaking of them will do me no favor in convincing themselves that I failed to spell out their names because of fear, for he who detests crime has no fear of speaking the truth, and if telling the truth meant that my life would be sacrificed, I would still do it gladly. I think that you know me well enough to convince yourself that I would know how to fulfill my duty.

I am well aware, my dear friend, that as I set out to vindicate the corrupted honor of the army, I will at the same time incur enemies within its ranks. I know that the inept never forgive having their errors published. Perhaps I shall incur further persecution and provoke fresh injustices in addition to those already perpetrated against me. But has this not always happened to those who swerve from the path of adulation and abide solely by the truth? I am determined to tell it, knowing full well that I cannot flatter everyone, but, schooled in adversity, I am prepared for anything, entrenched behind the bulwark of a clear conscience and the wise conviction of the Mexicans that nothing can frighten a man of honor.

I have heard some military personnel, especially those with rank, say that whatever happened in Texas should remain buried in the deepest silence because it is shameful; but those writers who have preceded me have surely convinced them that this is impossible. Others, who have heard about my diary, have been cruel enough to say that for the writing of it alone, I should be condemned to isolation in a fortress, and when they see that I have published it, they will no doubt think I should be shot. You and other sensible persons who read this will judge those who think thus as they deserve. As for me, I do not think that I should subject my ideas to those of everyone else.

Inclined as we all are to error, I wish to be judged impartially should I be guilty of it, as well might happen in the course of my narrative when I express my opinions, especially when I speak against the retreat, that shameful, unnecessary retreat. I sincerely desire that my statements be intelligently attacked, and that neither party loyalty nor adulation for the strong be the arms used against me, because impassioned language never convinces, but instead reflects unfavorably on the one who yields to it.

Through a series of unfortunate incidents detrimental to the Republic, one has been led to believe that only those in command have a right to think. It is taken for granted that men in high posts reason best, as if one did not know how these positions have been obtained up to now, pretending that the favoritism lavished on them could also endow them with talents. This sort of fanaticism engendered among members of the army and even among other classes of society produces a situation in which deeds are evaluated according to who is involved rather than by their own merits. Thus, my observations will have among other shortcomings that of not being those of a general. Another thing that will be noticed in my diary and that is common to all is repetition, though I have carefully tried to avoid it; but truly there are many things that have had to be repeated daily because they occurred daily.

I could have published my notes a few days after I returned from the campaign, but I was convinced that in order to be impartial, I had to take some time to verify those acts to which I was not an eyewitness and to obtain more accurate information about others, important objectives which I achieved by collecting the day-books from the various sections that constituted the army. On the other hand, since the campaign is still active, I have purposely kept from confronting the enemy with his faults, which were as gross as ours; for the same reason, I shall not mention those he committed lest he profit thereby, although I feel certain that the experience he has acquired by now and will acquire during the time he will have to recuperate will cause him to correct them.

Although there are many responsible people who honor me with their friendship to whom I might dedicate this work, I have preferred to dedicate it to my country, promising not to abstain from divulging everything I have seen, being fully convinced that truth is the most worthy homage I could render.

I must not conclude without reiterating for a third time that a person as unimportant as I, who has no aspirations, who expects no compensation, and upon whom no responsibility has been placed, would have no interest in distorting the facts. Whereas, on the contrary, those upon whom responsibility does rest, those against whom the nation will indignantly raise its voice to confront them with the opprobrium they have brought upon her, do have a great interest in presenting these facts in a manner most favorable to themselves.

If in bringing forth my notes I accomplish the noble objectives I have pursued in vindicating the honor of this unfortunate nation and its army, which has recently been tarnished, believe me, I shall feel amply rewarded for the insignificant services that I have been able to render it during my career and for the painful missions of this unfortunate campaign. I am well aware how difficult it is to write for the public and to fulfill the mission of a historian, but I also know that in order to narrate facts it is necessary to have integrity and steadfastness, qualities which, though it may be immodest to say, I do not lack.

JOSÉ ENRIQUE DE LA PEÑA
Matamoros, Tamps.
15 September 1836

*With Santa Anna in Texas*
A PERSONAL NARRATIVE OF THE REVOLUTION

THE political change which followed after eleven years of the nation's rule under a liberal system, and likewise the extension of its territory and the differences in climate and customs, were what provoked the Texas war or, better stated, were the pretexts of which the colonists took advantage. They would have legitimately presented to the nation a problem of justice in doing so under the banner of the 1824 Constitution, had it not been for the fact that their previous behavior had betrayed their distorted aims.[1]

The federal system, destroyed no less by the errors and the evils of its own liberals[2] than by the ignorance and bad faith of her antagonists, had established significant roots and created many interests, and there remained a strong and numerous party opposed to the new regime, which sooner or later would overcome its adversaries. It was this party which the revolutionaries in Texas attempted to flatter in order to encourage it to return anew to the cause in which it had just been overcome by perfidy after a long and bloody struggle in which it had always been victorious. Obviously they wished for us to destroy ourselves, the better to assure the success of their designs; but they were mistaken, because those same men to whom their cooperation was being offered rejected it, considering

[1] The Constitution of 1824, which created the federalist government, had brought little political stability to Mexico. Whichever party was defeated in an election promptly fomented a revolt. Ironically, Santa Anna, first elevated to the presidency by the liberals, put Mexico in a vise of conservatism. The old federalist guarantees rapidly gave way to centralist controls, and on December 30, 1836, a new Centralist Constitution was adopted, restricting power to the privileged classes. De la Peña is in sympathy with the liberal cause, but the colonists' frequent failures to comply with the terms of their contracts, together with the obvious interest of the United States in the territory of Texas, sullied their stated intent.—*Ed.*

[2] The Count of Ségur states: "Liberty is destroyed more frequently by its excesses than by its enemies."

the offer ignominious since it came from "newcomers." And in effect, it was, because after the triumph they would have demanded indemnities that would have been opprobrious to grant and that it would have appeared ungrateful to deny, had enough strength remained to do so. Those who had given themselves a country needed no help from foreigners in order to gain their freedom.

Circumstances forced them to remove their masks when it was least convenient; on the 2nd of March 1836, when the army had already invaded the territory, they declared the independence of Texas, because without this declaration the land speculators in New York and New Orleans and other points in the United States would have blocked the subsidies offered for the pursuit of the war.

This declaration was also useful to the Mexicans, for, once they saw these incidents in proper perspective, they knew exactly where they stood. The cry of independence darkened the magic of liberty that had misled some of the less careful thinkers, and the few who had cast their lot with the colonists, believing them to be acting in good faith, disassociated themselves immediately, there remaining with the colonists only Don Lorenzo de Zavala and the Béjar natives, Don Antonio Navarro and Don Juan N. Seguín, the only intelligent men who incurred the name of traitor, a label both ugly and deserved. At least they are the only ones that we know about.

Public documents had analyzed the events in Texas during the last months in 1835 and the telling of them alone sufficed to prove the injustice of the colonists' aggression. The insults lavished upon the nation as represented by the customs officials and commanders of military detachments, the disregard for laws, and the attitudes with which the colonists looked upon those who had given them a country were more than sufficient causes to justify war on our part. They were the aggressors and we the attacked, they the ingrates, we the benefactors. When they were in want we had given them sustenance, yet as soon as they gained strength they used it to destroy us.

The neglect, the apathy, or, even more, the criminal indifference with which all governments without exception have watched over the national interests; the failure to enforce the colonization laws; the lack of sympathy with which the colonists had been regarded and the loyalty that these still had for their native country; these things led us into these circumstances. Because of all this, war was

4

inevitable, for between war and dishonor there was no doubt as to the choice; however, it was necessary to prepare for it with mature judgment and to carry it out cautiously because the national honor was in the balance and it was less harmful to postpone the campaign than to expose the nation to ridicule by trying to carry it out contrary to the rules of the game.

It was necessary for all Mexicans of all classes and political parties to rally around the government in order to bring it forth successfully out of an undertaking that concerned everyone equally; but unfortunately this could not be.

The political scene had hardly changed when the cry of war was heard. The vanquished had been many; their wounds were still oozing blood. Directing affairs were the men least able to inspire confidence. The Ministries of the Treasury and of War were the most important posts at this time, but their duties were poorly discharged. The chief of the former [Rafael Mangino] was busy paying himself past-due debts which he maintained were long owed him; yet he claimed that there were no funds to cover the demands of the budget or to give the current pay to the corps and officers assigned to the campaign, when everyone knew that forced loans and taxes were being arrogantly demanded. There were several officers who, although designated to march with the army, did not do so, due to the lack of equipment. The latter ministry, it is true, was headed by a man of talent [José María Tornel], who is proficient in several subjects, who has lovely manners and a gift for captivating the good will of the people with whom he comes in contact, and who, in spite of his many inconsistencies and great defects, is gifted with other good qualities, such as that of expressing himself with ease, as well as his dramatic talent and oratory that have the appeal of a good actor on the stage. But he was not the ideal man to conduct the business of war. Having reached the rank of general without having gone through the lesser ranks, without having practiced his profession, without ever having seen the horrible scenes of the battlefield ( except those depicted in paintings), he could hardly be aware of the needs of the soldier during campaigns, estimate their sacrifices, temper the resilience of punishments and rewards, or select leaders who might better lead them in the presence of danger.

With such elements, the government found it impossible to

exercise the necessary moral influence; to this one must add the thoughtless violence with which forced recruiting was carried out and with which the other essentials needed by the army were taken. In spite of all this, it would have been more advantageous for the army had it first raised the curtain on the scene as represented on the 2nd of March. Nevertheless, enthusiasm was not lacking, and among the military classes it was great. As a whole, they were solidly behind the government because, united with the clergy and the friars, they had contributed the most toward the destruction of the old order.

War was the thing that could least frighten Mexicans, who seemed to have sworn not to live without it, but the distance of the country in which it would be waged, its climate, and the local conditions, not only in the general but in the particular topography as well, were factors of considerable weight in the eyes of the thinking person. It was the first time that our soldiers would be dealing with men of a different language and a different religion, men whose character and habits were likewise different from theirs. All was new in this war, and although it was happening on our own soil, it seemed as if it were being waged in a foreign land; but the government did not consider it so, for, as we shall see, it left everything to chance.

In an immense, open, and uninhabited country, it was necessary to take everything along and to proceed in a manner heretofore unknown. The Texas expedition should have been considered as a fleet taking to the high seas or, more strictly speaking, as a colonial enterprise. It was necessary to select the season, to assemble foodstuff beforehand, and to provide adequate means of transportation of all descriptions. The presence of good surgeons and well-equipped ambulatory hospitals was indispensable, not only for the wounded but also for the many illnesses caused by prolonged and difficult marches. But, as we shall see later, even if the entire operation suffered from negligence, this particular phase of it was done in a fashion so offensive to humanity as to appear incredible, were it not for the numerous testimonies attesting to it.

Since the soldier would be living constantly in a bivouac, the weapons had to be protected from the elements lest they be found useless when the time came to use them. This was even more necessary for the ammunition, which becomes as useless when rained on as when it is still being carried by the pack mules. There were wide rivers to be crossed, where it was necessary to leave at least two pontoon bridges in order to expedite crossings in the presence of the enemy and to carry out these movements with the speed so essential during war operations. It was necessary to know the depth of the rivers, their width, and the steepness of their slopes, as well as the force of their currents and the advantages and disadvantages of the woods surrounding them. This was not enough; it was also necessary to have companies with well-trained and well-paid swimmers. But we shall see later that all this was lacking, and what ill effects these deficiencies caused.

While these preparations were taking place and the supplies awaited, it was necessary to study the plans for the campaign with maps, to correct these, to spare no effort to inspect with absolute thoroughness the area where the action was to be, and to gather statistics that would accurately reveal every kind of resource that the country could supply so that the most adequate and economical type of transportation could be selected, as well as the roads that we ought to take.

The truth is that the public treasury was badly depleted, that all avenues of wealth had been blocked as a consequence of a civil war so barbarously prolonged; I can see everyone making this objection. But aside from the fact that this is not exactly true, the whole nation should know that more capital than was necessary has been invested in this disastrous expedition, and that the army, more unfortunate yet, has suffered great privations and has lacked many of the indispensable items, excepting courage and suffering, arms and munitions. But no wise use has been made of the former, and the latter has been pressed too much, both having been wasted as if they cost nothing. Thus, resources were not lacking; what was lacking was prudence, planning, order, foresight, clear and precise judgment. Said campaign, far from having drained the Republic, should, like the Italian campaigns, have increased the income of its treasury with considerable sums; but neither the director nor the executor recognized how valuable Texas was, nor did they know how to use the treasures that it contained. The Texans estimated their losses to be over ten million, and although to date one cannot say anything

7

positive regarding this, it is certain that no one utilized the wealth that the territory contained and that only an effort to destroy it was in evidence, as we shall see in time. The ministry and those in command deceived themselves and have endeavored to mislead the nation. Let us undeceive her!

The army had been infiltrated by a demoralizing force, which unfortunately was present in all classes. Although it absorbed all the taxes, leaving only meager crumbs for its employees, it was only a nominal army. It had been destroyed during the civil war, particularly during the years of 1832, 1833, and 1834. The flower of our veterans had perished without glory, killing each other, at times to uphold freedom, at others abuses, but most frequently tyranny; the errors and ambitions of the leaders of different parties have brought the country to ultimate ruin. Nonetheless, the same causes that had destroyed some soldiers had created others, perhaps less trained, less expert, less accustomed to withstanding dangers and labors. There were still experienced officers among the battalions and regiments, courageous and honorable and capable of leading their men to victory, but everything fell apart as one mistake led to another, and from error to error we went, giving new proof that as a thing is begun, so will it end.

The organization of the army that was to have performed brilliantly and was to have given the whole world an idea of the nation's power was generally defective. Its losses were filled by recruits snatched away from the crafts and from agriculture, by heads of families, who usually do not make good soldiers, by men in cells awaiting the punishment of their crimes, at times by men condemned by one corps yet finding themselves as part of another. Since so many men had been taken by force, the order of the commander in chief to execute any deserters was considered barbarous.[3] These

---

[3] See J. Sánchez Garza, ed., *La Rebelión de Texas*, vol. 1, *Manuscrito inédito por un oficial de Santa Anna* (Mexico City, 1955), appendix 6, an abstract of the general orders to the army of operations in Texas from December 18, 1835, in San Luis Potosí, to April 30, 1836, in Texas, section B of which excerpts from the general order to the Second Brigade of January 1 and 2, 1836, as follows: "A deserter from the Toluca Battalion has been apprehended and remains safely in prison, so that he may be executed in the brigade to which he belongs, thus complying with an

objections also were due to the fact that the government needed strong garrisons; its power had been created by bayonets and now had to be upheld by them.

Among the many abuses found within the army was the anxious desire of the commanders to increase their number, regardless of how weak or how incapable of resisting the hardships of a campaign these men might be; this occasion gave definite proof that numerical force did not correspond to individual force. There were many too young, some too old, some of these succumbing under the weight of their weapons and knapsacks, and although some have been transferred out and have returned again to their own ranks, this has become only a burden. How could these men withstand the long and tedious marches and rapid maneuvers they had to execute? This situation was more noticeable among the Sapper Battalion, where the men should be even stronger in order to withstand the demands of this unit.

The navy was the primary requirement for this campaign, and it was a grave error not to have made greater efforts to rehabilitate it. It is not out of place to say that the main operation of this enterprise should have been taken by sea, for it would have been much faster, especially for transport, and decidedly less costly. All the army corps closest to the northern parts should have been transported to the theater of war by sea, in order to have saved the men numberless leagues of march; a further advantage would have been fewer mouths to feed, since great numbers of squadrons of women and boys followed the army by land. But though it may have been thought more convenient not to transport the bulk of the army for attack by water, a discreet force should have been combined with those on land to protect our right flank, to cut off the enemy from his chief sources of supply, which entered through the ports, and also to prevent him from seizing our supplies that were coming by sea, whence they ought chiefly to have come in the final stages of the campaign. There was a delayed effort to correct this error; however,

---

order of his Excellency, the president, which provides that any individual caught committing a similar crime should be given the death penalty. All of which is transmitted through this order, so that it be read and understood by all members of this brigade, so that they may not plead ignorant of the law."—*Ed.*

the only thing accomplished has been to confess it, to increase costs greatly, to multiply the promotions, to advance the rank of a man without previous military record, without a country, lacking talents and virtues, disapproved of by many Mexicans who have grown old in the service of the navy and who above all are still Mexicans. This man is said to have the quality of courage, but this attribute is not unknown among us, and as he entered the service in 1832, being a first lieutenant is more than he deserved.[4]

The preparation for the campaign should have been secretly carried out; we should have been talking peace while preparing for war; but it might be said that this could not have been and that secrecy was of no importance inasmuch as the enemy had already taken the initiative. This granted, the government began its preparations by appointing a general, the selection amply confirming what was then being said, that the government trusted General Santa Anna's name more than its own strength, and that in this case as in many others it dared not take a single step without the approval of this commander. However, it is highly probable that he appointed himself; his interests were in war, for war would increase his fame, that chimera which so attracts the human heart, especially a soldier's heart.[5] The public press accused him of pursuing ambitious ends, going so far as suspecting him of promoting the war; however, when the time comes, I will not hide the thoughts and wishes of some of the military regarding this matter, much less his own, which can be read between the lines and in his actions.

General Santa Anna, having been named commander in chief by a free deliberation of the government, or perhaps on his own, presented himself in Tacubaya during November of 1835. This man was more renowned for the success with which he stirred up rebellions that tended to destroy his homeland than for his military feats, and because of the results of an uncertain and narrow-minded policy by which he had made himself indispensable, results brought

---

[4] The author probably refers to Brigadier General Pedro Lemus, a native of Cuba, whom he later mentions numerous times in derogatory terms.—J. S. G.

[5] Solís says: "The ambition of obtaining glory is a vice that must be forgiven in those who are worthy, and it approximates being a virtue among soldiers." But did our chief know how to be worthy?

about by force of a set of circumstances difficult to disentangle and irrelevant to our subject. All the courtiers, as usual, rushed to pay him homage; representatives, senators, generals, many distinguished members of society, ministers, and the chief executive himself ran into each other frequently in his palace. It is true that many were attracted by noble and patriotic purposes, but these did not constitute the greatest number. Meetings were held and long discussions took place because a war was being dealt with, a war that unfortunately was not a national one but that later on might become one. Each one presented his plans and rendered his opinion according to his talents, his wishes, his interest, or his manner of perceiving things, but all were idle words and empty discussions.

Santa Anna, while engaged in these debates, was in ill humor during the days he remained in Tacubaya. His irascible temperament did not lend itself to discussion, and he became especially annoyed when it tended to touch on the topic of taxes, at which time he would do nothing but make speeches, regret the shortage, and quarrel with everyone. Exceedingly well known are the reprehensible methods he used to obtain cash, and on this as on other occasions he abused the dignity of the laws; this reached its limit when a private person was permitted to introduce goods through Matamoros without previous registry, as in fact happened, and to no less a person than the one whose colossal wealth came about mostly through the shameful smuggling he has been carrying on for many years, thanks to the immorality of customs officials at ports of entry whom he had bribed, at the same time that the government knowingly paid their salaries, which should have been used to buy ropes to hang these public thieves.

San Luis Potosí was where General Santa Anna had decided to have his headquarters and to bring his forces together and organize them; but General Cos's capitulation made him change his plans.[6] It was here that the discussions of Tacubaya were renewed, although these became more heated at Leona Vicario [Saltillo]. The problem was to defend the country, to make sacrifices for national honor; a common interest was at stake and everyone thought himself entitled

---

[6] Martín Perfecto de Cos surrendered to the Texans at Béjar on December 10, 1835.—*Ed.*

to counsel what was best. Generals Juan Arago, Don Juan José Andrade, Eugenio Tolsa, and Antonio Gaona counseled wisely and gave the best advice. They were not counting on a great display of force or on favorable circumstances, for this would have prevented the campaign from ever being undertaken; they merely expected the more urgent and the more indispensable of factors. General Arago had twice before brought Santa Anna through with flying colors, and he wanted to do so again this time; he enjoys a well-deserved military reputation, as does Andrade, and they both merited an audience, but Santa Anna had become quite obsessed, as we shall have occasion to observe, and he refused to listen to reason, trusting only on his good fortune, which in a war does not play the major part. His inexperience cannot excuse him on this occasion. Some of his flatterers have had the audacity, for so it must be called, to compare him with the man of the century, although he is as distant from him as our planet is from the sun. It is true that he has the irascible character without which, Napoleon states, battles cannot be won, but of course he is incapable of the conceptions of that sublime, that daring and enterprising genius. To merit the title of general, according to military authorities, it is not enough to understand strategy and great tactics; a general needs knowledge of the exact sciences, pure and mixed, the natural sciences, and living languages; he must be acquainted with history, with the rights of peoples and the maxims of the best approved teachers of ethics. Furthermore, he must combine the strenth that good health provides, courage, steadfastness, audacity, and talent with a great reserve of patience, good manners, humanity, honor, righteousness, probity and purity of habits, all the qualities characteristic of wise men. Knowledge and ability are not enough to command an army, says an author; something more than prudent thinking, something more than wise measures, is necessary to inspire the army to action. At that moment when he is confronted with his opponent's genius, he must calmly and serenely elevate his own mind to a higher sphere that will not only rival but surpass his enemy's, responding to that creative power which superior resources grant, as well as courage and steadfastness. "What a terrible burden," he exclaims, "how superior to the men we know! What responsibility to carry on one's shoulders!"

During the course of this narrative it will become clear whether General Santa Anna is worthy of commanding and leading men to combat, whether he deserves the considerations bestowed on him.

All the efforts of the brigade chiefs to instruct the recruits and train them in firing were useless because the commander in chief maintained that they would become accustomed to gunfire during combat. If one tried to convince him that the cavalry could not be kept in a state of usefulness without feeding it grain, he replied that pastures along the road should be sufficient; and since the horses were fed with what served as beds to the horsemen, the cavalry branch of the army was rendered useless, and, as we shall see, its lack was greatly felt.

The general order of the day for the 18th of December 1835, given out at San Luis Potosí, distributed the army into two divisions. The First Division, under command of General Joaquín Ramírez y Sesma, comprised the battalions from Matamoros, Jiménez, and elements from San Luis Potosí, a regiment from Dolores, and eight pieces of artillery. The Second Division was made up of three small brigades. The first of these, under command of General Antonio Gaona, was composed of the Aldama, Toluca, and Querétaro battalions, light auxiliaries from Guanajuato, and six pieces of artillery. The second, under command of General Eugenio Tolsa, consisted of a battalion from Guerrero, the first active contingent from Mexico City, those of Guadalajara and Tres Villas, and six pieces of artillery; later on, the Morelos Battalion joined them. The permanent regiment from Tampico, the active from Guanajuato, and the auxiliaries from El Bajío formed a cavalry brigade under the command of General Juan José Andrade. The Sapper Battalion was attached to headquarters.

Division General Vicente Filisola was appointed second in command, and Brigadier Generals Juan Arago and Adrián Woll were appointed major general and quartermaster, respectively. Lieutenant Colonel Pedro Ampudia was appointed commanding general of the artillery, and Lieutenant Colonel Luis Tola was chief of the corps of engineers, which did not join the army until the end of May, 1836, when it was already in retreat. Don José Reyes López was in command of this army and Colonel Ricardo Dromundo, purveyor general.

13

This general order of the day stipulated among other things that: "His Excellency, the commander in chief, very emphatically recommends that the generals and the corps commanders zealously watch so that the armaments be in good condition; that infantrymen be provided knapsacks, two changes of wearing apparel, capes, spare shoes, canteens, and plates; that the cavalry corps be provided with the best horses possible; that the officers be supplied with spare horses, which should be placed in advance in good pastures. His Excellency recommends the greatest precision in the service, being well convinced that there is no need to try to inflame the troops with ardor for a campaign in which national honor is involved and in which the nation will not be compelled to weep over the triumphs obtained by the army."

This zeal was most praiseworthy, and one can sense in this order noble sentiments, for love of his country had become almost an obsession with General Arago, who dictated it; but there was no way to carry out what was ordered. For a moment his friendship for General Santa Anna had cooled off, but not during the Texas campaign, which he intended to write about. One night, when Santa Anna visited Arago, who was confined to quarters by illness, he outlined briefly the details of the assault on the Alamo; he praised the Sapper Battalion, knowing that General Arago was concerned for its good name, and derided the liberal government for having brought about so much bloodshed. He referred here and there to the legion of honor and then, addressing himself to several commanders and officers present at the time, said that it had become necessary that the campaign should be recorded. He who is the author of this narrative had already planned to do so and now took the commander at his word, but without acquainting him of it.

General Cos had been hemmed in at Béjar, 480 leagues from the capital, with a small garrison and in need of both munitions and foodstuff; desperate because he never received the help so frequently offered, he was compelled to capitulate on the 10th of December 1835.

Those who were not within range of his compromising situation and those accustomed to find fault in others that they failed to see in themselves have judged this commander a weakling. But he has exonerated himself before the government that abandoned him, that

14

instead of munitions and food, instead of trained soldiers, sent him replacements who only increased his needs; had he been aided at the time, he unquestionably would have overcome the enemy from the very beginning and would have had no need of showing himself as daring and brave, but the ministry considered it more important to defeat those Mexicans who opposed political changes than to defend the common homeland.

General Ramírez y Sesma received orders to come to the aid of General Cos, and on the 17th of November the part of the forces placed under his command left San Luis Potosí. He was advised to reach Béjar by forced marches, but this order was ill-timed and the general made no special efforts to comply with it. Several of the military personnel felt certain that Sesma had had time to come to the aid of this garrison and that his own apathy was the cause of its loss. Others accused him of cowardice. Later we shall see that this was not lacking in truth.

On the 26th of December Ramírez y Sesma's division joined with that of General Cos, who had already arrived at Laredo following the capitulation at Béjar. On the 27th, Generals Filisola and Ramírez y Sesma joined forces, remaining at this point until the 3rd of January 1836, when they received orders to march, the latter with his forces to the Río Grande, and Cos with his toward Monclova, in which direction Filisola also countermarched. Ramírez y Sesma had suffered much during the 24th, 25th, and 26th of December, when he marched between twenty-seven and thirty leagues without finding a drop of water and for the last two days without any food.

In the meantime the rest of the army had begun to mobilize, for the capitulation at Béjar had aroused the indignation of its leader and of each one of the men who were part of the army. Some had friends to avenge, and their threats ran before their vengeance; few were revenged but many were sacrificed.

The First Brigade left its general headquarters on the 22nd of December in the direction of Leona Vicario, carrying with it two twelve-pounders, two six-pounders, and two howitzers, one hundred boxes of gun cartridges, one thousand flintstones, supplies for the artillery pieces, a field blacksmith shop, a wagonload of supplies, two blacksmiths, two carpenters, and a company of artillery. During an inspection at arms ordered for this brigade on the 21st, it was

15

specially recommended that each soldier should have an extra pair of shoes and a pair of sandals. On the 24th of the same month the Second Brigade began its march, and with it the Sapper Battalion, the six remaining artillery pieces, and the equipment belonging to it. In the order of the day were included the same admonitions given the First Brigade. On the 26th the Cavalry Brigade left San Luis Potosí.

On the 6th of January, the commander in chief arrived at Leona Vicario, followed by the different brigades, so that by the middle of the month all of the Second Division had converged at this point. Here the campaign plan to be adopted was discussed again more earnestly: the supervision of supplies, the replacements, and the transportation to bring them. The map of Texas itself indicated the path to be followed. The political plan was no less important than the military one and the latter should have been subordinated to the former; but the ministry, which always operated in a dilatory manner, had neglected a rather important political point, which was to ascertain that the cabinet in Washington would not give support to the enemy; and much too late it tried to remedy this unpardonable oversight by sending Señor Manuel E. de Gorostiza as minister extraordinary to that government. But regarding the plan and its military aspects, from what has been observed up to now, the commander in chief seems to have been left absolutely free to act according to circumstances, which was a wise provision, for as the author previously quoted [Solís] so well states, "Plans conceived at great distances and based on fallible data regularly cause enormous errors, terrible consequences to the nation and to the honor of the commander of armies and the army itself." Convinced of this fact, Eugenio Turena, Condé, Moreau, and many other wise military minds always refused to take command of an army if they were not allowed the freedom to alter the plans of the cabinet according to the circumstances and the competence or error of their opponents; but General Santa Anna would have needed a century of indoctrination (as Alexander said during the Battle of Austerlitz, that he needed an army to fight Napoleon) in order to resemble any of these great captains. Nor can one say what the great Cyrus did, when he was asked what plans he was contemplating against his enemies, after having pledged the necessity of guarding this secret even from

16

his sovereign, to whom he had to answer for its success with his honor and his head: "If you have no trust in my ability and in my proficiency, dispose of this insignia to which all pretend that I am entitled."

At Leona Vicario our generals made new recommendations and presented again their earlier observations, supported by the strength given by reason and experience, the foresight of some, and the good wishes of the majority. To the observations of the commanders already mentioned were also added those of Generals José Urrea and Martín Perfecto de Cos. The latter had just been fighting the enemy we were soon to engage and had covered part of the territory in which we were to fight, and he should have been listened to.

## ❧ 2 ❧

ALL the advance information that had been gathered was unreliable and there were conflicting estimates of the size of the forces about to be engaged and the resources in their possession. In the general order of the 8th and 9th of January, there was an enclosed circular from the government stating that war preparations were being carried out in the United States and an effort being made to aid the Texans with all kinds of resources; this caused rumors to the effect that public meetings were being held to arm expeditions at the same time that assurances were being given that these acts were condemned by the government of that nation, with which we were on the best of terms and harmony. At the proper time we shall call attention to this circular, which opened the doors for the perpetration of great crimes against humanity.

The enemy did not expect our forces until the middle of March, and since our march had been accelerated by a month, the enemy was taken by surprise, an added reason why he could have been vanquished. He expected us to march on Goliad, the key position that would have opened the door to the principal theater of war. In fact, we should have attacked the enemy at the heart instead of weakening ourselves by going to Béjar, a garrison without any political or military importance. This was the unanimous opinion of all the military, and the commander in chief heard it from all those of any significance in the army; but he was not willing to gain the devotion of his subordinates by persuasion and by convincing them; he disdained their approval and contented himself with their obedience. General Santa Anna becomes irritable with discussions; he dislikes to make comparisons in search of the truth, which is always withheld from those most entitled to know it but certainly on this occasion was not withheld from him.

Not only were the military of this opinion but also all influential persons who knew the country, among them, for instance, the governors of Nuevo León, Coahuila, and Texas. General Pedro Lemus traveled from Monterrey to Leona Vicario with the object of supporting along with his colleagues the adoption of this plan, but nothing could influence Santa Anna to change his plan to march on Béjar, for which there was no further necessity after its capitulation. This march was a great mistake, an error that brought serious consequences; however, I do not wish to anticipate events, but rather to proceed with them, presenting them by date in the order in which they happened.

Once this important question was decided, the general order for the 22nd completed organizing the army (if what was done could be called organization), and on the 26th the army continued its march toward Monclova, the First Brigade and the Sapper Battalion having left on this day, the Second Brigade on the 28th, and the cavalry on the 30th. The general staff gave the brigade commanders the itinerary they should follow, freeing them to modify it as circumstances might demand. This order admonished that our soldiers should have with them the necessary equipment, for the commander in chief wanted our soldiers to act brilliantly once the time came to salute the Sabine and plant our eagles on its banks. Doubtless our armies would have been reflected by its waters had there been no further imprudence, or if the mournful song of a bird that appeared from Italy [Filisola] had not held back the flight of those who were marching to the right and to the rear of those who had been caught in a moment of surprise. So, having taken these supplies to Texas served only to tax the treasury, because of the tremendous expense of transporting them, only to have them destroyed or to lose the greater part of them.

The same order provided for a military hospital for the sick who could not continue but who should follow after the army as soon as they were rehabilitated, but what establishments lacking surgeons and medicines could one properly call hospitals?

It also ordered that each brigade should have with it a month's supply of food in the charge and under the responsibility of a private purveyor, who should be aided by a sergeant from its unit. The necessities had been poorly estimated and incompetent management caused many of these supplies to be lost, for in trying to save ten a hundred would be lost. Items such as crackers, rice, and salt, which should have been transported in barrels or boxes, were carried in gunny sacks, so that the rains or the ropes that held the loads to an animal ruined them. It is true that this was largely the result of lack of equipment, but with better methods and some foresight this shortcoming might have been counteracted.

The expedition, the most important and risky, the most difficult and most far-reaching in consequences of any heretofore undertaken by the Republic, depended on the wealth of a private person; the army which left San Luis Potosí under the protection of Don Cayetano Rubio would never have gone beyond Monclova without the help and the patriotic efforts of the departments of Nuevo León, Coahuila, and Tamaulipas and the timely and beneficial aid of landowner Don Melchor Sánchez, who gave it the necessary impetus to reach Béjar. The general order of the 23rd furnished the details that were to precede the grand parade that took place the following day commanded by General Juan José Andrade. The presence of the commander in chief with the select part of his general staff contributed to the success of this brilliant dress parade. It reportedly consisted of about five thousand men. It is impossible to ascertain precisely the number of combatants that entered Texas, because desertions occurred in great numbers up to the time the Río Bravo del Norte was reached; the reported status of the forces was inaccurate because among these were reported the ill. But since it is necessary to have some idea, I will do it, if only approximately, begging the reader to forgive me for being so meticulous.

Let us assume that no more than 4,500 men left Saltillo and that the losses had been replaced at Monclova by the forces coming from Béjar; General Ramírez y Sesma had 1,500 men at the Río Grande, and General Urrea pulled 300 infantrymen and 200 horses out of Matamoros. Included in this total of 6,500 men of all branches of the army were 1,000 horses plus companies made up of convicts; although, as I have said before, this estimate may be only an approximation, it is not far from the truth. Many of the military agree, among them General Andrade.

I am willing to suppose that up to the moment hostilities broke out there might have been 500 losses from illness and desertions, and that 6,000 men were sufficient to overcome an enemy that did not reach even half this number, an enemy inexperienced and untried in the science of war.

I should not go any further without mentioning that the companies of convicts from the northern frontier were in a worse state than the rest of the army, but as they were made up of men well acquainted with the terrain and skillful in waging war, it was important to reorganize them. The commander in chief, however, could not be persuaded of the importance of this, and instead of providing adequate protection for them, he contributed to their destruction, even taking away horses from some of these men. The soldiers forming these companies, though having little knowledge of the tactical use of their arms, were less demoralized than the rest of the army. They generally make good subordinates, are industrious, can be maintained at a minimal cost, and are good hunters. They can fight better on foot than mounted and thus have great advantage over our infantrymen because their aim is accurate. All that these soldiers have of honorable behavior is lacking to the majority of their officers, many of whom have carved out fortunes at the expense of their subordinates.

Once our small army was prepared to engage in battle, great eagerness and enthusiasm was evident, aroused by patriotism, moved by a feeling inspired by ingratitude and revenge, and exalted by glory and ambition. Some individuals were incited by their desire for pillage and by ambition, and it was quite easy to recognize those moved by this ignoble sentiment, not only from their previous conduct, but also from the language they used and by their actions. The sentiments of each man in the army were guided for the most part by his respective situation. General Santa Anna tried to foster ambitions and to look for new stimuli, and it was therefore natural that he would recommend to the honorable General Arago the creation of a legion of honor, a recommendation sent to the proper ministry for its approval; but obviously Señor José María Tornel appropriated it as his own idea.

The army was flattered by its commander during its actions in our country, but tyrannized when it was embarked in the immense desert. He prohibited the distribution of campaign bonuses in spite of the fact that a general order given on the 22nd of January at Saltillo had informed the commanders and officers that they were entitled to it. At Béjar, he deprived the soldier of his extra pay; he suppressed the *masita* fund,[7] the allowance for lights and paper, and all classes of allowances, ordering the payment of only one real for each man from the rank of sergeant down, a measure that produced a general feeling of disgust and provoked ill will. To deprive an officer during a campaign of allowances granted by law would have been praiseworthy, had communities not been burdened with heavy demands and had the funds not been used to let a few rascals live in luxury. But one cannot recall how the soldier was deprived of his due when he in turn was offering his life and was receiving only the bare necessities to sustain him, without feeling the most profound indignation and wanting to curse the perpetrators of such sufferings.

The armies of all nations, no matter how disciplined, always carry licentiousness with them wherever they march, and the greater their number, the greater the disorders committed and the greater the difficulties of preventing them.

General Ramírez y Sesma had preceded us in these things; permitting many violent acts and committing some himself, he had left behind him grim memories that were still fresh. As we went along, we heard only bitter complaints against this commander and were looked upon as enemies. At least three-fifths or one-half the number of our soldiers were squadrons composed of women, muledrivers, wagon-train drivers, boys, and sutlers; a family much like the locusts that destroy everything in their path, these people perpetrated excesses difficult to remedy, and naturally all hatred fell on the army and those who commanded it.

In the conclusion of a diary kept [by an officer] in the division of Señor Ramírez y Sesma, who was able to judge things for himself and whose integrity and circumspection would place him beyond all suspicion in speaking of this general, one reads, among other things, the following: "Putting aside the brusque and arrogant character with which he shows himself to those who do not know how to exercise the privileges to which they are entitled, I will speak of the behavior he displayed during the march toward Béjar, where I

---

[7] Traditional money for soldiers, withheld from their pay in advance and issued as an allowance for purchasing necessities.—*Ed.*

severed myself from his command. From Matehuala to the Río Grande, he demanded pack mules and horses for the division without compensation. The town of Pesquería made a gift of a considerable number of mules and horses for the benefit of the army corps,[8] but certainly none were given to mine by the general. At Salinas he gave an order for the troops to be paid one real, assuring them that he would furnish them food. In fact, in the towns of Aldama, Candela, and Lampazos and at the hacienda of Carrizal he demanded bread or tortillas and meat, and although here and elsewhere the inhabitants cheerfully granted whatever they could for the soldier, these same troops were ordered to issue receipts stating the amounts and the quality of the rations taken, all of which was then charged to us, perhaps for the benefit of the treasury, though I seriously doubt it. Nevertheless, I will admit in his behalf that the supreme government, as always, did not furnish him the necessary resources; still, the general placed the division at Béjar with 30 thousand and some-odd pesos, which he received as follows: at Saltillo toward the end of November 1835, 14 or 15 thousand, and at the Río Grande during the beginning of February 1836, 19 thousand. But the country paid for it, the country in which we have lived at times at the mercy of the generosity of townships and landowners, and at other, more frequent times, when these and the others are compelled to give us their stock, their flour, their corn, etc., in exchange for receipts they will never redeem from our most discredited treasury department."

These and what will be seen later will be sufficient proof that General Ramírez y Sesma, with his errors and abuses, really harmed us more than the enemy did; it is impossible to excuse him of the latter, the more so since he had received 43 or 44 thousand pesos for his division; the author of the diary did not know that he had received 10 thousand pesos at Zacatecas for Jiménez and Matamoros. On the 2nd of February, the First Brigade reached Monclova and subsequently the two remaining ones. The commander in chief arrived between the 4th and 5th of February. On the 8th they con-

---

[8] I have been assured by an eyewitness that the gift consisted of four hundred mules.

tinued their march toward Béjar, the First Brigade having left on that same day, the Second on the 11th, and the cavalry on the 13th. The rest of the garrison from that post, together with a four-pounder, joined the Second Brigade by general order of the 6th. According to the same order, each one of the two infantry brigades was to be increased by one sergeant and ten soldiers from the presidial companies to guard their respective equipment. This small escort was certainly inadequate to guard at night the immense multitude of beasts under their care; but fortunately the savages who frequently roam these areas omitted their bothersome visits this time. They were in the habit of roaming the camps where we had spent the previous night to see what could be found there, sometimes venting their cruelty on those left behind or on deserters. These fierce people customarily scalp their victims, sometimes before sacrificing them, sometimes after, and then have a celebration during which many hours are spent dancing around the scalp.

In order to suppress the strong, well-founded reasons that had been given in favor of marching to Goliad and to diminish the aversion that the whole army felt about marching to Béjar, the commander in chief had conceived the idea of establishing a general headquarters at Río Grande [Guerrero] and operating from there as circumstances demanded. But, unable by temperament to concentrate on any one thing and, on the other hand, eager and anxious to commence the hostilities, he advanced first, leaving behind at Monclova his second in command, his major general, and his quartermaster to expedite the movement of all elements that should follow the army; he gave his orders, and on the 11th of February the First Division left the Río Grande to rejoin him on the 19th at the Frío River, continuing together until they reached Béjar.

Thus, we now have our small army crossing a desert of more than one hundred leagues in order to reach Béjar, where it could depend on no more provisions than those it carried and often had no water to quench its thirst, which was parching at times and is always a need that irritates and depresses the unfortunate one who suffers from it. It is, therefore, now time to introduce my diary, in order to make those observations that occur and those which naturally present themselves, although this may not be done in the order that I might wish. This diary begins the 8th of October 1835, a date on which, by a despotic act, I was expelled from the capital on short notice, to prevent my demanding satisfaction for an offense done to me by an infamous foreigner; but I must not include anything not relating to Texas and the movements and operations there.

## ❧ 3 ❧

WITH the intention of joining the Sapper Battalion, to which I had been assigned on the 13th of February, I left Monclova some hours after the Cavalry Brigade, and in following their tracks I got lost; but I noticed the error before they realized that the road they had taken was not the right one. The Tampico Regiment countermarched first, but at a time when night had already extended its mantle, so pitch dark that objects were not discernible at five paces. Advancing by myself and not knowing what path I was following, I decided to spend the night at the foot of a palm tree; I was bent on making a fire with part of some ragged clothing belonging to some wretched women and boys who had gathered there, when the aforesaid regiment arrived, having had to follow my example for the same reasons. We had set out with a fierce norther and had suffered all day long, facing its cutting winds and rain, and by seven that night the rain had turned to snow. Since, as I have mentioned, the counter-march had been executed in the dark, in a wooded area, and on a narrow road, all was confusion and chaos. Some muledrivers took advantage of the disorder to escape, and those who did not neglected their mules because the agonizing cold kept increasing and dire necessity forced the men to neglect their duties, to think only of taking care of themselves. We were halfway up a hill, and darkness prevented us from finding wood for warming ourselves; and if it were located, the men were so numbed with cold that no one could gather it. Sometime later, through the efforts of the colonel of the Tampico Regiment and other officers, a few fires were started, which served as a converging point to the wandering multitude. Officers, soldiers, women, and boys, all shivering, gathered around the fires; circumstances had made equals of us all, and the soldier could crowd against his officer without fear of being reprimanded. But these fires were insufficient, and furthermore, no one wanted to volunteer to find wood to keep them going. The wood, moreover, green and very wet, resisted the fire, which the snow suffocated. The snowfall increased and kept falling in great abundance, so continuous that at dawn it was knee-deep; it seemed as though it wished to subdue us beneath its weight. Indeed, one could not remain standing or sitting, much less lying down; those not taking care to shake their clothes frequently soon were numb with cold and, immobilized by the weight that had been added to their bodies, were obliged to beg the help of others in order to move, but help was given only with great reluctance. This horrible night when surprisingly few could sleep; this night of agony, which our soldiers spent around the fires, adding to the clamor the curses desperation evoked from many; this night, which the torment of cold and hunger made longer, was followed by the day, which, so longed for and looked for, presented to our eyes an indescribable spectacle, the most enchanting that can be imagined. What a bewitching scene! As far as one could see, all was snow. The trees, totally covered, formed an amazing variety of cones and pyramids, which seemed to be made of alabaster. The Tampico Regiment had left its cavalry saddled, and the mounts, covered to the haunches, could not be distinguished by their color. Many mules remained standing with their loads; others, as well as some horses, died, for those that fell and tried to get up inevitably slipped from being so numb, and the weight of their loads would make them crack their heads. The snow was covered with the blood of these beasts, contrasting with its whiteness. Colonel González y Pavón, wishing to save some of these mules, had removed their loads the night before at the same place where they had found them, and all these packs were so completely buried beneath the snow that to identify them it was first necessary to dig them up. Thanks to the zeal of General Andrade, those containing the money were not lost. This officer of the Guanajuato Regiment had spent this memorable night a league from our rear guard. Travel toward his camp or toward ours had to be done by reckoning, for the roads had completely disappeared; fortunately nobody fell into a precipice that was close by and completely hidden. An abundant slush, formed by the melting snow, had by eight o'clock in the morning revealed by the tracks the route that the vanguard, guided by experts who knew the terrain, was following. We could not help recalling on this

27

date those illustrious conquerors of many nations who in 1812 had succumbed beneath the snows of Russia—but what a difference! Those heroic warriors, in the midst of the rigors of a cruel winter, naked, shoeless, weakened by disease, and unbelievably hungry, had to endure bloody battles every day, while their firearms were falling from their lifeless hands; scarcely half alive, had to tax their valor in order to confront more numerous and well-acclimated armies; had to face a whole nation, fanatical and powerful and aching to avenge many insults. What a notable difference between us and those who had to struggle against so many great misfortunes in enemy country, devastated by those enormous masses and by the inevitable confusion, and worse yet, crushed by winter or devoured by the flames that Russians and Englishmen fed by turn; with what universal compassion and admiration did they render unto ashes such populous cities as Moscow, Smolensk, Vilna, and other great cities!

The snow continued falling without interruption, though less abundantly, through the 14th until five o'clock in the afternoon. On this day we arrived at Las Adjuntas, a large rural settlement situated seven leagues from Monclova; the previous night some of us had been two and a half leagues away, others, three or four leagues. This unexpected storm did not cause the other brigades the damage that it caused the cavalry, but its snows brought dismay and sadness to the whole army, leaving unpleasant memories not yet erased. Even the most enthusiastic had let their hearts be frozen by these snows and were predicting dire results for our expedition. If we lose a few horses today, they would say, there are still some left, but within a few days all of us will have to march on foot, and there will be no replacements for any men we lose. On the 13th the First Division found itself about thirteen or fourteen and a half leagues beyond the Río Grande. The First Brigade of the Second Division, forty-nine leagues away, left the Sauz Creek and camped at the haciendas of Soledad and San Juan, which are separated by the Sabinas River. The Second Brigade was at Las Dos Hermanas, whence it did not move. Nevertheless, all lost men, horses, mules, and oxen, but if the losses suffered by the First Division and the infantry brigades of the Second were unavoidable, those of the cavalry could have been prevented if General Filisola had not compelled them to leave on the day of the storm; a day's delay would have made no difference, since even greater delays occurred later on account of this error. Our soldiers, especially the cavalrymen, suffered cruelly from the intense cold, so foreign to them and for which their clothing was not suitable, and needed to remain in bivouac.

On the 15th I left Las Adjuntas, leaving behind the cavalry, which could not go forward without replacing its losses. I halted at Dos Hermanas, a hacienda eight or nine miles distant from the aforementioned place, where the Lipan, Castro, was staying with part of his tribe in their wigwams. I continued my march and a short time later overtook the battalion from Tres Villas, which made up the rear guard of the Second Brigade, which I found encamped at Lampazos Creek around five o'clock in the evening. The placements of their battery and of the units was so well done and in such accordance with the nature of the terrain, the tents of the commanders and officers formed such a beautiful perspective, that I was delighted at the sight of the camp. It is indeed a pleasant experience to see an encampment laid out according to the rules. The march of the mules and carts that were carrying the munitions of war and food and equipment was so slow, their drivers had to overcome so many obstacles, and there were so many causes for exasperation that the rear guard did not arrive until eight o'clock that night, having spent ten hours to travel fourteen or fifteen miles, that is to say, five leagues.

On the 16th the brigade was already in motion when I began my march; I lost some time apprehending and delivering some deserters, and after traveling about twelve miles I arrived at El Aura, a river of beautiful water, which seemed to me the more beautiful as it contrasted with the unhealthy and pestilent water of the Lampazos. After the troops arrived and when the heat of the sun had relented and my mounted men had rested somewhat, I continued my march. I spent the night in a spot along the Sauz, where I was welcomed by some ranchers who were herding cattle for the brigades on the march and who sheltered me in their hut of hides and branches as a protection against the rain that was beginning to fall. From El Aura to Sauz, my companion and I had the pleasure of having one of these ranchers sell us, as a special favor, some poor corn biscuits and a little *pinole* to appease our hunger and that of our aides.

29

On the 17th I left Sauz, where there was only a pool of rainwater for men and beasts, going toward the Soledad hacienda owned by Don Melchor Sánchez. However, no food was found there, but I was assured that I would find everything at San Juan and was furnished with a guide who would show me a pass along the Sabinas, a river beautiful and picturesque, not only because of its clear and abundant waters but also because of the magnificently tall, straight cypress trees along both its banks. I arrived at San Juan, and Señor Sánchez, who had without charge given much help to the First Brigade, was not at all willing to do likewise for me, even at a fair price, because this good patriot had perhaps been antagonized by the many sacrifices he had already made. So after I had napped for two hours, I had to continue to the Los Alamos River, arriving at nightfall and directed by a stupid guide, which made the crossing difficult, but it had to be done in order to pasture the animals. However, the next day I was aware that this had been a mistake. Here I also apprehended three deserters, two of whom I delivered to the units to which they belonged. These, traveling in gangs, belonged to the group of men who had been forced into a military uniform. I feared that they might attack me, but it was my duty to apprehend them, for had I not done so it would have set a bad example for those around me. Later, when I saw them enduring so much fatigue and making so many useless sacrifices, I repented having contributed my part in adding to the number of unfortunates. On this day we traveled eighteen miles from Sauz to La Soledad, two from this point to the Sabinas, and five or six from the Sabinas to the Los Alamos, where we met some carts with families coming from Béjar. Later I overtook others belonging to Don Ramón Múzquiz, political chief of the place; he had had the misfortune of being attacked by the savages, who had destroyed and set fire to everything they could not take with them and had murdered the leaders of the group, among them a nephew of Múzquiz; only one had escaped to bring news of the disaster. In San Juan we ran the risk of meeting the Comanches along the Los Alamos, for this was reported to be their favorite crossing. My companion, who was much wiser than I, gave me many reasons, all in vain, why we should not spend the night at this point, but I resolved to stay. I redoubled my vigilance and nothing happened, only a dream I had, that they were stealing our beasts. I awakened as we were defending them, and this experience served to double our precautions.

On the 18th between six and seven in the morning we left Los Alamos, and after traveling sixteen or seventeen miles, we arrived about eleven o'clock at the mudholes of San José, which are actually pools of rainwater, and after we had given the mounts two hours' rest, we traveled twenty more miles. I managed to arrive between five and six in the afternoon at the upper end of the Santa Rita, the place from which the First Brigade had departed; I had decided to join them this same day at their place of encampment, and there I had the pleasure of embracing my friends and companions, with whom I continued reunited.

The First Brigade had the same great number of poorly tended mules and carts as the Second, which slowed and encumbered the march. Unity and mobility bring victory to armies, and perhaps it was these important qualities that brought so many distinguished victories to the immortal genius of war, but we are far from achieving them. Our army marched in a single column, its echelons particularly irregular if one considers the smallness of the whole; each of its parts concerned with its own needs, as if isolated in a desert without ties, without points of contact, and without communication with the rest; its commander many leagues to the vanguard, its second in command and its rear guard all equally unaware as to what happened in the center and at both extremes of the column. The usefulness of military posts seemed to be unknown to the commander in chief, for he completely neglected this point, attention to which is more or less necessary in order to facilitate the frequent communication that becomes indispensable in war; without these posts intercommunication became impossible in the great and unpopulated distances we were traversing.

The oxen pulling the carts, by nature cumbrous animals and used to working only certain hours of the day, were being needlessly worked to death, harnessed even before sunrise until some hours after sunset, with no care taken to pasture them during the night, and left most of the day without any water. These animals, weakened by fatigue, hunger, and thirst, became still more sluggish, and their drivers, irritated by their slow pace, would mistreat them further by striking them or would simply let them perish through

31

neglect. This cruelty was the result of having to use soldiers instead of drivers, who had deserted and left their charges behind to be cared for by the army. The soldiers, not satisfied with striking the oxen, would torment them with the points of their bayonets or their sabers.

On the 19th between seven and eight in the morning the brigade continued its march toward San Juan de Allende, a small, sad, and miserable village, where we arrived early, having traveled barely twelve miles. On the 20th we went to the township of Nava, as wretched and unpleasant in aspect as the former, and the same distance. There we had the satisfaction of receiving mail from Mexico City.

On the 21st we left Nava between eight and nine in the morning and had not traveled very far when a cloud charged with hail and lightning descended on us with all its fury. A wild wind kept us from advancing, holding men and horses back by its force, but the rain, which was more copious, hit even harder. Between five and six in the afternoon we encamped on the prominence of Armadillo, spending the night in the mud and tormented by thirst, having found not a drop of water to drink. We must have traveled between eighteen and twenty miles. On the 22nd, after traveling about fifteen miles, we went toward the presidio at the Río Grande, that is, the village of Guerrero, third and last town after Monclova. On the 23rd we made a stop to give the troops time to clean their weapons and dry their clothes, and on the 24th we traveled four or five miles before arriving at Río Bravo del Norte, a stream quite wide at this point, beautiful without being picturesque, somewhat shallow and slow of current. Infantrymen crossed without incident in water up to their waists, and the pack beasts with their loads crossed without difficulty; only here and there was a load of equipment and supplies ruined. Nevertheless, a few oxen that had been poorly driven drowned, and it was necessary to abandon some of the carts, overloading others or placing the loads on the mules.

On the 25th between twelve and one in the afternoon we left the Río Bravo and traveled about eight or ten miles to camp at San Ambrosio, a place without water but with such an abundance of rabbits that the soldiers could catch them by hand as easily as chickens from a hen. Through carelessness the stores of powder belonging to the Aldama Battalion caught fire, an accident that caused considerable alarm in camp.

On the 26th we camped at Peña Creek, which was no more than a big puddle of water, and we traveled about twelve or fourteen miles. Those of us traveling with the vanguard saw more than two hundred jack hares on the road within two hours. It gave us much pleasure to see them jumping in all directions. On the 27th, unaware of what was happening ahead and to our rear, we were hampered in continuing the march by a considerable loss of oxen, by the worsening condition of those remaining, which could hardly be driven even by shouts and blows, and by the total desertion of their drivers, when suddenly a message arrived from the commander in chief. He communicated that on the 23rd he had entered Béjar and that the enemy had retreated and had barricaded themselves in the fortress of the Alamo. He ordered the sapper battalions from Aldama and Toluca to start forced marches, and these orders were fulfilled between one and two o'clock in the afternoon under command of Colonel Francisco Duque, the rest of the brigade remaining with General Gaona. This sullen man, irritable and haughty in character, who never commands except in an imperious way, at times verbally offending those under his command, something natural to him but improper for a commander, is vigorous and tenacious when responsibility is placed on his shoulders, a commendable quality that makes one overlook his defects. On several occasions we saw him driving the carts and helping them to yoke the oxen. General Santa Anna, who at San Luis Potosí had already had a serious disagreement with him, during which General Arago had acted as mediator, reprimanded him for his slow march when he arrived at Béjar, but this reprimand was unjust because General Gaona had done everything in his power to overcome all obstacles on the way, and there was not a single person under his immediate command that did not share this opinion.

Thinking that the twelve-pounders were adequate for the attack on the Alamo and that with good mule teams these could move with the same speed as the infantry, I suggested this before we began the march, but the general answered that since they had not been requested, obviously they were unnecessary, and that if by an unforeseen accident they should impede the march, he would be blamed for this advice. He was right.

I was designated officer in command in Colonel Duque's section and received orders to remain with the rear guard in order to speed the march of all elements belonging to it; at nightfall I arrived at Espantoso Creek, where I encamped nine miles distant from where we had spent the previous night. It was a short creek that appears to be a branch of the Nueces River, but there is nothing frightening [*espantoso*] about it; on the contrary, it is picturesque because of the charm of the woods surrounding it. It is said that the Comanches gave the creek this name after an incident that occurred when they spent the night there once; they believed that one of their women had been turned into an alligator, and this superstition so horrified them that since then they have never even gone near the creek, it is said.

On the 28th at seven in the morning we set out from Espantoso, and after traveling three miles we crossed the Nueces, a stream narrow and deep, its banks a lovely sight. On a tree situated to the left of a wooden bridge linking its two banks was a neatly carved inscription, recording that "on the 16th of February 1834 the first colony from the Villa de Dolores passed by here." Under this there was another, hurriedly carved, which said that "the 15th of the same month in 1836 the First Division of the army bound for Texas had passed," which actually happened. On this day the troops took possession of the first ranch in a place called La Tortuga, where there were a few puddles of water, and we camped at the glen called El Negro, where there was not a drop of water but good pasture for the animals. We must have traveled between eighteen and twenty miles when General Cos, who had joined us during the halt we made, pitched his tent in our camp.

On the 29th, the last day of February, the troops took the ranch on Leona Creek, which dominates the scene as it courses over a beautiful plain, an inviting site that begs to be inhabited; were a great city to be built there, it would have a most enchanting view, the description of which alone would fire the most frigid soul. The whole belt between this creek and the Nueces River is pleasant and rather beautiful and varied, and as one explores it the soul expands and fills with joy; the sight of nature in its brilliant splendor brings an indescribable sense of wonder; the most delightful feelings follow one another to converge all at once and leave the recipient in a state of sublime ecstasy. Those who may have enjoyed the pleasures of love during the flower of youth and the heat of a passion irritated by obstacles and stirred up by desires might be the only ones who could feel what my soul felt on this day in the midst of nature so full of beauty and life.

After the troops had eaten and rested, the march continued until eight in the evening, when we camped on the right bank of the Frio River, which did not betray its name, for a bitter cold was brought on by a blustery norther. To arrive there, we had traveled a stretch of approximately forty to forty-five miles.

When we invaded Texas, the enemy was scattered in the interior of the colonies and along the banks of the Brazos, Colorado, Guadalupe, and San Antonio rivers, with observation posts on the latter and in the forts of Goliad and in the Alamo; these forces later advanced against our right flank as far as the Nueces River. Mr. Samuel Houston was the commander in chief of the Texas armies, and Mr. Thomas J. Rusk acted as secretary of war.

The enemy should have begun to harass the army at the Frio River, for this is an advantageous position, easy to defend with slight loss, since a forest more than five leagues long covers the left bank, adding to the advantage. There is not the least doubt that the foe should have limited himself to a defensive war, which the nature of the terrain indicated, but he was too inexperienced and thus could not utilize its advantages.

Fannin, who acted as second in command for the Texans, was stationed at Goliad with somewhat less than eight hundred men, waiting for reinforcements that were to arrive through the port at Cópano, some of which later fell into our hands. Part of those forces were divided between San Patricio and the mission at Refugio. Dr. James Grant, perhaps the most active of the Texas leaders, reconnoitered the country with a company of rifles. Our commander, with General Ramírez y Sesma's division, had advanced more than fifty leagues away from the closest forces that might have come to his aid, a great error, for when he proceeded thus he was in complete ignorance of the enemy's number, and in spite of what is now said to the contrary, he was as ignorant as the enemy was of our movements. Fannin, in command of a force that was rested and barely thirty-eight miles from Béjar, should have reinforced Travis, who with a handful of brave men had barricaded himself at the Alamo; or he should have staked out at the Frio River in order to divide the force which, already in the vicinity, was marching to attack this point. We would have been separated from our vanguard, which might have countermarched to aid us, thus giving Travis a chance to withdraw, while Fannin, better acquainted than we were with the terrain, could have marched away between our forces. Thus a sacrifice useless to both parties could have been prevented, but the folly of our commander, that of the enemy, and a lack of foresight caused us to consummate it. It has been said that Fannin went so far as to leave Goliad to execute this plan, but for this he needed the daring of our commander, for which reason he countermarched, fearing attack on the way. Be that as it may, we shall soon see that this sacrifice should have been avoided by us in various ways.

To continue the diary, on the 1st of March we crossed the Frio River and traveled from twenty-five to twenty-seven miles to reach the Tinaja de Arroyo Hondo, where we found water but, as in the previous journey, no pasture for the beasts. The troops passed the night along a riverbed that protected them somewhat from the north wind but not from the snowfall, which was rather abundant and prevented the unfortunate soldier from enjoying his rest. Written messages could not be sent the next day, because the ink had frozen in the inkwells and bottles. It was along this creek that we saw for the first time the wild turkeys that abound in that territory.

On the 2nd, after we had buried a soldier of the Toluca Battalion against whom the excessive cold and severe pain had conspired together, and after I had ordered the mules to be reloaded to make up for some that had strayed the night before, I marched to join my group, which I caught up with at the Chacón Creek, where they had halted. The march continued, and between five and six in the afternoon we crossed the Medina River, a little stream whose banks were rich with pecan trees. This was the place where General Arredondo had fought against the colonists who had rebelled during the Spanish regime. Here we spent the night, having received orders from the commander in chief that we could rest and arrive in Béjar the next day. This day we traveled between twenty-eight and thirty miles, and that night a captain of the grenadiers from Aldama died of a pain, no help being available for him. On the 3rd of March between eight and nine in the morning, after the troops had put on their dress uniforms, we marched toward Béjar, entering between four and five in the afternoon within sight of the enemy, who observed us from inside their fortifications. They calculated accurately the number of our forces, which differed by no more than a hundred men from their estimate; in the message Travis sent about this incident, he placed the number at around a thousand. There were 846 combatants, which, with the commanders, officers, and drivers, came to that number. We entered Béjar just as the roar of cannon and martial music were announcing General Urrea's victory.[9]

---

[9] The Mexican forces at Béjar had just been informed of Urrea's defeat of the Texans at San Patricio four days earlier. See chapter 6, p. 68.—*Ed.*

## ⚜ 4 ⚜

BEFORE going on to describe what happened at that post during our sojourn there, we will speak of what happened between the arrival of the First Division and our commander, and our division. The relevant section of the diary is transcribed as follows:

On the 23rd General Ramírez y Sesma advanced at dawn toward Béjar with one hundred horsemen; although he had approached them at three o'clock in the morning, the enemy was unaware of our arrival. The rest of the division came within sight between twelve and one, but by then the enemy had sounded the call to arms and had withdrawn to his fortification at the Alamo. There they had fifteen pieces of artillery,[10] but not all were mounted and ready to use, because of a shortage of cannon balls. They had an eighteen-pounder and an eight-pounder pointing toward town. After the division had rested for about half an hour at the foot of the Alazán Hill, two miles from Béjar, the president-general mounted his horse and started toward this city with his general staff, three companies of light infantry under command of Colonel Morales, three of grenadiers under command of Colonel Romero, two mortar pieces, and General Ramírez y Sesma's cavalry; he ordered the rest of the division to march with General Ventura Mora to Missión Concepción. The president, unaware upon entering Béjar that the church was abandoned, ordered Colonel Miñón to take it with half the chasseurs. As the column entered the plaza, from the Alamo came a cannon shot from the eighteen-pounder; immediately the artillery commander was ordered to set up two howitzers and to fire four grenades, which caused the enemy to raise a white flag. The firing ceased and Bowie sent a written communication addressed to the

---

[10] There were nineteen, of different calibers.

38

commander of the invading troops of Texas, stating that he wished to enter into agreements.[11] The president ordered a verbal answer that he would not deal with bandits, leaving them no alternative but to surrender unconditionally. Then he ordered the placement of the troops, and that they eat and rest, and summoned to Béjar the forces attacking Concepción.

On the 24th at nine o'clock his Excellency appeared and ordered that shoes be distributed in his presence among the preferred companies, and that the frontal advance proceed immediately toward the Alamo and commence the firing, which had been interrupted the previous afternoon. A battery of two eight-pounders and a howitzer was properly placed and began to bombard the enemy's fortification. The enemy returned fire without causing us any damage. On this day, inventories were also taken of stock in the stores belonging to Americans. At eleven, his Excellency marched with the cavalry in order to reconnoiter the vicinity.

On the 25th at nine-thirty his Excellency appeared at the battery and had the column of chasseurs and the battalion from Matamoros march to the other side of the river, he himself following. Our soldiers fought within pistol range against the walls, and we lost two dead and six wounded. During the night some construction was undertaken to protect the line that had been established at La Villita[12] under orders of Colonel Morales. On the 26th, 27th, and 28th nothing unusual happened; the artillery and rifle fire had been brought into play as needed without any misfortune to the division. On the 29th the siege continued, and about seven-thirty at night the enemy killed a first-class private belonging to the first company of the San Luis Battalion, Secundino Alvarez, who on orders of the president had got in close to reconnoiter the Alamo.

On the 1st, 2nd, 3rd, 4th, and 5th of March, the siege continued without anything of note happening, except that on the 2nd the chasseur from San Luis, Trinidad Delgado, drowned, and on the 3rd the sapper battalions from Aldama and Toluca arrived.

---

[11] William Barret Travis was commander at the Alamo, James Bowie his second, and a certain Evans a commander of artillery.

[12] A small village near the Alamo and on the left bank of the San Antonio River.

On the 17th of February the commander in chief had proclaimed to the army: "Comrades in arms," he said, "our most sacred duties have brought us to these uninhabited lands and demand our engaging in combat against a rabble of wretched adventurers to whom our authorities have unwisely given benefits that even Mexicans did not enjoy, and who have taken possession of this vast and fertile area, convinced that our own unfortunate internal divisions have rendered us incapable of defending our soil. Wretches! Soon will they become aware of their folly! Soldiers, our comrades have been shamefully sacrificed at Anáhuac, Goliad, and Béjar, and you are those destined to punish these murderers. My friends: we will march as long as the interests of the nation that we serve demand. The claimants to the acres of Texas land will soon know to their sorrow that their reinforcements from New Orleans, Mobile, Boston, New York, and other points north, whence they should never have come, are insignificant, and that Mexicans, generous by nature, will not leave unpunished affronts resulting in injury or discredit to their country, regardless of who the aggressors may be."

This address was received enthusiastically, but the army needed no incitement; knowing that it was about to engage in the defense of the country and to avenge less fortunate comrades was enough for its ardor to become as great as the noble and just cause it was about to defend. Several officers from the Aldama and Toluca sappers were filled with joy and congratulated each other when they were ordered to hasten their march, for they knew that they were about to engage in combat. There is no doubt that some would have regretted not being among the first to meet the enemy, for it was considered an honor to be counted among the first. For their part, the enemy leaders had addressed their own men in terms not unlike those of our commander. They said that we were a bunch of mercenaries, blind instruments of tyranny; that without any right we were about to invade their territory; that we would bring desolation and death to their peaceful homes and would seize their possessions; that we were savage men who would rape their women, decapitate their children, destroy everything, and render into ashes the fruits of their industry and their efforts. Unfortunately they did partially foresee what would happen, but they also committed atrocities that we did not commit, and in this rivalry of evil and extermination, I do not dare to venture who had the ignominious advantage, they or we!

In spirited and vehement language, they called on their compatriots to defend the interests so dear to them and those they so tenderly cherished. They urged mothers to arm their sons, and wives not to admit their consorts in their nuptial beds until they had taken up arms and risked their lives in defense of their families. The word liberty was constantly repeated in every line of their writings; this magical word was necessary to inflame the hearts of the men, who rendered tribute to this goddess, although not to the degree they pretend.

When our commander in chief haughtily rejected the agreement that the enemy had proposed, Travis became infuriated at the contemptible manner in which he had been treated and, expecting no honorable way of salvation, chose the path that strong souls choose in crisis, that of dying with honor, and selected the Alamo for his grave. It is possible that this might have been his first resolve, for although he was awaiting the reinforcements promised him,[13] he must have reflected that he would be engaged in battle before these could join him, since it would be difficult for him to cover their entry into the fort with the small force at his disposal. However, this was not the case, for about sixty men did enter one night, the only help that came. They passed through our lines unnoticed until it was too late. My opinion is reinforced by the certainty that Travis could have managed to escape during the first nights, when vigilance was much less, but this he refused to do. It has been said that General Ramírez y Sesma's division was not sufficient to have formed a circumventing line on the first day, since the Alamo is a small place, one of its sides fronting the San Antonio River and clear and open fields. The heroic language in which Travis addressed his compatriots during the days of the conflict finally proved that he had resolved to die before abandoning the Alamo or surrendering unconditionally. He spoke to them thus: "Fellow citizens and compatriots, I am besieged by a

---

[13] Fannin was still expected to come with aid from Goliad. Not until several days after the Alamo fell was he ordered to Victoria instead. See his letter from Fort Defiance on March 14, 1836, to Colonel A. C. Haton [Albert C. Horton].—*Ed.*

thousand or more of the Mexicans under Santa Anna. I have sustained bombardment and cannonade for twenty-four hours and have not lost a man. The enemy has demanded a surrender at discretion, otherwise the garrison are to be put to the sword, if the fort is taken. I have answered the demand with a cannon shot, and our flag still waves proudly over the walls. *I shall never surrender or retreat.* Then, I call on you in the name of Liberty, of patriotism, and everything dear to the American character, to come to our aid. If this call is neglected, I am determined to sustain myself as long as possible and die as a soldier who never forgets what is due to his own honor and that of his country."[14]

Twelve days had passed since Ramírez y Sesma's division had drawn up before the Alamo and three since our own arrival at Béjar. Our commander became more furious when he saw that the enemy resisted the idea of surrender. He believed as others did that the fame and honor of the army were compromised the longer the enemy lived. General Urrea had anticipated him and had dealt the first blow, opening the first campaign, but we had not advanced in the least during the twelve days that our vanguard stood facing this obstinate enemy. It was therefore necessary to attack him in order to make him feel the vigor of our souls and the strength of our arms. But prudent men, who know how to measure the worth of true honor, those whose tempered courage permits their venturing out only when they know beforehand that the destruction they are about to wreak will profit them and who understand that the soldier's glory is the greater, the less bloody the victory and the fewer the victims sacrificed; these men, though moved by the same sentiments as the army and its commander, were of the opinion that victory over a handful of men concentrated in the Alamo did not call for a great sacrifice. In fact, it was necessary only to await the artillery's arrival at Béjar for these to surrender; undoubtedly they could not have resisted for many hours the destruction and imposing fire from twenty cannon. The sums spent by the treasury on the

---

[14] De la Peña's Spanish translation of the Travis letter is accurate except for three omissions: the reference to Mexican reinforcements in the body of the letter, the closing words "Victory or Death" and the postscript. The original letter, with those omissions, is used here.—*Ed.*

artillery equipment brought to Texas are incalculable; the transportation alone amounts to thousands of pesos. Either they did not wish or did not know how to make use of such weaponry; had it been judiciously employed, it would have saved us many lives, and the success of the campaign would have been very different indeed.

There was no need to fear that the enemy would be reinforced, for even though reinforcements had entered because of our lack of vigilance, we were situated so as to do battle with any other possible arrivals one by one. We were in a position to advance, leaving a small force on watch at the Alamo, the holding of which was unimportant either politically or militarily, whereas its acquisition was both costly and very bitter in the end. If Houston had not received news of the fall of the Alamo, it would have been very easy to surprise and defeat him.

During a council of war held on the 4th of March at the commander in chief's quarters, he expounded on the necessity of making the assault. Generals Sesma, Cos, and Castrillón, Colonels Almonte, Duque, Amat, Romero, and Salas, and the interim mayor of San Luis were present and gave their consent. The problem centered around the method of carrying it out. Castrillón, Almonte, and Romero were of the opinion that a breach should be made, and that eight or ten hours would suffice to accomplish this. Field pieces were coming up and Colonel Bringas, aide to the president-general, had left with the idea of activating them. It was agreed to call the artillery commandant and to alert him to this, and although the artillery would not arrive for a day or so, and that solution was still pending, on the 5th the order was given for the assault.[15] Some, though approving this proposal in the presence of the commander in chief, disagreed in his absence, a contradiction that reveals their weakness; others chose silence, knowing that he would not tolerate opposition, his sole pleasure being in hearing what met with his wishes, while discarding all admonitions that deviated from those wishes. None of these commanders was aware that there were no field hospitals or surgeons

---

[15] The disposition of the troops for the assault is specified in the general order for March 5, 1836, marked secret and issued under the signature of Juan Valentín Amador and certified at Béjar, March 6, 1836, by Ramón Martínez Caro, Santa Anna's secretary (see *La Rebelión de Texas*, appendix 8).—*Ed.*

to save the wounded, and that for some it would be easier to die than to be wounded, as we shall see after the assault.

When in this or some other discussion, the subject of what to do with prisoners was brought up, in case the enemy surrendered before the assault, the example of Arredondo was cited; during the Spanish rule he had hanged eight hundred or more colonists after having triumphed in a military action, and this conduct was taken as a model. General Castrillón and Colonel Almonte then voiced principles regarding the rights of men, philosophical and humane principles which did them honor; they reiterated these later when General Urrea's prisoners were ordered executed, but their arguments were fruitless.

We had no officers of the engineers' corps who could estimate for us the strength at the Alamo and its defenses, because the section in this corps appointed for the army had remained in Mexico; however, the sappers were not lacking in personnel who could have carried out this chore, and, furthermore, information given by General Cos, by wounded officers he had left at Béjar, and by some townspeople of this locality was considered sufficient. The latter made clear to us the limited strength of the garrison at the Alamo and the shortage of supplies and munitions at their disposal. They had walled themselves in so quickly that they had not had time to supply themselves with very much.

Travis's resistance was on the verge of being overcome; for several days his followers had been urging him to surrender, giving the lack of food and the scarcity of munitions as reasons, but he had quieted their restlessness with the hope of quick relief, something not difficult for them to believe since they had seen some reinforcements arrive. Nevertheless, they had pressed him so hard that on the 5th he promised them that if no help arrived on that day they would surrender the next day or would try to escape under cover of darkness; these facts were given to us by a lady from Béjar, a Negro who was the only male who escaped, and several women who were found inside and were rescued by Colonels Morales and Miñón. The enemy was in communication with some of the Béjar townspeople who were their sympathizers, and it was said as a fact during those days that the president-general had known of Travis's decision, and that it was for this reason that he precipitated the assault, because he wanted to cause a sensation and would have regretted taking the Alamo without clamor and without bloodshed, for some believed that without these there is no glory.

Once the order was issued, even those opposing it were ready to carry it out; no one doubted that we would triumph, but it was anticipated that the struggle would be bloody, as indeed it was. All afternoon of the 5th was spent on preparations. Night came, and with it the most sober reflections. Our soldiers, it was said, lacked the cool courage that is demanded by an assault, but they were steadfast and the survivors will have nothing to be ashamed of. Each one individually confronted and prepared his soul for the terrible moment, expressed his last wishes, and silently and coolly took those steps which precede an encounter. It was a general duel from which it was important to us to emerge with honor. No harangue preceded this combat, but the example given was the most eloquent language and the most absolute order. Our brave officers left nothing to be desired in the hour of trial, and if anyone failed in his duty, if anyone tarnished his honor, it was so insignificant that his short-comings remained in the confusion of obscurity and disdain. Numerous feats of valor were seen in which many fought hand to hand; there were also some cruelties observed.

The Alamo was an irregular fortification without flank fires which a wise general would have taken with insignificant losses, but we lost more than three hundred brave men.

Four columns were chosen for the attack. The first, under command of General Cos and made up of a battalion from Aldama and three companies from the San Luis contingent, was to move against the western front, which faced the city. The second, under Colonel Duque and made up of the battalion under his command and three other companies from San Luis, was entrusted with a like mission against the front facing the north, which had two mounted batteries at each end of its walls. These two columns had a total strength of seven hundred men. The third, under command of Colonel Romero and made up of two companies of fusiliers from the Matamoros and Jiménez battalions, had less strength, for it only came up to three hundred or more men; it was to attack the east front, which was the strongest, perhaps because of its height or perhaps because of the number of cannon that were defending it, three of them situated in a battery over the church ruins, which appeared as a sort of high fortress. The fourth column, under command of Colonel Morales and made up of over a hundred chasseurs, was entrusted with taking the entrance to the fort and the entrenchments defending it.

The Sapper Battalion and five grenadier companies made up the reserve of four hundred men. The commander in chief headed this column, according to the tenor of the secret order given for the assault, and its formation was entrusted to Colonel Amat, who actually led it into combat.

This was the general plan, and although there were several minor variations proposed, almost all were cast aside.

Our commander made much of Travis's courage, for it saved him from the insulting intimation that the critical circumstances surrounding Travis would have sufficed to spare the army a great sacrifice.

Beginning at one o'clock in the morning of the 6th, the columns were set in motion, and at three they silently advanced toward the river, which they crossed marching two abreast over some narrow wooden bridges. A few minor obstacles were explored in order to reach the enemy without being noticed, to a point personally designated by the commander in chief, where they stationed themselves, resting with weapons in hand. Silence was again ordered and smoking was prohibited. The moon was up, but the density of the clouds that covered it allowed only an opaque light in our direction, seeming thus to contribute to our designs. This half-light, the silence we kept, hardly interrupted by soft murmurs, the coolness of the morning air, the great quietude that seemed to prolong the hours, and the dangers we would soon have to face, all of this rendered our situation grave; we were still breathing and able to communicate; within a few moments many of us would be unable to answer questions addressed to us, having already returned to the nothingness whence we had come; others, badly wounded, would remain stretched out for hours without anyone thinking of them, each still fearing perhaps one of the enemy cannonballs whistling overhead would drop at his feet and put an end to his sufferings. Nevertheless, hope stirred us and within a few moments this anxious uncertainty would disappear; an insult to our arms had to be avenged, as well as the blood of our friends spilled three months before within these same walls we were about to attack. Light began to appear on the horizon, the beautiful dawn would soon let herself be seen behind her golden curtain; a bugle call to attention was the agreed signal and we soon heard that terrible bugle call of death, which stirred our hearts, altered our expressions, and aroused us all suddenly from our painful meditations. Worn out by fatigue and lack of sleep, I had just closed my eyes to nap when my ears were pierced by this fatal note. A trumpeter of the sappers (José María González) was the one who inspired us to scorn life and to welcome death. Seconds later the horror of this sound fled from among us, honor and glory replacing it.

The columns advanced with as much speed as possible; shortly after beginning the march they were ordered to open fire while they were still out of range, but there were some officers who wisely disregarded the signal. Alerted to our attack by the given signal, which all columns answered, the enemy vigorously returned our fire, which had not even touched him but had retarded our advance. Travis, to compensate for the reduced number of the defenders, had placed three or four rifles by the side of each man, so that the initial fire was very rapid and deadly. Our columns left along their path a wide trail of blood, of wounded, and of dead. The bands from all the corps, gathered around our commander, sounded the charge; with a most vivid ardor and enthusiasm, we answered that call which electrifies the heart, elevates the soul, and makes others tremble. The second column, seized by this spirit, burst out in acclamations for the Republic and for the president-general. The officers were unable to repress this act of folly, which was paid for dearly. His attention drawn by this act, the enemy seized the opportunity, at the moment that light was beginning to make objects discernible around us, to redouble the fire on this column, making it suffer the greatest blows. It could be observed that a single cannon volley did away with half the company of chasseurs from Toluca, which was advancing a few paces from the column; Captain José María Herrera, who commanded it, died a few moments later and Vences, its lieutenant, was also wounded. Another volley left many gaps among the ranks at the head, one of them being Colonel Duque, who was wounded in the thigh; there remained standing, not without surprise, one of the two aides to this commander, who marched immediately to his side, but the other one now cannot testify to this. Fate was kind on this occasion to the writer, who survived, though Don José María Macotela, captain from Toluca, was seriously wounded and died shortly after.

It has been observed what the plan of attack was, but various arrangements made to carry it out were for the most part omitted; the columns had been ordered to provide themselves with crow-bars, hatchets, and ladders, but not until the last moment did it become obvious that all this was insufficient and that the ladders were poorly put together.

The columns, bravely storming the fort in the midst of a terrible shower of bullets and cannon-fire, had reached the base of the walls, with the exception of the third, which had been sorely punished on its left flank by a battery of three cannon on a barbette that cut a serious breach in its ranks; since it was being attacked frontally at the same time from the height of a position, it was forced to seek a less bloody entrance, and thus changed its course toward the right angle of the north front. The few poor ladders that we were bringing had not arrived, because their bearers had either perished on the way or had escaped. Only one was seen of all those that were planned. General Cos, looking for a starting point from which to climb, had advanced frontally with his column to where the second and third were. All united at one point, mixing and forming a confused mass. Fortunately the wall reinforcement on this front was of lumber, its excavation was hardly begun, and the height of the parapet was eight or nine feet; there was therefore a starting point, and it could be climbed, though with some difficulty. But disorder had already begun; officers of all ranks shouted but were hardly heard. The most daring of our veterans tried to be the first to climb, which they accomplished, yelling wildly so that room could be made for them, at times climbing over their own comrades. Others, jammed together, made useless efforts, obstructing each other, getting in the way of the more agile ones and pushing down those who were about to carry out their courageous effort. A lively rifle fire coming from the roof of the barracks and other points caused painful havoc, increasing the confusion of our disorderly mass. The first to climb were thrown down by bayonets already waiting for them behind the parapet, or by pistol fire, but the courage of our soldiers was not diminished as they saw their comrades falling dead or wounded, and they hurried to occupy their places and to avenge them, climbing over their bleeding bodies. The sharp reports of the rifles, the whistling of bullets, the groans of the wounded, the cursing of the men, the sighs and anguished cries of the dying, the arrogant harangues of the officers, the noise of the instruments of war, and the inordinate shouts of the attackers, who climbed vigorously, bewildered all and made of this moment a tremendous and critical one. The shouting of those being attacked was no less loud and from the beginning had pierced our ears with desperate, terrible cries of alarm in a language we did not understand.

From his point of observation, General Santa Anna viewed with concern this horrible scene and, misled by the difficulties encountered in the climbing of the walls and by the maneuver executed by the third column, believed we were being repulsed; he therefore ordered Colonel Amat to move in with the rest of the reserves; the Sapper Battalion, already ordered to move their column of attack, arrived and began to climb at the same time. He then also ordered into battle his general staff and everyone at his side. This gallant reserve merely added to the noise and the victims, the more regrettable since there was no necessity for them to engage in the combat. Before the Sapper Battalion, advancing through a shower of bullets and volley of shrapnel, had a chance to reach the foot of the walls, half their officers had been wounded. Another one of these officers, young Torres, died within the fort at the very moment of taking a flag.[16] He died at one blow without uttering a word, covered with glory and lamented by his comrades. Something unusual happened to this corps; it had as casualties four officers and twenty-one soldiers, but among these none of the sergeant class, well known to be more numerous than the former.

A quarter of an hour had elapsed, during which our soldiers remained in a terrible situation, wearing themselves out as they climbed in quest of a less obscure death than that visited on them, crowded in a single mass; later and after much effort, they were able

---

[16] The only flag proved to have flown over the Alamo is that of the New Orleans Greys. It is the one Santa Anna sent home, and it can be seen at the museum in Chapultepec Castle in Mexico City.—*Ed.*

in sufficient numbers to reach the parapet, without distinction of ranks. The terrified defenders withdrew at once into quarters placed to the right and the left of the small area that constituted their second line of defense. They had bolted and reinforced the doors, but in order to form trenches they had excavated some places inside that were now a hindrance to them. Not all of them took refuge, for some remained in the open, looking at us before firing, as if dumbfounded at our daring. Travis was seen to hesitate, but not about the death that he would choose. He would take a few steps and stop, turning his proud face toward us to discharge his shots; he fought like a true soldier. Finally he died, but he died after having traded his life very dearly. None of his men died with greater heroism, and they all died. Travis behaved as a hero; one must do him justice, for with a handful of men without discipline, he resolved to face men used to war and much superior in numbers, without supplies, with scarce munitions, and against the will of his subordinates. He was a handsome blond, with a physique as robust as his spirit was strong.

In the meantime Colonel Morelos with his chasseurs, having carried out instructions received, was just in front of us at a distance of a few paces, and, rightly fearing that our fire would hurt him, he had taken refuge in the trenches he had overrun trying to inflict damage on the enemy without harming us. It was a good thing that other columns could come together in a single front, for because of the small area the destruction among ourselves could be partially avoided; nevertheless, some of our men suffered the pain of falling from shots fired by their comrades, a grievous wound indeed, and a death even more lamentable. The soldiers had been overloaded with munition, for the reserves and all the select companies carried seven rounds apiece. It seems that the purpose of this was to convey the message to the soldier not to rely on his bayonet, which is the weapon generally employed in assault while some of the chasseurs support the attackers with their fire; however, there are always errors committed on these occasions, impossible to remedy. There remains no consolation other than regret for those responsible on this occasion, and there were many.

Our soldiers, some stimulated by courage and others by fury, burst into the quarters where the enemy had entrenched themselves, from which issued an infernal fire. Behind these came others, who,

50

nearing the doors and blind with fury and smoke, fired their shots against friends and enemies alike, and in this way our losses were most grievous. On the other hand, they turned the enemy's own cannon to bring down the doors to the rooms or the rooms themselves; a horrible carnage took place, and some were trampled to death. The tumult was great, the disorder frightful; it seemed as if the furies had descended upon us; different groups of soldiers were firing in all directions, on their comrades and on their officers, so that one was as likely to die by a friendly hand as by an enemy's. In the midst of this thundering din, there was such confusion that orders could not be understood, although those in command would raise their voices when the opportunity occurred. Some may believe that this narrative is exaggerated, but those who were witnesses will confess that this is exact, and in truth, any moderation in relating it would fall short.

It was thus time to end the confusion that was increasing the number of our victims, and on my advice and at my insistence General Cos ordered the fire silenced; but the bugler Tamayo of the sappers blew his instrument in vain, for the fire did not cease until there was no one left to kill and around fifty thousand cartridges had been used up. Whoever doubts this, let him estimate for himself, as I have done, with data that I have given.

Among the defenders there were thirty or more colonists; the rest were pirates, used to defying danger and to disdaining death, and who for that reason fought courageously; their courage, to my way of thinking, merited them the mercy for which, toward the last, some of them pleaded; others, not knowing the language, were unable to do so. In fact, when these men noted the loss of their leader and saw that they were being attacked by superior forces, they faltered. Some, with an accent hardly intelligible, desperately cried, *Mercy, valiant Mexicans*; others poked the points of their bayonets through a hole or a door with a white cloth, the symbol of cease-fire, and some even used their socks. Our trusting soldiers, seeing these demonstrations, would confidently enter their quarters, but those among the enemy who had not pleaded for mercy, who had no thought of surrendering, and who relied on no other recourse than selling their lives dearly, would meet them with pistol shots and bayonets. Thus betrayed, our men rekindled their anger and at every moment fresh skirmishes broke out with with renewed fury. The

51

order had been given to spare no one but the women and this was carried out, but such carnage was useless and had we prevented it, we would have saved much blood on our part. Those of the enemy who tried to escape fell victims to the sabers of the cavalry, which had been drawn up for this purpose, but even as they fled they defended themselves. An unfortunate father with a young son in his arms was seen to hurl himself from a considerable height, both perishing at the same blow.

This scene of extermination went on for an hour before the curtain of death covered and ended it: shortly after six in the morning it was all finished; the corps were beginning to reassemble and to identify themselves, their sorrowful countenances revealing the losses in the thinned ranks of their officers and comrades, when the commander in chief appeared. He could see for himself the desolation among his battalions and that devastated area littered with corpses, with scattered limbs and bullets, with weapons and torn uniforms. Some of these were burning together with the corpses, which produced an unbearable and nauseating odor. The bodies, with their blackened and bloody faces disfigured by a desperate death, their hair and uniforms burning at once, presented a dreadful and truly hellish sight. What trophies—those of the battlefield! Quite soon some of the bodies were left naked by fire, others by disgraceful rapacity, especially among our men. The enemy could be identified by their whiteness, by their robust and bulky shapes. What a sad spectacle, that of the dead and dying! What a horror, to inspect the area and find the remains of friends—! With what anxiety did some seek others and with what ecstasy did they embrace each other! Questions followed one after the other, even while the bullets were still whistling around, in the midst of the groans of the wounded and the last breaths of the dying.

The general then addressed his crippled battalions, lauding their courage and thanking them in the name of their country. But one hardly noticed in his words the magic that Napoleon expresses in his, which, Count Ségur assures us, was impossible to resist. The *vivas* were seconded icily, and silence would hardly have been broken if I, seized by one of those impulses triggered by enthusiasm or one formed to avoid reflection, which conceals the feelings, had not addressed myself to the valiant chasseurs of Aldama, hailing the Republic and them, an act which, carried out in the presence of the commander on whom so much unmerited honor had been bestowed, proved that I never flatter those in power.

Shortly before Santa Anna's speech, an unpleasant episode had taken place, which, since it occurred after the end of the skirmish, was looked upon as base murder and which contributed greatly to the coolness that was noted. Some seven men had survived the general carnage and, under the protection of General Castrillón, they were brought before Santa Anna. Among them was one of great stature, well proportioned, with regular features, in whose face there was the imprint of adversity, but in whom one also noticed a degree of resignation and nobility that did him honor. He was the naturalist David Crockett, well known in North America for his unusual adventures, who had undertaken to explore the country and who, finding himself in Béjar at the very moment of surprise, had taken refuge in the Alamo, fearing that his status as a foreigner might not be respected. Santa Anna answered Castrillón's intervention in Crockett's behalf with a gesture of indignation and, addressing himself to the sappers, the troops closest to him, ordered his execution. The commanders and officers were outraged at this action and did not support the order, hoping that once the fury of the moment had blown over these men would be spared; but several officers who were around the president and who, perhaps, had not been present during the moment of danger, became noteworthy by an infamous deed, surpassing the soldiers in cruelty. They thrust themselves forward, in order to flatter their commander, and with swords in hand, fell upon these unfortunate, defenseless men just as a tiger leaps upon his prey. Though tortured before they were killed, these unfortunates died without complaining and without humiliating themselves before their torturers. It was rumored that General Sesma was one of them; I will not bear witness to this, for though present, I turned away horrified in order not to witness such a barbarous scene. Do you remember, comrades, that fierce moment which struck us all with dread, which made our souls tremble, thirsting for vengeance just a few moments before? Are your resolute hearts not stirred and still full of indignation against those who so ignobly dishonored their swords with blood? As for me, I confess that the very memory of it makes me tremble and that my ear can still hear the penetrating, doleful sound of the victims.

To whom was this sacrifice useful and what advantage was derived by increasing the number of victims? It was paid for dearly, though it could have been otherwise had these men been required to walk across the floor carpeted with the bodies over which we stepped, had they been rehabilitated generously and required to communicate to their comrades the fate that awaited them if they did not desist from their unjust cause. They could have informed their comrades of the force and resources that the enemy had. According to documents found among these men and to subsequent information, the force within the Alamo consisted of 182 men; but according to the number counted by us it was 253. Doubtless the total did not exceed either of these two, and in any case the number is less than that referred to by the commander in chief in his communiqúe, which contends that in the excavations and the trenches alone more than 600 bodies had been buried. What was the object of this misrepresentation? Some believe that it was done to give greater importance to the episode, others, that it was done to excuse our losses and to make it less painful.[17]

Death united in one place both friends and enemies; within a few hours a funeral pyre rendered into ashes those men who mo-

---

[17] See the accompanying documents, the second of which states exactly the number of losses sustained by us. Most of the wounded died on account of poor care, lack of beds, shelter, surgical instruments, etc., etc. All of the enemy perished, there remaining alive only an elderly lady and a Negro slave, whom the soldiers spared out of mercy and because we had established that only force had kept them in danger. The enemy dead, therefore, were 150 volunteers, 32 inhabitants from the township of Gonzales who had entered the fort two days before the assault under cover of darkness, and about 20 or so townspeople or merchants from the township of Béjar. [De la Peña included two documents (see *Rebelión de Texas*, appendix 9). The first, an excerpt from Santa Anna's official report of March 6, 1836, states that 600 Texans had been killed, among them Bowie and Travis, and that Mexican losses were 70 dead and 300 wounded, including 2 commanders and 23 officers. The second, Juan Andrade's tabulation of Mexican losses by rank and brigade, lists 8 officers dead and 18 wounded, 252 soldiers dead and 33 wounded, a total of 311.—*Ed.*]

ments before had been so brave that in a blind fury they had unselfishly offered their lives and had met their ends in combat. The greater part of our dead were buried by their comrades, but the enemy, who seems to have some respect for the dead, attributed the great pyre of their dead to our hatred. I, for one, wishing to count the bodies for myself, arrived at the moment the flames were reddening, ready to consume them.

When calm opens the way for reflection, what sad and cruel thoughts rush to the sensitive soul contemplating the field of battle! Would anyone be the object of reproach, who, after having risked his life to comply with his duty and honor, for a brief period unburdens his feelings and devotes some time to charitable thoughts?

The reflections after the assault, even a few days after it had taken place, were generally well founded; for instance, it was questioned why a breach had not been opened? What had been the use of bringing up the artillery if it were not to be used when necessity required, and why should we have been forced to leap over a fortified place as if we were flying birds? Why, before agreeing on the sacrifice, which was great indeed, had no one borne in mind that we had no means at our disposal to save our wounded? Why were our lives uselessly sacrificed in a deserted and totally hostile country if our losses could not be replaced? These thoughts were followed by others more or less well based, for the taking of the Alamo was not considered a happy event, but rather a defeat that saddened us all. In Béjar one heard nothing but laments; each officer who died aroused compassion and renewed reproaches. Those who arrived later added their criticism to ours, and some of these, one must say, regretted not having been present, because those who obeyed against their own judgment nonetheless attained eternal glory.

All military authors agree that battles should be undertaken only in extreme situations, and I will take full advantage of these opinions; they affirm that as a general rule, so long as there is a way to weaken and overcome the enemy without combat, it should be adopted and combat avoided. Civilization has humanized man and thanks to its good effects the more barbarous methods that were prevalent before, to kill the greatest number of men in the least possible time, have been abandoned; murderous maneuvers to destroy a whole army at a single blow have been discarded. It has been established as an axiom that a general entrusted with the command of an army should devote as much zeal to sparing the blood of his army as to the enemy. The opinion of the military sages, together with that of the moralists, states that the general who is frugal with the blood of his soldiers is the savior of his country, whereas he who squanders and sacrifices it foolishly is the murderer of his compatriots. One of these authors states that Louis XIV, at the time of his death, was inconsolable because of the blood spilled during his reign; that the memorable Turenne, in the last moments of his life, could not be quieted by the priests, in spite of all the consolation religion offers. As a matter of fact, false feelings of glory are not sufficient to suppress the remorse that the useless spilling of blood always brings about. If General Santa Anna were to see gathered together at one place the bodies of all the Mexicans he has sacrificed in all the revolutions he has promoted and in all the ill-directed battles over which he has presided, he would be horrified, no matter how insensitive he may be. The most renowned captains have always feared the day of battle, not so much because of danger to their lives as because of the interests and the soldiers entrusted to their care; but ignorance fears nothing because it foresees nothing. Some of our generals, particularly the conqueror of the Alamo, seemed not to have heeded these authors, for the latter, in his long career, has always separated himself from principles and has cast aside wise counsel. He has acted capriciously, uselessly sacrificing the life of the soldier, the honor and interests of the Republic, and the decorum of its arms, certain that no accounting will be required of him, or else that were this to be brought about, he would be acquitted, as experience has demonstrated. He would certainly act differently were he to be punished for his errors, but since he is lavished with honors even after his defeats, regardless of how shameful these may be, he could care less about losing or winning battles so long as they serve the interest of his party.

The responsibility for the victims sacrificed at the Alamo must rest on General Ramírez y Sesma rather than on the commander in chief. He knew that the enemy was at Béjar in small numbers and in the greatest destitution; he had scarcely had news of our march before our vanguard reached the gates of the city; he ordered the vanguard to surprise the enemy with a force of sixty horsemen, and to effect the march quickly and without the enemy's knowledge; he ordered the officers at the Medina River to yield their own horses to the dragoons that lacked good mounts. When General Ramírez y Sesma sighted the town, the enemy was still engaged in the pleasures of a dance given the night before; he therefore could have and should have prevented their taking refuge in the Alamo. Several came to inform him, indicating to him the points through which he might enter and the orders he should give, and urging him earnestly, but he turned down these recommendations and the repeated requests, conducting himself with extraordinary uncertainty and weakness; we have seen how dearly his indecision was paid for. At the very moment that General Ramírez y Sesma was advised to enter Béjar, there were only ten men at the Alamo, and it would have required an equal number to take it. Had he just placed himself at the bridge over the San Antonio that connects the fort to the city, as he was advised, he would have prevented the enemy from taking refuge there, thus avoiding the painful catastrophe that we witnessed. Later on we shall see how this same general made another great mistake that strongly influenced the fatal outcome of the campaign, and that the commander in chief noticed his lack of skill too late, although it was common knowledge among the expeditionary army, for he had certainly revealed his worthlessness through the censurable conduct we have just described.

## ⤫ 5 ⤭

Two days after the events at the Alamo, forces that had been on the march began to arrive at Béjar. On the 8th of March General Gaona arrived with the remainder of the First Brigade and I, as officer in command of its first section, reported to him the status of the force, with an account of the wounded and dead sustained during the attack by the troops it comprised, and the order given, that they were to be again under his command. On the 9th the second in command, the major general, and the quartermaster arrived, on the 10th General Andrade and his brigade arrived, and on the 11th Tolsa, with the Second Infantry Brigade.

The morale of the army had changed completely since the taking of the Alamo, because of the errors committed in that undertaking and the sufferings they were undergoing and had undergone en route; on the march the soldier could count on only half his rations and the officer had only enough pay to provide himself with food, which was sold at prices quoted in gold by the very people who were responsible for providing these necessities. The critical situation in which the army found itself at Béjar and the exasperation of its members is faithfully expressed in several letters of that period, written at that city, and also in various printed articles. Since these documents exist, authenticating the facts, and since no one can label them as false, because they were written by eyewitnesses, I take the liberty here of quoting some passages, obviously with some repetition.

Dated the 18th of March 1836, from Mexico City, it was written: "It is difficult to foresee what will happen; commanders and officers find themselves in a state of excitement; the campaign has hardly begun and many of us who have come will not see its end; General Santa Anna is opposed by those who know more than he; he has not fixed on any plan, we find ourselves without a base of operations, and he seems unaware of the importance of determining one. The army should not have taken this route, but should have followed instead the path where resources were available, where we could have taken them from the enemy. Béjar was of no importance after Cos's capitulation, and the suffering that we endured there was very great. At present, a cartload of corn is worth forty-eight pesos, one of beans seventy-two pesos, a pound of poor sugar one peso, and a *piloncillo* [a cone-shaped sweet made of brown sugar] four reales. Flour is not to be had, so only his Excellency can eat bread. A few days ago, in order to satisfy my desire to have some, I had to coerce the baker who makes it to give me a small loaf, which did not weigh over eight ounces but cost me four reales. I distributed this among my three comrades as a reminder of past times, and although it was really bad, it seemed delicious to us. It is true that few among us are sick, but we have 257 wounded with no surgeons to treat them, no medicines, no bandages, no gauze, and very meager food.

"The conduct that was followed in handling items of prime necessity was generally scandalous, especially regarding food, and it was publicly said, in sharp accusation, that General Santa Anna had plotted with the provisioner general, his brother-in-law, to exploit the sufferings of the soldiers. There is no doubt that in spite of the scarcity prevailing among the officers in Béjar, they were not even partially paid until the Dromundo's canteen arrived in the city, but even this continued toward the Brazos River, in two carts that were daily costing the nation ten pesos apiece for freight charges; nor was any effort made to put an end to the shamelessness with which the sutler took advantage of the circumstances to rob them. Allowing them to operate this way was not in consideration of individual freedom, but sometimes because it suited the private interests of those in command, and at others because of indifference toward the consumers; that is to say, there was no one to look after the soldier's interests."

In an article sent from Matamoros on the 11th of July 1836 by several of the military who witnessed the events, what was said on the subject is as transcribed in the accompanying document.[18]

In the diary we will see at what exorbitant prices articles of prime necessity were sold and what criminal acts tolerated.

---

[18] See *El Cosmopolita* (Matamoros), February 23, 1837.—*Ed.*

Scarcity and the high price of food were certainly not the only causes that produced such great disgust among all army classes. There were many others, as we will continue to note, but nothing shows more the lack of foresight of the government and the general in chief and nothing stirred up more hatred than the cruelty with which they treated those shedding their blood as an offering to their country. They committed a crime against humanity in leading men to war without having those resources which science offers for the saving of lives of those not perishing in the assault. For that reason indignation was aroused when the minister of war assured the nation that the only thing lacking in the Texas army was Italian opera, and when public eulogies were showered on him for his charlatanism while men were dying for lack of surgeons, medicine, and food. If cursing could kill, Señor Tornel would not be living, for so many were heaped upon him then by everyone from the general to the most insignificant soldier.

No one in the army is unaware that the surgeons assigned to its corps are generally indifferent men of meager education, wretched, many of them ignorant, who have taken no notice of the advances in their profession that would make them proficient in carrying out their duties; for when these positions are poorly provided for, there is no stimulus to attract good surgeons and they are sought instead by those who have no acceptance among the public. Thus no able professional is going to exchange the comfort he enjoys in society or the fees he derives there for the fatigues of the camp or the miserly salary. How many times before the Texas campaign have men elsewhere lamented this flaw! Among the few in the medical corps that finally found themselves in Texas, perhaps only Don José F. Moro is entitled to the name of surgeon. The letter he addressed from Matamoros to Don Pedro del Villar, chief surgeon, on the 6th of August 1836, concurrently published in *El Mercurio*, in the same place and the same month and year, is authentic testimony of the inhumanity dealt the sick and the wounded in the army, particularly those at the Alamo. For that reason I have judged it appropriate to insert it here[19] and to recommend its contents to the

---

[19] See *El Mosquito Mexicano*, September 30, 1836, vol. 3, no. 51, pp. 1–4.—*Ed.*

reader. No sensitive soul could read this communication without being moved, without cursing the pitiless man who would immolate so many victims, both friends and enemies. Dr. Moro has stated: "I arrived at Béjar and was simply appalled to learn all that happened there. Without any thought that there were no resources to set up a field hospital, an assault was mounted, but there was no place in which to house the more than two hundred wounded, although up to the last efforts were made to locate one; meanwhile the suffering patients wandered from one place to another, their suffering made greater by thoughts that naturally occurred to them in their pitiable situation. Hurtado, Reyes, and the practitioners with them did not arrive at Béjar until many days after the events, and Arroyo, who was there at the time, had exhausted the little I had left him during the month of December of the previous year.

"He had neither bandages nor material for making them, no gauze for the initial dressings, and nothing had been ordered or prepared for him; lacking everything, he made repeated requests, to no avail. The bandages finally given to him were of cotton material which, as your Excellency well knows, is noxious to wounds. Many had been admitted, among them two superior officers and some twenty others, to whom not a single surgeon could attend. Was the medical corps of the army at fault in this, or was it the persons who had these things so ordered?"

In fact, the plight of our wounded was quite grievous, and one could hardly enter the places erroneously called hospitals without trembling with horror. The wailing of the wounded and their just complaints penetrated the innermost recesses of the heart; there was no one to extract a bullet, no one to perform an amputation, and many unfortunates died whom medical science could have saved. General Santa Anna doubtless thought that he could alleviate the sufferings of his victims by appearing frequently among them, smiling at those miserable men who scarcely had the energy to see him, offering them their full pay with one hand but ordering it not to be disbursed with the other. There were many fools who were encouraged by his words, but to mislead them was an insult to their misfortune.

From among the goods and the tents found which the enemy had abandoned when they took hurried refuge in the Alamo, one of the tents erected was called the president's tent because it was placed in the premises occupied by his Excellency. These goods were sold at four times the market price after the best part of it had been picked out for the personal use of his Excellency and his favorites. Even the pecans, which are usually abundantly harvested in Béjar, were sold to us four dozen for a *medio real*. With what has been said, let the whole world wonder that when officers had to give up their linens for bandages for the soldiers in their respective corps, the commander in chief refused to yield any linen materials available for such a noble purpose; let humanity judge this general, who had no concern at all for the soldier.

Colonel Don Esteban Mora, one of the many who died at San Jacinto, was finally appointed director of the hospital and the Toluca captain, Don Francisco Martínez, comptroller. Those who were acquainted with the former knew him as a cossack, devoid of all human feeling, so that his appointment for a post requiring great reserves of patience and sensibility, in addition to scientific knowledge, gave rise to many comments. Fortunately for the patients, he did not remain there long; but, to be truthful, one must say that Mora did more for them than one would have expected from as bloodthirsty a man as he. In addition to him, the lieutenant from the Guerrero Battalion, Don Trinidad Santos Esteban, had been appointed to discharge this same duty, and he presented a contrast with Mora because of his positive attitude in the care of the unfortunates entrusted to him and, furthermore, because he did have some practical knowledge of surgery.

On the 30th of June 1836, when I visited the military hospitals at Matamoros, my feelings were considerably affected on seeing the poor patients left on the floor, given no more care than at Béjar. Officers met the same fate as the soldiers in this city, and some who could have been saved died because of the lack of aid. There was an officer, Second Lieutenant Villasana from the Aldama Battalion, who died because there was no one to ligate an artery. These are deeds that many of us have witnessed and that no one will dare to deny. Among the victims who perished because of General Santa Anna's faults and lack of resources, one finds the name of Don José María Heredia, a sapper officer. From the very outset of the campaign, this amiable youth had predicted his end and would often repeat his certainty of never seeing his family again. The reputation Texans have for marksmanship is well deserved. Heredia and I were going to appear in white hats, which gave me a presentiment hours before the assault that he and I would die in the attempt; but he laughed good-naturedly when I mentioned this to him. Urging on the platoon he commanded, at times scolding with sword in hand the soldier who showed little courage as the Sapper Battalion advanced, he received a mortal wound two inches above the right nipple in one of the last enemy barrages; this courageous officer could have been saved by the services of a good surgeon, but the lack of such and of medicine took him to his grave after thirteen days, during which, with admirable courage, he suffered intense pain. Perhaps it would have been enough to save him had he been placed in the proper position, and not flat on his back with a wound on his chest, so that the pus could have drained naturally toward the internal organs, for although there was suppuration, it did not drain adequately. Death did not surprise Heredia, for he realized his critical condition and awaited it calmly; having chosen death as a Catholic rather than as a philosopher, he received the sacrament of the Eucharist to the sound of martial music and surrounded by a flashy entourage. His funeral, though not sumptuous, was the most moving I have seen in my life, because he was a well-beloved officer and the army lamented his loss. General Gaona, the artillery commanders, a corps to which Heredia had belonged, that of the sappers, and all his comrades and friends from the other branches of the service were present, carrying his remains alternately on their shoulders to the place where he was interred; I had the privilege of being one of the pallbearers. This happened on the very day of his birthday. And after the appropriate honors were rendered him according to military code, we gave him our last adieu, turning away as if by force from the place where we were leaving him forever. I could not desist from visiting the cemetery where the remains of my friends were buried during the time I remained in Béjar, and the most tender emotions were with me as I contemplated the end of miserable human existence. Health, talents, courage, happiness, and love may all be ended at once by a lead bullet. Only the memory of virtues survives him who possessed them. I hope I may be forgiven the digression that friendship has led me to take.

The captain of the Toluca contingent, Don José María Macotela, and other officers met the same fate as Heredia, and those who were able to escape death, such as Colonel Don Francisco Duque of the same corps and Lieutenant Colonel Don Manuel González of the Matamoros, owed it more to their strong constitutions than to the healing arts.

## ✎§ 6 ̊৯৶

THE masters of the science state that when the invasion of enemy territory is undertaken, it is most desirable to avoid slowness of operations and not to dally in the original established bases. One should keep advancing, but wisely.

As we have already seen, the First Division had been at Béjar since February 23rd, and it was not until the 11th of March, after being there twenty days, that General Ramírez y Sesma marched with orders to take San Felipe de Austin, having under him seven hundred infantrymen from the Aldama, Matamoros, and Toluca battalions, two field pieces with their crews, one hundred horses chosen from the Dolores and Tampico regiments, fifty cases of rifle ammunition, and food for fifteen days.

On the same day the permanent Jiménez Battalion and the active one from San Luis, with a twelve-pounder, an eight-pounder, and a howitzer, together with those things required to man them and accompanied by sixty-five cases of rifle cartridges and sufficient supplies, all under command of Colonel Morales, marched to Goliad to place themselves under orders of General Urrea.

On the 15th general headquarters received news that General Ramírez y Sesma had entered the township of Gonzales the day before, a distance of about twenty-five leagues, after the enemy had set fire to it and had retreated, taking with him men, women, and children. Our soldiers arrived in time to see the flames. Moved by this incident and the exaggeration during those days of the value of what the enemy had left behind, a letter written to Mexico City on that same date, which we have before us, stated: "General Sesma entered the village of Gonzales yesterday, and five hundred armed men who were there had had no news of what had happened at the Alamo. Even the children fled, and they have set on fire and abandoned what they could not take with them. It is feared that

Ramírez y Sesma will permit pillage, as he has been accused of doing here and in all other places, for all the inhabitants of places or sites through which his division has passed have complained bitterly about it. On account of this commander and others like him lacking refinement, the army, aside from having renown for its courage, will also have acquired the reputation of banditry, a bitter feeling for those of us who sacrifice ourselves for the good name of the Republic." Another letter further states: "With this type of war and the errors that our commander in chief has committed up to now, we are lost, because as the enemy reorganizes and provides himself with supplies, the spirit of our soldiers will necessarily diminish. The reasonable men among us become highly indignant upon seeing that action is taken contrary to principles and that unnecessary sacrifices are undertaken." "I am the humblest of soldiers," an army officer was telling us, "but if I had been in command there would have been no doubt as to the success of the campaign"; it looks more like our general is determined that this be the last one.

On the 17th General Tolsa marched with the battalions from Guerrero and the first active from Mexico City, a force of six hundred men, to reinforce General Ramírez y Sesma, and, although the marching orders indicated that a hundred horsemen selected by the general commanding this branch should march first, only half this number did so because all the horses were almost useless from lack of grain, something that General Andrade and other commanders had anticipated before it happened. General Tolsa was carrying twenty cases more of rifle cartridges, a thousand flintstones, and supplies for only six days, for there were none to be had at Béjar and he had been assured that he could provide himself with these at Gonzales. The active battalions from Guerrero and Tres Villas under Colonel Don Cayetano Montoya marched on the same day, carrying with them a twelve-pounder and supplies for eight days, with the object of reinforcing Urrea's division.

Let us, for the moment, leave General Ramírez y Sesma marching to San Felipe de Austin, let us forget for a moment the critical situation of our wounded in Béjar, their intense pains, the wretchedness that touched everyone equally, and the predictions and conjectures that were circulating, and turn our gaze to our right and see the commander at the head, full of life, energy, courage, and

1. Fannin criticized for not responding to Travis's plea for reinforcements. See text, page 36. (Holograph manuscript, courtesy of Mrs. John Peace.)

2. Signature of José Enrique de la Peña, at conclusion of the prologue, authenticated by the Military Archives in Mexico City. See text, pages xxviii–xxix. (Holograph manuscript, courtesy of Mrs. John Peace.)

DEPARTAMENTO DE ARCHIVO
CORRESPONDENCIA E HISTORIA
Archivo de Cancelados

Confronté la firma  del extinto Tte. Corl.
de Caballería JOSE ENRIQUE DE LA PEÑA
EL TTE. CORONEL AUX.OFTA.J. DEL ARCHIVO.

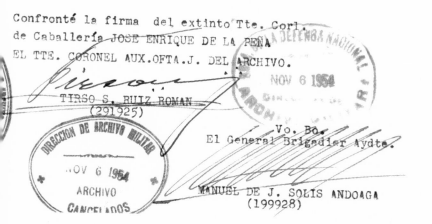

TIRSO S. RUIZ ROMAN
(291925)

Vo. Bo.
El General Brigadier Aydte.

MANUEL DE J. SOLIS ANDOAGA
(199928)

3. Bowie's offer to discuss a truce and Santa Anna's refusal. See text, pages 38–39. (Holograph manuscript, courtesy of Mrs. John Peace.)

Alamo é hizo romper el fuego sus-
pendido desde la tarde anterior.
Se tiró una barería de 2 piezas de
a 8 y un obus y te comenzó a batir
~~el Alamo~~ la fortificacion enemiga, q.
contestó los fuegos sin hacernos ningu.
daño — En ese dia se ~~abrieron las~~ comenzaron
~~tiendas de los americanos~~ por inventa-
riar las existencias de las tiendas de
los americanos — A las once S.E. marchó
con la Caballería p.ª reconocer las cerca-
nias."

"El 25 a las nuebe y media se presentó
S.E. en la barera, hizo marchar al
otro lado del rio la columna de
Caradores y al B.n de ~~Matamoros~~, pasan

4. Santa Anna orders the troops to attack the Alamo. See text, page 39. (Holograph manuscript, courtesy of Mrs. John Peace.)

militarmente; cuando su adquisicion fué costosa y produjo resultados muy amargos. No teniendo Houst.. noticias de la rendicion del Alamo, hubiera sido facil sorprenderle y batirlo.

En un consejo de guerra tenido el 4. de Marzo en casa del gral en gefe, manifestó este la necesidad de dar el asalto. Los grales Sesma, Cos, Castrillon y los coroneles Almonte, Duque, Amat, Romero, Salas, y el Mor accidental de S. Luis que asistieron á él, prestaron su deferencia. La cuestion roló principalmente sobre el modo de hacerlo. Castrillon, Almonte y Romero estubieron conformes con que se abriera brecha, que ocho ó diez horas bastaban para hacerla practicable. Benian en marcha piezas de batir y el coronel Bringas ayudante del gral Presidente, habia marchado con el objeto de avivarlas. Se acordó llamar al comandante de artilleria y ponerse de acuerdo con él y no obstante, que la Artilleria estaba para llegar de un dia á otro, y que la resolucion habia quedado pendiente, el 5. se dio para el asalto la orden que se halla en el n.º de documentos. Algunos que aprobaron esta resolucion en presencia del gral en Gefe, la desaprobaban cuando no estaban delante de él, ~~cuy~~ cuya

4

5. Santa Anna convenes a council on March 4 to plan the final assault. See text, page 43. (Holograph manuscript, courtesy of Mrs. John Peace.)

á buscar una muerte menos oscura que la
qe recibían apiñados en una sola masa
y cuando / despues de mucha afuerza
logaron en num.º suficiente coronar el
para pero sin distinción de cuerpos, los
defensores aterrados se encerraron atro-
pelladamᵗᵉ en unos cuartos colocados á
derecha e izquierda de la pequeña plora
qᵉ formaban de 2.ª linea de defensa.
Se habian aspillerado y atrincherado las
puertas, pᵉ pᵃ formar esa trinchera habian hecho unos fosos interiores qᵉ les e-
ran perjudiciales. No todos se encerraron
pues algunos se quedaron al descubierto.
mirándonos antes de tirar y como asom-
brados de nuestra audacia. Se vió a Tra-
vis tirotear pᵒ uno sentado en la muralla qᵉ legisⁱⁱ.
Daba algunos pasos y se paraba, volviendo á
nosotros la cara alrada i para descargar
su fuego, pues se batia como soldado: Mu-
rió al fin pero murió despᵉˢ de haber vendido muy cara su
vida: ninguno de los suyos murió con mas heroismo y todos
murieron. — Travis se portó como un heroe es necesario ha-
cerle justicia epues que con un apuñado de hombres sin diciplii-
na se resolvio ha hacer frente a hombres acostumbrados a la
gᵘᵉʳʳᵃ y en numero muy superior al suyo sin viveres con pocas
municiones y contra la voluntad de sus subordinados. Era un
..ío bien apersonado de un fisico tan robusto cual era

6. Travis's heroism praised. See text, page 50. (Holograph manuscript, courtesy
of Mrs. John Peace.)

De estatura, bien formado y de facciones regulares, en cuyo semblante estaba impreso el sentim.to de la adversidad, pero en el cual se notaba cierta resignacion y nobleza q.e le recomendaban. Era el naturalista David Croket, muy conocido en el Norte-america por un original y aventurero, q.e habia venido a recorrer el pais y q.e hallandose en Bejar en los mom.tos de sorpresa se habia encerrado en el Alamo temeroso de no ser respetado por su calidad de extrangero. S. A. ma corrido a la in
tervencion del Castillon con un gesto de indignacion y dirigiendose en seguida a los Zapad.r que era la tropa q.e tenia mas serca mando q.e los fucilaran. Sargentos y oficiales &c.a

7. Description of David Crockett and his execution. See text, page 53. (Holograph manuscript, courtesy of Mrs. John Peace.)

enthusiasm, inviting the emulation of all the generals and commanders of the army, including its chief. The feeling among commanders and officers at Béjar following the victories of General Urrea were varied. Some attributed to luck what was really due to the patriotism, the tireless zeal, and the foresight of this commander, while others did justice to him and enthusiastically proclaimed him the greatest champion. Later, when he left his command, evil tongues converted his laurels into objects of hatred and persecution, and we have seen in the ranks of his enemies those very ones he had most singled out by his esteem and those who had been the loudest in praises for him at the very site where he had acquired immortal fame.

While General Santa Anna did nothing but sacrifice our soldiers at the Alamo, while he ordered useless executions, inviting the enmity of the army as well as that of his military family, dishonoring it and consummating his errors by allowing himself to be surprised at four in the afternoon, General Urrea was marching rapidly from victory to victory, provisioning the soldier abundantly, even in the non-essential items, and acquiring glory more by his generous and humane actions, which attracted the admiration and respect of the enemy, than by the brilliancy of his victories.

On the 15th of January news was received at Saltillo general headquarters that 300 colonists were marching on Matamoros with the taking of that port as their objective, so the commander in chief ordered General Urrea, with 250 cavalrymen, to come to its aid. During his transit through the townships of the north he noticed extraordinary agitation for the Constitution of 1824, and since the inhabitants thought that the Texans upheld it in good faith, they maintained relations with them and were disposed to take up arms and follow them. Colonel José María González and a section of the convict companies had already taken up arms. On the 22nd of the month General Urrea went toward Mier, where González had taken refuge with the force he headed; the city council had declared itself in favor of the malcontents and had entered into talks with Urrea in order to give González and his soldiers time to save themselves. Señor Urrea nevertheless took twenty-four prisoners and, after reproving them, incorporated them into the section under his command, a group that rendered very useful services afterward. This commander omitted no means to convince the inhabitants of those townships of the bad faith with which the Texans were acting; he advised them to remain calm, then went toward Matamoros, where he remained until the middle of February waiting for the auxiliaries to carry on and to fulfill the instructions he had been given.

All the news arriving at Matamoros indicated that an invasion of that place was being planned, and there were rumors about the number of forces marching against it. General Urrea decided to go out and meet it, even though he lacked the necessary resources, and on the 17th he ordered out a section made up of 300 aborigines recently recruited in Yucatán who did not know the language and could hardly handle a rifle, some infantrymen from small scattered groups in the garrison, a field piece, 230 dragoons from several corps, and among all these a few from the convict companies. This was the respectable force with which he initiated his operations and which General Filisola pondered over so much, adding in his second folio that for each one of the engagements Urrea had undertaken he deserved a courtmartial; but on the 18th of March in the neighborhood of Goliad, he joined the first section, which had left Béjar for this purpose, and on the 26th, at Guadalupe Victoria, part of the second section.

General Urrea was eager to meet with the enemy and, with the knowledge that the force marching toward Matamoros had countermarched toward San Patricio, he forced a march with part of the cavalry, leaving the infantry and the convoy behind. On the 25th, 26th, and 27th of February, the soldiers were exposed to a severe storm, during which six from Yucatán, being from a tropical climate and unable to withstand the excessive cold, perished. Taking advantage of the bad weather and marching through forests and creeks, General Urrea was able to surprise the enemy at San Patricio at three o'clock in the morning, inflicting a loss of twenty dead and thirty-two prisoners, with no losses to himself other than one dragoon dead and four wounded. The general order of the day, given at Béjar on the 3rd of March, acquainted the army with this episode.

On the first day of this month General Urrea had news that Dr. James Grant was returning from Río Bravo, where he had marched with a party of select riflemen in an exploratory excursion to round up horses, and during the night General Urrea started moving with eight dragoons to encounter him, but since the weather was so harsh and so excessively cold, it was necessary to await him at a point called Los Cuates de Agua Dulce. The next morning he dealt Grant a decisive blow; forty-two men were killed, including Grant and Major Morris; some prisoners, firearms, and horses in their possession were the fruit of the day's labor. Dr. Grant was a landowner in Coahuila, a person well known and prominent. His capture would have been more useful than his death because many advantages could have been derived from it; so General Urrea thought, and he recommended that no attempt should be made against his life and every effort exerted to make him a prisoner, but the bait of his silver saddle, of his flashy firearms and other valuable jewels, provoked one of the "cossack" officers shamefully to murder him, thus bringing ignominy upon himself. Eyewitnesses assert that Grant defended himself courageously, and on many occasions have we heard General Urrea lament his death.

According to the orders Urrea had received, the principal objective of his operations was to explore the coast and to clear it of enemy forces. After he returned from the expedition against Grant, he stayed at San Patricio awaiting that part of his section which had remained at Matamoros and which joined him on the 7th. He spent his time in disciplining it and making it carry out continuous exercises, in some reconnoitering exploration, and in forecasting the intentions of the enemy at Goliad.

I should not proceed further without saying that while the commander in chief disapproved and even disdained the convict soldiers, General Urrea, on the contrary, flattered the few whom he had and found them quite useful, for they were well acquainted with the country, and he had in them excellent guides, skillful scouts who would lead him along suitable routes and would give him timely and important reports. A good part of the success of his operations depended upon this. Marching where the main body of the army should have marched, he had ample occasion to prove his skill, his energy, and his courage. Any other general possessing these qualities would have done exactly the same.

Because of his alert scouts, General Urrea learned that the enemy was planning to move on San Patricio on the 8th, so he marched to this colony with three hundred men to set a trap; he waited there for the enemy until the 9th, but by the 10th he learned that the enemy had changed his plans and had decided to march to the aid of the Alamo, although as previously stated in the explanatory part, this march never took place.

Thinking that it might still take place, General Urrea decided to prevent it, and on the 13th, marching to Goliad, he learned that the enemy had detached a strong escort to protect the force that was due to arrive from the port of Cópano, which a few days later fell into our hands. On account of this he ordered Captain Pretalia with a small party of soldiers and thirty fellow townsmen to advance and delay the enemy until he could arrive with the force selected to give battle. He chose 100 horsemen and 180 infantrymen, and, with the only field piece he had, started the march; he traveled all night, and at dawn on the 14th he found himself facing the enemy, who had been forced to halt at the mission of Refugio by the party in pursuit. The general's conduct on this occasion was the only time he merited censure during the course of his operations in Texas. Letting himself be misled by the excitement of some of those rash men who never foresee consequences, and as if he could by this justify useless bloodshed, he ordered an assault on the enemy, two hundred in number, who occupied a defensible position. It could not be taken because of the poor infantry destined for the sacrifice, who had been exhausted by the forced marches.

One of the things that a general should bear in mind is not to tire out the soldier with inconsiderate marches, lest he be found useless when the moment comes; those whom General Urrea thrust into combat had marched without interruption the previous day and night and had spent the 14th engaged in fighting without any food. These errors would be unpardonable even in a corporal, but much more so in a person carrying the insignia of a general. The result of General Urrea's attempt was a significant loss to us and none to the enemy, except six wounded. According to a communiqué that we intercepted,[20] the latter had contemplated uniting all his forces in order to initiate his retreat, and the importance of obstructing

---

[20] The author refers to a letter from W. Fannin at Fort Defiance to Captain Samuel A. White, March 14, 1836.—*Ed.*

this reunion and, still greater, of preventing the retreat may serve to excuse the general for the precipitate manner in which he acted, because the circumstances in which he found himself later were quite critical. While he was bent on fighting the force that had entrenched itself in the mission church, another one appeared at his rear guard, compelling him to send part of his reserve to face this new enemy. The latter had deployed himself in a wood, where a creek made him less accessible, so the general had to give up yet another part of his force; he ordered Colonel Garay to dislodge the enemy with sixty infantrymen. The thickness of the brush and density of the woods allowed us no further advantage than killing eleven and capturing seven, because daylight soon faded and the enemy, favored by darkness, fled. Those who had remained enclosed had no food or water, and the general promised that they would surrender the next day or come out in open field and fight. They managed to escape nonetheless, for the measures we took to prevent it were inadequate; nor could we have done so with our small number of extremely fatigued troops on a gloomy night made even more dismal by a strong north wind and copious rain. Our losses for this day were eleven dead and thirty-seven wounded, among these, three officers. At dawn on the 15th, when we took possession of the abandoned point, we found our wounded, some families of the colonists, and four of the enemy who had chosen not to follow their companions, as well as some compatriots of ours who had been impressed into the enemy ranks. The general ordered all the cavalry at his disposal to chase the fugitives, costing the enemy sixteen dead and thirty-one prisoners on this day and fourteen on the following.

General Urrea, certain that the enemy force enclosed within the fort at Goliad was attempting to abandon it and to concentrate itself at the colony of Guadalupe Victoria, hastened to prevent it. He left his convoy and the wounded at Refugio with a garrison to defend them and to keep watch at Cópano. On the 16th he moved on Goliad with only two hundred men at his disposal, sending ahead a detachment of cavalry to intercept any communication with the enemy and to observe his movements at short range.

The vigor and precision with which General Urrea conducted himself on this occasion is beyond all praise; surprised and astounded by his rapid movements and unaware of the dispersal of the troops they had had outside the fort, which they still awaited, the enemy did not decide to abandon the fort and retreat until too late. If, on the 17th, Fannin had known the insignificant number facing him, he could have retreated without General Urrea being able to prevent it, but when he attempted it on the 19th, the latter had already received three field pieces, ammunition, and a reinforcement of five hundred men.

General Urrea had established his camp three miles to the north of the fort. On the morning of the 19th, the advance posts reported all quiet, unaware that the fort had been abandoned until the enemy was three or four miles away, retreating toward Victoria. This commander, eager to adorn his brow with new laurels, hurried to seize this chance of fighting the enemy in open battlefield. Although he did not know his adversaries' numbers, he was soon within range and hastily confronted the foe with 360 infantrymen and 80 cavalrymen, leaving orders with Colonel Garay to take possession of Goliad and to have the artillery and ammunition follow; had Urrea wanted to march with all of his convoy, he would have given the enemy time to escape. He encountered the enemy between one and two o'clock in the afternoon at the headland of Encinal del Perdido just as the enemy was taking possession of a thickly wooded area from which it would have been very difficult to dislodge him; but the maneuver that General Urrea executed to prevent it gained us the advantage. During his rapid march this commander had been informed by his spies that the enemy seemed to have fewer troops than it had had at Goliad; he was thus impelled to order a countermarch of 100 infantrymen to protect the artillery. On facing the enemy, however, he found himself inferior in numbers, for he had only 260 infantrymen and 80 cavalrymen with which to combat over 400, who had nine artillery pieces and a great advantage over our soldiers in the quality of their ammunition, their superior firearms, and their good marksmanship; but, on the other hand, they did not adhere to the rules of the art but relied instead on special tactics. Although endowed with great courage, which he demonstrated until the moment of death, Fannin also demonstrated his lack of knowledge of the principles of strategy and grand tactics, for otherwise he would have fought while retreating, which would have been the best choice. Having decided to stand firm, he deployed his troops in battle formation as soon as our forces were near and awaited them with resolution. Our soldiers, most of them veterans of the Alamo, believed that overtaking and fighting the enemy would be one and the same, but it is difficult to say which of the two contending forces fought with greater ardor, for both showed tenacity and valor. Our commander, abandoning his general's post, placed himself at the head of two infantry companies attacking the enemy's right flank, while Colonel Morales attacked the left, Colonel Salas the front, and our cavalry harassed the rear guard; but it was all in vain, for courage could not overcome the numbers or the energy and steadfastness of the enemy, who brought into action all means at his disposal to render himself formidable. He formed a square with his cargo and wagons, which provided good protection as he fought; our soldiers, on the other hand, had no other protection than their breasts. Impetuous as the first blow was, it failed, but the general, wishing to prevent the enemy from completing his entrenchment, tried to disconcert him by charging his rear guard with the cavalry; these individual efforts, however, were fruitless, for the enemy, having foreseen this maneuver, had prepared himself, and furthermore, the cavalry, besides being few in number, was poorly equipped. Urrea's position was precarious; when he first engaged the enemy, he was counting on the artillery and munitions arriving on time, but these lost the way and did not arrive until the following day; moreover, since the order given at the beginning of the march, that the troops be supplied with four rounds apiece, had not been properly implemented, ammunition soon became scarce and finally was exhausted completely. The enemy seemed unaware of this, for he did not take advantage of a situation that was invaluable to him.

Although the handful of our brave ones was quite fatigued and not a few of them disabled, and though their efforts had been fruitless up to then, they were neither dismayed nor any less determined to gamble their lives again. The general, seizing on this enthusiasm, decided to make a last effort before the already scarce munition was exhausted. He placed himself at the head of the cavalry, in which he had served early in his career, and at the sound of the *diana* our small columns advanced on the double against the enemy entrenchment, approaching within a few paces of it, but such a courageous effort apparently was useless. The enemy made a vigorous defense with his artillery, which flanked our weak columns; he handled it masterfully and the rifle fire was very intense, forcing Urrea to sound the retreat, which was carried out in orderly fashion but not without losses. Appearing before his reassembled troops, he addressed them in a fashion intended to stir up their spirit; since his bad luck and his frustrated efforts had not diminished it, he felt sure of victory, which was predicted for the next day.

Night put an end to battle, but it was very cruel for the wounded of both sides, the more so for the enemy's, who could not quench their thirst as ours could. Fannin lost still another chance; he could have taken advantage of darkness to continue his retreat, since our own force was too weak to prevent it, being, as we have said before, smaller in number and much fatigued by the forced marches made to overtake him and by the many attempts made that afternoon. But noble sentiment and over-generous consideration dissuaded him: he would not abandon his wounded. The great excitement among his subordinates was not sufficient to tear him away from those who had already shed their blood, and he chose to share their misfortune rather than abandon them. More than on victory, he was counting on being able to obtain a reasonable agreement the next day that would save all. Poor wretch! Had he foreseen his tragic end, he would have preferred death on the battlefield, though he died with no less heroism nor has he descended to his grave with less glory. The generous acts of some of these men seemed to be inspired by the noble spirit of freedom, for they could have come only from free souls; or perhaps my own sentiments make me judge them thus. When Fannin was overtaken he was accompanied by about fifty mounted men, some of whom, not daring to confront our cavalry, escaped, thanks to their excellent horses, while others resolved to accept the fate of their comrades.

General Urrea, justly fearful that the enemy would escape during the night, spent all night reconnoitering his opponent's advance guard, making his aides watch in their turn; he sent his scouts forward to a point where they could observe the slightest movement, and by means of different bugle calls he was able to keep the enemy forces in a continuous state of alarm.

At dawn on the 20th the enemy, retaining the position he had the previous night, had also reinforced his trenches with dead horses and oxen and a narrow excavation. General Urrea received reinforcements of one hundred infantrymen, two field pieces, and the ammunition he so badly needed. He immediately ordered the resumption of the battle interrupted the previous day and had hardly opened battery fire when the enemy hoisted a white flag in reply. The general ordered a cease-fire and an inquiry as to the enemy's intentions. Learning that he wished to capitulate, Urrea dispatched a message through Colonels Morales and Salas that he could accept only unconditional surrender. There were requests and refusals and the discussion was prolonged; time was passing, so the general, wishing to end this business, approached the enemy camp in person, informing its commander of the impossibility of conceding anything other than what had been previously stated. After a brief discussion, he addressed himself to Fannin and his comrades and, in the presence of the aforementioned commanders, added: "If you wish to surrender unconditionally, this is ended; if not, I will return to my camp and the attack will continue." The frankness and dignity of this language pleased Fannin very much, for General Urrea's sentiments were inspired by a noble soul. The two commanders got along well together and would have developed great esteem for each other had they had the chance to do so. The suavity of their manner, their gentlemanly sentiments, their courage and other qualities made them much alike. Fannin recognized in our commander a noble enemy and resolved to entrust him with his own life and that of his comrades; the latter, for his part, saw in Fannin an unfortunate but courageous man worthy of all consideration. His heart yearned to accord him guarantees that were not within his power to grant, so he limited himself to offering to intercede with the commanding general, and he kept his word, as we shall see later.

After a brief conference among the enemy commanders, they surrendered their arms; there were 365 prisoners of whom 97 were wounded, among these Fannin himself. Three flags, nine field pieces of various calibers, about a thousand guns, many rifles, over forty pairs of excellent pistols, abundant ammunition, and several draw-carts were the trophies for this day. The enemy sustained 27 dead, and we had 11 dead and 49 wounded, among whom were 5 officers, one of them in serious condition.

This feat, in itself of minor importance and not too costly, yielded great results: it lifted the spirits of the army and it spread terror and dismay among the enemy, who would flee in fear at the mere mention of the name Urrea. But it bore future consequences, and it would have been better to have lost it, if not for Urrea, for the rest of the army, because its commander in chief would not then have fallen into a false sense of security after this victory, and would have conducted himself in a manner more circumspect and more appropriate to the rules of war and the country in which it was being waged. But this is not yet the time to speak of the feeling that the victory at Perdido brought to General Santa Anna, nor of its consequences.

We have said before that General Urrea had expert guides and excellent explorers among the presidial soldiers, but not that he had attracted through his policy and consideration a great multitude of countrymen from Lipantitlán, San Patricio, Refugio, Goliad, and Victoria, who rendered important services; the most outstanding among these were Don Guadalupe de los Santos[21] and his sons, whom the general will never be able to recompense adequately. Knowing that Goliad had been occupied by Colonel Garay, that no enemy had been left to his rear, and that the pass at Guadalupe Victoria could be challenged by those dispersed from Refugio and the rest of the force that Fannin had called to his aid, General Urrea, having just effected the surrender of that commander, and with no rest at all, marched toward the colony of Guadalupe Victoria, leaving Colonel Morales with instructions as to how the prisoners, the armaments, and the supplies that had been taken should be conducted to the fort.

On the 21st at seven in the morning he took possession of that colony, which was made up of Mexicans, French, and Irish, who had been in touch with the general and had apprehended six stragglers before his arrival. His rapid march was not fruitless, for after he had been there for two hours, part of the enemy force was seen approaching the town from the lower river, but all were killed

---

[21] This person died in the capital, asking to be remunerated for his services; as a result of the war he had lost everything, and his worthy family was left in great poverty and fatherless.

or taken prisoners. Sergeant Calzada of the Cuautla Regiment had apprehended seven on that same morning and Captain Rafael Pretalia ordered them executed before they reached Victoria, at the very moment that he heard the shots of those approaching the town.

The officers who shared in the bloodthirsty spirit of the commander in chief were pointed out, as we shall see later.

At eleven o'clock the same morning another enemy detachment of one hundred men was seen at the upper river, which approached after it had joined the former, but being well acquainted with the country, they were able after a short skirmish to evade the precautions that had been taken to prevent them from taking refuge in a wide and thickly wooded area.

The general took some precautions regarding the safety of Cópano, Victoria, and the prisoners he had sent toward Goliad and advised Colonel Morales to join him with the remainder of the battalions from Jiménez and San Luis; on the 22nd of March, at the head of two hundred infantrymen, fifty horsemen, and a field piece, he moved to intercept the retreat of the enemy who had escaped the previous day.

At two o'clock in the afternoon he arrived at a point thirty miles from Victoria, called Las Juntas because four creeks meet there, at the very moment that the enemy force he was pursuing arrived. Four men belonging to it were captured, who revealed that the enemy was hiding in the woods nearby. The general, who had secured all possible exits and made sure that the enemy could not possibly escape without stumbling upon his soldiers, sent one of the prisoners to acquaint their commanders with the situation, warning that if they did not surrender unconditionally, they would all perish by the sword. This arrogant insinuation was sufficient for Mr. Ward, who commanded this force, to request words with the general, and a conference lasting a few minutes was enough for him to surrender with nearly one hundred men under his command, including ten of officer's rank. The general spent the night at this place and designated the cavalry to reconnoiter the port of Lint, where they found abundant supplies that were sent to Victoria and distributed free of charge among the troops.

On the 23rd he countermarched toward Victoria with his prisoners, eighty of whom he dispatched on the 25th; he sent scouts to Lavaca Bay, Lavaca Bayou, and Navidad Bayou. Receiving news that one of his detachments had taken eighty enemy prisoners at Cópano, he issued new orders for the safety of this port and the prisoners, and for employing the latter in the rebuilding of the fort, with the exception of officers. He provided means of initiating a summary investigation to ascertain their reasons for having taken up arms and to determine what their future views would be, and he also issued orders for the rest of the force, which included artillery and munitions, to join him in order to continue the campaign.

The general spent from this day to the 27th reorganizing his division, as well as repairing and cleaning the armaments, setting in order both munitions and food supplies, providing measures for the security of the points to be left at his rear guard, and arranging for his wounded to be cared for in the best way possible with only a poor surgeon and a lack of the necessary materials; but since there were skilled practitioners among the prisoners, he made use of their knowledge to establish a field hospital and even sent two or three of them to the hospitals at Béjar, which was later to save his life.

By the 28th he had collected the entire force with which he was to continue his operations and had begun to move his first brigade, composed of the Jiménez and Querétaro battalions and a twelve-pounder under orders of Colonel Salas, toward Lavaca Bay. On the 29th he marched his cavalry to reconnoiter the banks of the Lavaca and Navidad bayous; on the 30th the Second Infantry Brigade, under orders of Colonel Morales and composed of the active battalions of San Luis and Tres Villas with two field pieces, headed for the village of Santa Anna; and on the 31st he himself marched to join them. Let us then leave General Urrea to continue his ever-victorious march, leaving nothing behind him without the stamp of honor and performing his duties with the greatest zeal and enthusiasm, and turn our eyes toward a general whose conduct contrasts with his, and look upon the dismal scenes that were taking place meanwhile at Béjar and Goliad.

WE left General Ramírez y Sesma on the march to San Felipe de
Austin, and we shall now see how the errors he committed were in-
strumental to the fatal outcome. Arousing the hatred of influential
persons is painful and harmful to me, but no consideration should
cause me to shrink from stating the truth, however harsh, regardless
of how it might affect me personally. General Ramírez y Sesma is a
timid and irresolute commander, dilatory in his judgment and apa-
thetic in his movements, and since with this poor attitude he worries
about every possible difficulty, his plans are always exaggerated.
Certainly boldness should not go beyond the limits of prudence, for
whoever so dares steps into certain failure, as General Santa Anna
has demonstrated. But it is likewise true that prudence should never
degenerate into weakness, and General Ramírez y Sesma (may his
lordship forgive me) fails in this respect. The commander in chief
never took a step that was not the wrong one; he did not even have
the good judgment to use his lieutenants according to their abilities.
General Ramírez y Sesma's previous deeds were well known, so he
could mislead no one. The conduct observed during the march toward Béjar, the purposelessness and the folly he manifested within
sight of this city, refusing to enter it at the stipulated hour, spoke
against him and foreshadowed what he would do later, but General
Santa Anna was determined to do what was not to be. Sesma foolishly compared Santa Anna with Napoleon and tactlessly styled himself as his Murat, as he sometimes was ironically called in the army.

We have already noted that our soldiers were able to see the
flames at Gonzales. The enemy had retreated shortly before carrying
this out; his march had been slow and cumbersome, as he took with
him a great number of covered wagons, which carried all the families
in the village and their possessions. Since General Ramírez y Sesma
had under him seven hundred infantry, two field pieces, and one

hundred horses, he could have easily dispersed the enemy, who was inferior both in numbers and discipline. He should have pursued him between the Guadalupe and the Colorado to prevent his joining reinforcements on the left bank of the latter stream; it was a great mistake not to have done so. General Woll, who was under General Ramírez y Sesma's command, realized the importance of such a maneuver and requested the use of the choice companies and the cavalry to carry out this scheme, but he was refused for the useless reason one may see in the communiqué from that commander, a copy of which is inserted here.[22]

On the 24th of March General Tolsa joined General Ramírez y Sesma, augmenting the division to 1,300 infantry, 2 field pieces, and 150 cavalry.

At that time the enemy had only 1,000 men and was suffering numerous desertions, but since there was a wide river in between and no resources for making a rapid crossing, General Ramírez y Sesma could not maneuver successfully, limiting himself to the role of spectator and making this known to the commander in chief, having for this purpose addressed a communication on the 28th which brought the number of the enemy up to 1,200. In order to dislodge the enemy from the position he was holding and to fight him with the advantage, it was necessary for General Ramírez y Sesma to engage his attention frontally while a second force crossing at some other point threatened one of his flanks or attacked him from the rear; it was so stated by that general, so the commander in chief advised General Urrea to follow this plan. However, on the 6th of April at San Bernardo Creek a counter-order was given; the enemy, alert to General Urrea's rapid movements, abandoned the Colorado and took a position on the left bank of the Brazos at Gross Pass, several miles above San Felipe de Austin, for Houston figured that anyone who had fought Fannin, who had such good troops, could more easily fight him, who had less able combatants.

If General Andrade, whose military talents, energy, and good judgment are so well known, had been sent instead of General Ramírez y Sesma, the result of this march would have undoubtedly been a happy one. Not only would he have engaged the enemy at

---

[22] This communication cannot be located.—*J. S. G.*

Gonzales and pursued him between the Guadalupe and the Colorado, thus preventing his joining the force at Austin, but if that had failed, he could also have pursued the enemy between the Colorado and the Brazos, which would have almost ended the campaign had the maneuver been executed rapidly and resolutely. In war, time is invaluable, but not everyone knows how to take advantage of it; courage, foresight, and energy are indispensable qualities that General Ramírez y Sesma obviously did not possess, and his obtuse conduct opens a vast field for criticism; any other army commander would have acted differently than he did. The fault was that of the commander in chief for having selected him.

The preference given General Ramírez y Sesma contributed significantly to the increasing general disgust noted at the headquarters at Béjar. We were a long way from that union inspired by love or friendship or that trust which rests on the talents, the probity, and the sound judgment of the leader. Nearly all the commanders and officers who were then serving under the orders of our commander had fought against him when they had been in the ranks of the people; hatreds were not completely extinguished, and there were many reasons why they were aroused again.

On the 23rd of March news reached Béjar of the important action at Perdido, and good wishes were extended to the commander in chief. Varied were the feelings that this produced, many the conjectures made, and many the estimates of its consequences. Some, among them the commander in chief, believed the campaign to be at an end, with little left to be done; others expressed contrary opinions, saying that it was just beginning, and even went as far as to predict an ill-fated end. While General Urrea speeded up his operations and triumphed over the enemy, he gained the esteem of the majority of the army but at the same time revived the jealousies of its commander and the other generals: "Urrea does everything," they would cry out, "he alone has the glory, while we just sit watching his victories."

The language that General Santa Anna employed when he was congratulated for the victory of the 20th gave a very unfavorable idea of his genius, for he displayed the most unfortunate ideas regarding Texas, expressing in the strongest way his opinion that it should be razed to the ground, so that this immense desert, he said,

81

might serve as a wall between Mexico and the United States. In the communications he addressed on that day to Generals Urrea and Ramírez y Sesma,[23] he satiated them with these ideas, and some of us who witnessed this act could only be astonished and saddened to think that such a man was at the head of a great people. When he spoke thus, he was completely ignoring the importance of the country, its prodigious fertility, its geographic situation, and its channels of communication to the sea. When Texas is populated and governed by good laws, it will be one of the most enviable places in the world, in which it doubtless will play a brilliant role. Often, as I admired its beauty, I had the thought, perhaps not so preposterous, that military colonies should have been established, a distribution made among those members of the army who wished to participate in the plan of part of the land and equipment that had served only to encourage pillage and rapacity among certain commanders, some of the Béjar townspeople, and others of the sparsely inhabited places close to the colonies. Among the army there were many individuals who desired it, and they would have been satisfied, because the land was inviting.

Doubtless politics should have influenced the success of the campaign more than arms, but that pursued by the cabinet and the commander in chief was stupid, miserly, ill-conceived, and censurable from all angles. The war to the death that the latter undertook to follow left the enemy the harsh alternatives of vanquishing or perishing, and forced the colonists to unite with the enemy, though the majority were not for independence but rather for the re-establishment of the 1824 Constitution. These were in disagreement with the adventurers who had come from the north because they would attack the colonists' possessions, since, as they had nothing to lose, for them everything was a gain. If General Urrea's pattern of behavior had been followed, the colonists would have submitted without any difficulties, for by his policy he had gained their good will, and as a consequence they gave him important information that

---

[23] Santa Anna's letters of March 23, 1836, two to Urrea and one to Ramírez y Sesma, included as appendix 13 in *La Rebelión de Texas*, declare harsh treatment for the rebels, whose behavior has invalidated the colonization agreement, and give detailed military instructions.—*Ed.*

lead to the success of his campaign, and offered to contribute, by persuading and convincing those of their comrades who still remained in the ranks to leave the armed bands. How much more honorable and expedient would this have been for us than to kill, desolate, and destroy.

Officers who were present when Béjar was besieged in 1835 by the same enemy that we later fought tell of some generous acts he performed: among other things, interrupting hostilities at times to give us a chance to pick up our wounded when he had no way of saving them. After the capitulation, Lieutenant Colonel José María Mendoza, who was later to lose a limb from a cannonball wound received defending the Alamo, was saved, together with other officers, thanks to the diligence and assistance given them by Dr. James Grant. Certainly this conduct is in contrast to that followed by our commander in chief: "I neither ask for nor give quarter," he used to say at Béjar, and he was known to have said once to one of his aides that he would authorize him to strike him with a pistol were he to deviate from his resolution. Certainly he did not maintain this attitude at San Jacinto, where he changed his tune and debased himself to the extreme. In order to save his life, he signed an ignominious agreement that degrades him and is in every way shameful. He has lacked the courage nobly to withstand the misfortune into which his insane vanity drove him; he has shown himself unworthy of the great role that he represented; he has foolishly ruined himself and has tried to involve the nation in his own downfall. Its honor and his own have carried no weight in his mind. By all his deeds he has proved that he deserves his misfortune and that he is far from meriting all the praise bestowed on him; he has shown himself to be of small stature and ignorant of the fact that virtue, even in misfortune, commands the respect of the enemy and that disdain is brought about by lowly deeds.

We now come to one of the incidents that these days has focused the shocked attention of the civilized world, presenting us Mexicans as Hottentots, as savages who do not know how to respect any right. I want to speak of the brutal execution at Goliad, as unnecessary as it was censurable, which so greatly tarnished the noble cause we were defending.

Fannin and his comrades surrendered with the understanding

that their lives would be respected, and although General Urrea had given them no guarantee and the capitulation that they signed was invalid since the latter had not wished to ratify it, they did, nevertheless, trust our overrated generosity in the belief that the intercession of the victor would not be ignored; for if one gave credence to this, they were not so weak that they could not have continued their defense; they could have resolved to die fighting, and such a resolution would have made victory, if not problematic, at least very costly. General Urrea kept his word and interceded for them efficaciously and was particularly interested in Fannin, but the commander in chief denied this reasonable demand, basing his refusal on frivolous pretexts, which he gave in his answer from Béjar on March 24. In the official communication of March 3,[24] he spoke to General Urrea as follows concerning the prisoners at San Patricio: "Regarding the prisoners to whom your Excellency refers in the aforementioned communication, I must remind you of the circular of the Supreme Government stating *That any foreigners invading the Republic be treated and tried as pirates whenever found armed,*' and since, in my estimation, the Mexican who engages in the traitorous act of joining adventurers, as described, loses his rights as citizen according to our laws, the five prisoners to whom your Excellency refers should also be treated likewise."

General Santa Anna, who has always introduced or ignored the law according to his own insidious designs, believed he should respect the barbarous decree that Señor Tornel had made public on the 30th of December 1835. But even this he distorted, declaring on his own that these Mexicans participating in the war had no rights, even though the ostensible purpose of this war was to proclaim the Constitution of 1824, for on the 3rd of March neither we, nor those already taken prisoners, nor those we were fighting at the time could possibly have known that the instigators of the war had on the previous day declared independence. Including the circular that provoked such a misdeed and served as a basis for the perpetration of

---

[24] See *La Rebelión de Texas*, appendix 15, for the texts of both letters. The "frivolous pretexts" to which de la Peña refers are Santa Anna's appeal to the national outrage that would follow if he spared even one of the "foreigners" and his statement that the war is not between brothers, but between nations.—*Ed.*

such horrible crimes, I have deemed it appropriate also to include the comments made about that decree in one of the newspapers of the period,[25] because the arguments with which the writer has opposed it are in my estimation conclusive, and I would not be able to present them with as much precision as the arduous task I have undertaken demands of me. Furthermore, allowing without conceding that the government had the authority to issue such a decree, which, as has been rightly stated, was merely a means by which the legislative power initiated an act contrary to policy and advantage in order to carry out an action in opposition to international law, to humanity, and to the spirit of the century in which we live, an effort should have been made at least to identify the persons. But General Santa Anna completely ignored this, and among those who were led to this barbarous sacrifice were many colonists, among them those who unquestionably enjoyed the rights of Mexican citizens. That is to say, it involved eighty of the ninety-two who on the 22nd had presented themselves to General Urrea without having fired a shot and several Irishmen from the colony of San Patricio who unquestionably supported the Mexican cause and whom the enemy had kept within its ranks by force. General Santa Anna became as furious as a tiger when its prey is taken away, when Captain Don Manuel Sabariego informed him that eighty of the adventurers apprehended at Cópano by a section of General Urrea's division had been spared from the general slaughter. Heroic Fannin! Noble Ward! The barbarity with which you were immolated has been more than avenged! Your blood so infamously spilled has reawakened the crushed spirit of your compatriots. It has stirred in them sufficient wrath, it has inspired them with a desperate resolve to obtain victory, which has cast shame on us and which they would have never accomplished without your sacrifice.

General Santa Anna gave the order in triplicate that the pris-

---

[25] The government circular of December 30, 1835, signed by Santa Anna and Tornel, speaks of open meetings held in the United States to recruit for armed expeditions to Texas, and declares those "crossing our borders or disembarking on our parts, . . . armed for the purpose of attacking us" to be pirates and treated as such (see *La Rebelión de Texas*, appendix 16). Sánchez Garza remarks that the commentary to which de la Peña refers could not be found.—*Ed.*

oners at Goliad be executed. Not satisfied with this, he sent by stagecoach one of his aides, Colonel Miñón, to witness the execution, for he had reached the point of doubting that his bloodthirsty order would be obeyed. But unfortunately it was not so, for in the person of Lieutenant Colonel Nicolás de la Portilla he found a blind and willing servant, as he desired. The latter should have answered as that illustrious commander of Bayonne answered an order of Charles IX, regarding the barbarous St. Bartholomew executions: "My Lord, I have transmitted your Majesty's order to the faithful inhabitants and soldiers of this garrison; among all of them I have found only good citizens and brave soldiers but not a single executioner. They and I humbly beg of your Majesty that you deign to employ our arms and our lives in positive things, no matter how dangerous, and we will sacrifice our last drop of blood." If a reply like this given to an absolute monarch merited universal applause, as Vattel relates, with much more reason should such a reply have been made to a commander in chief in a republic where everyone, from the chief magistrate to the least of citizens, is subject to law. "Obedience should never be absolutely blind," says the same author, "for no superior officer can require or authorize a hundred men to violate natural law, and no one should obey orders obviously in violation of this sacred law."

The order was limited only to those who had surrendered in the action at Perdido and was couched in clear and definite terms; but de la Portilla, wishing to have his zeal recognized and being a man cut out for the duties of an executioner, extended the decree to include the eighty that had arrived with Ward on the very day that he had received the first order. He exempted from the massacre those captured at Cópano, who were invaders and to whom the government's circular really applied, because he believed it his duty to inquire what fate should befall them, but he did not have the same consideration for those prisoners who had just arrived from Victoria, among whom were colonists and the circumstances surrounding whose capture he ignored. What ignorance can be capable of! How true it is that in order to follow the honorable profession of arms men should know more than how to obey blindly. Truth is the most desirable demand of history, but I have been unable to ascertain until now the exact number of men with whose sacrifice the Passion of

Christ was commemorated on Palm Sunday, the 27th of March 1836. In spite of all the investigations that I have carried out, I have not obtained a satisfactory result, so I am obliged to present facts only, in order for the reader to decide for himself.

According to General Urrea's communiqué those surrendering on the 20th were about 400 men, and according to my investigations there were 365, but the commander in chief in the report mentioned above mentions barely 234 men. However, it may be that all the prisoners had not arrived when Colonel Garay reported in advance, according to instructions he had received from General Urrea at the battlefield, since it was impossible for Urrea to dispatch it at that moment. Lieutenant Colonel de la Portilla, in that part of his diary which is included in the documents and which one should consult,[26] says that at dawn on the 26th he resolved to comply with the order issued by the commander in chief, considering it to take precedence over everything (doubtless also over humanity and the laws), that he ordered all the garrison into formation and the prisoners, who numbered 445 and were still asleep, to be awakened and the 80 apprehended at Cópano to be separated, for the reason already mentioned. I am inclined to believe that this number 80 is not included in the 445, because, allowing that only 234 had been sent from Perdido, with 80 sent from Victoria and a like number from Cópano, the total reaches 394, a number less than that Portilla refers to. Now adding the 375 that surrendered at Perdido with the 80 from Victoria, the total comes to 445, the number here referred to; if we add those from Cópano, it yields a total of 525, a figure over the one mentioned. Let the reader thus judge from what has been said; and since I have already referred to the immorality of this action, let him permit me to relate the cruel way in which it was carried out and share with me the sorrow that always seizes me whenever I must recall this bloody scene. I described it at the very scene, after interviewing many eyewitnesses, and for that reason I consider sufficient what is found in my diary, which is as follows.

Goliad, May 22nd. Until today (a month ago, according to the date, we received news of the disaster at San Jacinto) I have not

---

[26] See *La Rebelión de Texas*, appendix 16, document 2, for the extract from de la Portilla's diary, March 24–27, 1836.—*Ed.*

been able to assemble the data that would allow me to speak with truth about the enemy prisoners who were executed at this place. According to all opinions, there were 425 or 427 in all, of whom 80 or 90 were wounded. These, among whom was their commander, were executed within the fort. Lamenting their sufferings, most of them dragging themselves along, they were taken out of the hospital one by one and thrown into the clutches of death. There were some, unable to stand upright, to kneel, or to sit, who were killed in their own beds, which is quite credible, since most of the wounded could keep themselves in no other position than lying in bed. The rest, divided into three parties, were led in different directions, having been told at the moment they were led out of their beds, for some were still asleep, that they were going to be taken to Matamoros. They were requested to take their knapsacks to make them believe this unworthy falsehood, which they so trusted that they started singing as they began their march; these poor unfortunates little suspected that they were marching to their execution. Upon arriving at a certain place, they were lined up in rows with their backs to the troops, but since these were in equal number, or perhaps fewer than the prisoners, there was hardly one man for each victim, so the scene was most horrible. One of the officials in charge of the execution acted in advance of the agreed hour, and since he was close to those who were to be made victims, they heard the firing clearly enough to know its cause; the rest, growing suspicious, were overcome with terror, suffering the anguish and cruel torments inspired by their situation. It is rather strange that they did not decide to fall upon the troops and to die fighting, as other men would have done in similar unfortunate circumstances. Some chose to run away at the first shots, but the infantry and dragoons pursued them on the plain, hunting them as wild beasts, so that some died at a distance from the assigned place. One hundred and twenty-five of these unfortunates being tied up when the others fled, and during this operation they witnessed the flight of their companions who were trying to escape the infamous death so closely threatening them. Cavalry Captain Don Pedro Balderas, in charge of the executions, spoke to them to inform them of the savage decree that condemned them, but ignorant of the language, they died unaware of its contents, which added further injury to their misfortune. Their gesticulations and signs were the only language they could employ to arouse the sympathy of their executioners and to implore the mercy of the Mexicans. They trusted that their lives would be spared, and for that reason they did not attempt flight, which they could have accomplished on earlier days, for some were free to enter and to leave the fort and not a single one forfeited his word. They trusted our generosity too much, but they were misled.

The soldiers from Tres Villas and Yucatán and some pickets from the regiments of Cuautla, Tampico, and the active from Durango, whose unlucky lot it was to be the executioners, say that they were greatly moved upon being required to perform a duty so alien to their rules, so degrading to brave soldiers, but in my opinion they should not be blamed for having obeyed. Doubtless none of this group had to do with the execution of Fannin. When he was informed of the order for his execution, he received it calmly and merely asked for enough time to write a farewell letter to his wife and another to General Santa Anna, in which he declared that he was not for the independence of Texas and that he died a victim of his love for the Constitution of 1824, under the auspices of which he had come to the country and for which he went to the sacrifice gladly.[27]

Fannin marched to the place of execution, a few paces from the room where he was lodged, with great courage and firmness, which brought on the admiration of those who led him to the sacrifice and who witnessed it. There he requested that they call Lieutenant Colonel Nicolás de la Portilla, commander of the post, so that he could give him his watch and request that it, together with the letter he had written, be sent to his wife as his last manifestation of tenderness; but the captain of Tres Villas, Don Carolino Huerta, who was to order the execution, cruelly denied him this favor, though he knew that all requests should be granted to those agonizing in their last moments. Adding to his baseness, not to call it crime, he kept for himself the watch and also the ten pesos Fannin gave him to comply with the request that they aim at his head and his

---

[27] There is no doubt that this took place, although I have found it impossible to locate copies of these documents and I do not know that they reached the persons to whom they were addressed. Write to Portilla concerning them.

89

heart. Some have increased this amount to seventy, and I have been assured of this by a captain belonging to the same corps as Huerta, but depositions taken from several persons reaffirm the first statement. Fannin was one of those who had trusted our supposed humanitarianism; one had often heard him say, "Oh, I have great faith in the honor and character of all Mexicans."

William Ward, Fannin's second in command, and seventy-nine of the men under his orders, including those with officer's rank, who had been captured on the 22nd of March at Las Juntas Creek without firing a shot, were included in the sacrifice made to the Divinity on the same Palm Sunday of the same month.

Among all these men so inhumanly sacrificed there were colonists, but the majority were volunteers, among whom there were some in fair economic position. In general, they were men of good stature, robust and well built, but in the description given by those who knew them, special attention is given to two very young men who appeared to be as dainty as two damsels because of their fine-textured skin and delicate features. There were also many craftsmen who could have been most useful had they been placed in public shops for the education of our craftsmen and for the production of uniforms, supplies, and armaments for the army; keeping these men as prisoners would have been an advantageous victory for the commander in chief. One had to possess the heart of a tiger to be able to sign three times an order to immolate so many victims, and that of a wild beast in order to execute it. Among those who perished were some Irishmen, whom the enemy had held in their ranks by force.

Among the few who were saved from the catastrophe were two surgeons who took care of our wounded, one of whom experienced the grief of seeing two of his sons perish; when the same man who had given the order of execution conveyed his good wishes to that surgeon for having been spared, the latter, his eyes clouded with tears and moved by paternal love, answered that he wished he had been executed with them or in their stead. Other surgeons were shot at a time when general headquarters and the whole army were in need of their services, a topic about which so much could be said that it is better to pass over it now and do so another time. Some of the colonists were accidentally saved: those whom General Urrea took with him, who were very useful during the march, acting as sappers, a few others hidden by Colonel Garay, and those who were able to flee at the moment of sacrifice; to speak the truth, it would have been better had they not escaped so they would not have been able to paint such a horrible picture for their comrades.

The same general who had vanquished and made prisoners of these men tried to save them because, as his bravery in combat is outstanding, so also is his humanity away from it praiseworthy, and because he foresaw both the infamy that would mar his country's history with so many cold-blooded murders and the consequences of war to the death. With this in mind, he wrote the commander in chief, presenting his respects and referring to the services he had just rendered; he was interested in all, and particularly in Fannin, but he was ignored and in reply he received nothing but reproach. Nevertheless, the enemy will respect his memory and posterity will do him justice. Seventy-eight or eighty men taken prisoners at Cópano under the same terms as Ward and his companions had the good fortune to escape and remained during this incident under cover of some peach trees facing the fort and in the very center of the places of execution.

The friendship that I bear Señor de la Portilla has not released me from the obligation of denouncing him before the whole world for having committed a crime against humanity, for it has been shown that he exceeded himself in carrying out the order he received. He could have won honorable renown had he refused to serve as an executioner, but since he felt it his duty to carry out such a painful office, he could have and should have done it in a less cruel fashion. Moments afterward he apparently repented, for he confessed later in a personal communication addressed to General Urrea to have been horror-stricken and lamented the fact that such an odious role should have been his lot.[28]

I am glad to say that there were few who gave approval to the carnage at Goliad and other similar instances. The army in general was stirred up and raised its voice to condemn it, for it wished

---

[28] Portilla's letter to Urrea dated March 27, 1836, from Goliad appears as document 2 in *La Rebelión de Texas*, appendix 17.—*Ed.*

to distinguish itself, to make its wrath and power known at the moment of combat, but to exercise clemency and moderation with the vanquished. It recognized that the nation it defended should make itself respected and obeyed because of illustrious worth, for its gestures of compassion and humanity and not for its cruelty and terror. The cry of horror that the Republic raised and the indignation of the civilized world made us tremble and look upon each other with disdain. So many and such cold-blooded murders tarnished our glory, took away the fruits of victory, and would prolong the war and make its success doubtful, because it provoked the enemy and placed him in the difficult dilemma of vanquishing or dying. What opprobrium, it was said, to appear in the nineteenth century as barbarous as the Middle Ages! Much like a horde of Hottentots and assassins. In the communication of the 21st that General Urrea transmitted from Victoria regarding this encounter, he concluded thus: "For the present there is only one thing left for me to do: to emphasize, in general, the fearlessness and valor of the brave leaders, officers, and soldiers who with such great honor and determination were able to bring to the action of the 19th that courage which characterizes the Mexican Army, following this courage with the most admirable indulgence toward a vanquished enemy. This gesture of generosity after such a hard-fought battle is most worthy of the most singular commendation, and I can do no less than commend it especially to your Excellency, begging you at the same time to have due consideration for the families of the brave men who gave up their lives in defense of their country's rights, an account of which I will dispatch to your Excellency in due time."

Some of our wounded soldiers gave worthy lessons in humanity to our leader and his obedient agent, laudably resolving to place in their beds and cover with their own bodies three or four of the enemy who happened to be in the hospital with them. What a pity that such commendable actions were so few in number, and what a pity likewise not to know the names of those charitable souls who did this. The ladies at Matamoros also rendered homage to humanity by signing a petition in behalf of the captives that General Urrea had imprisoned, by this means not only postponing the execution but in the end saving them.

It is very painful to me to acknowledge that this general

tarnished his laurels by giving in to the excitement of some of the officers regarding the fulfillment of the government decree and the orders of the commander in chief affecting some thirty of those taken prisoner at the mission at Refugio. It is true that this took place under difficult circumstances, since he was being threatened by the enemy from several points and could not muster more than a small force, of which he could not possibly relinquish even a small portion for the custody of these prisoners; and also that only those who fell under the government decree were executed; the colonists and Mexicans were set free.

We have mentioned earlier that the commander in chief had already brought upon himself the ill will of the army; the hatred for him was found even among his friends and intimates, for his aides frequently would try to avoid serving as his guards or being near him. General Castrillón had been one of the men most loyal to General Santa Anna, and he met death against his will, ultimately expressing himself acridly against him and wishing not to follow him anymore.[29] The same could be said about Colonel Don José Batres and others. When, on the 21st of March, general headquarters rendered tribute to the kindly General Barragán, interim president of the Republic, the commander in chief rebuked all his aides and insulted even those closest to him in the presence of all the leaders and officers who attended this ceremony. General Castrillón was the only one who had the courage to confront him with the indecorous treatment that he was giving them, so his Excellency appeared as having repented, admitting that it was not within his power to control his irascible character, which circumstances had only made worse. He lamented the indifference with which his military family looked upon him and begged indulgence, and thus succeeded in quieting animosities and in winning over to his side his aides-de-camp, so that they would not be drawn to opinions other than those his acts had led them to entertain. Some of the military, though few in number, spoke of crowning him at the conclusion of the campaign and presented this extravagant idea as something right and necessary; but they soon changed their minds after the subsequent conduct of their hero. The ideas of his parasites were flatter-

---

[29] Manuel Fernández Castrillón was killed at San Jacinto.—*Ed.*

ing to him, but he nevertheless expressed himself in favor of establishing a government just and ready to act; he ridiculed the idea of establishing a power that would be responsible only to God for its operations and spoke bitterly against liberal principles because they had caused so much blood to be shed; and perhaps he might have reached the heights to which he aspired if the framework had not collapsed on the fields of San Jacinto. The bloody scenes at Goliad and their like seemed to have been designed to terrorize the Mexicans or to condition them to such horrible spectacles.

Because of his decision in favor of the Texas campaign, General Arago joined it in spite of his ill health, which was further aggravated during the marches, and from Monclova on he was prostrate and in pain. With many difficulties he arrived at Béjar, where he remained constantly bedridden. At night the generals and top-ranking army leaders would visit his quarters, and General Filisola lived with him, and the commander in chief himself would come occasionally, so I had an opportunity of becoming acquainted with the opinion of the army. At such times, all would speak freely; subjects of importance arose and were heatedly discussed, and most of the time well-founded arguments came forth. Most of the visitors there would criticize the decisions of the general in chief, and rarely did anyone concur with his opinions. General Arago, if I may be permitted to render tribute to the memory of the virtuous man whom I esteemed and who in turn esteemed me, might be compared, in regard to General Santa Anna, to the illustrious Laudon, who so efficaciously contributed to the glory of the wise Joseph II, worthy successor of the great Frederick, for he could be a conqueror at the same time that he attracted esteem and commanded respect. The success of the Texas campaign would certainly have been different had this unfortunate general not been prevented by his illness from influencing it.

Also, if the commander in chief had returned to Mexico as he had thought of doing, and which was taken as a foregone conclusion after the death of the interim president and the engagement at Perdido, very probably the campaign would have ended successfully, because the second in command would have given ear to the recommendations of his colleagues and would have conducted himself wisely, if slowly; he would not have been bewildered, as our commander in chief was, with the death blow that we received, nor would he have incurred the grave errors that the latter committed as a result of this; the misfortune at San Jacinto would never have happened, with so much shame and such opprobium following it; so many sacrifices would not have been in vain nor so much precious blood shed uselessly.

It must be noted that the commander in chief, with no pre-arranged plan and no firm base of operations, did not believe the campaign to be ended until he learned of the action on March 19, which is proved by his order of the 25th that the cavalry brigade, the artillery, the munition dump of the corps and their pickets return to San Luis Potosí, as well as by instructions given to the generals the 23rd of that month.

It was at least believed, and it was so stated in the army, that the jealousy inspired by General Urrea and the reproachable conduct of General Ramírez y Sesma forced him to alter the decision he had made to return to Mexico and leave General Filisola in command. He well knew how much he was being censured because of the costly and unnecessary sacrifices at the Alamo, and the wish to forget this blot, the fear that General Urrea would bring the campaign to an end, since up to now he had done almost everything, and the uneasiness brought on by the exaggerated news about Ramírez y Sesma are probably the causes that forced him to continue the march.

## ৺৪ 8 ৪৵

THE Sapper Battalion and the active from Guadalajara were the only infantry corps remaining at Béjar, but on the 27th of March orders were received to march toward Austin under the command of Colonel Agustín Amat. On the 28th a review of the army was held, and on the 29th, after the commanding general himself had reviewed the troops, the march was initiated at four o'clock, with one howitzer, twenty dragoons, and the pickets of all the corps that had already marched, a total force of 550 men. We had with us fifty boxes of ammunition, half rations of *condochi* [a thick corn tortilla] and beans, and one hundred *fanegas* [about 250 bushels] of corn, with a definite order not to touch them. On that day we camped at the Salado Creek after a march of seven miles.

Before continuing the entry from my diary and making the reflections that this always bring about, I must declare that on the 31st the general in chief left Béjar with his second in command and his general staff. On the 2nd of April he arrived at the Guadalupe River and on the 3rd marched toward the Colorado, leaving General Filisola with the brigade that Colonel Amat led. The disorder with which the advance was made was great; no military posts or communication points were established. Our soldiers suffered great privations as a result of the criminal indifference with which they were looked upon, when their needs could have been remedied by gathering the corn that was plentiful all around and by the herds of pigs and cattle found in abundance. In spite of all this and the fact that the soldiers were poorly attended, they were forced to work unfairly, and without the least consideration. These chores were exceedingly arduous, especially at the river crossings, during which the Guadalajara Battalion was outstanding in its perseverance and patience. This group was the worst provided for; the majority of its soldiers wore their jackets next to their skins, and their shoes and uniforms, whether worn out in their toil or taken because of a lack

96

of police vigilance, were never replaced. There was no consideration whatever for the excess loads with which the soldier was burdened, and it is public knowledge how much these unfortunates were the object of constant exploitation.

As a proof of what has been stated, I now insert verbatim what is found in my diary, beginning with our departure from Béjar until our arrival at the Brazos River.

On the 30th of March, the day began with abundant rain but our march continued; by three o'clock in the afternoon we had had several violent storms, which made the road impassable and the march cumbersome. As commanding officer of the brigade, I advanced to Cibolo Creek in order to reconnoiter the ground, and during two hours in the afternoon, in the neighborhood of the road, I saw hundreds of buffalo in herds. I arrived at the creek at nightfall; by eight o'clock the brigade had arrived after a march of over twenty miles.

On the 31st, Maundy Thursday, we left Cibolo, camping at a spot with an unknown name, where there were only a few puddles of rainwater for man and beast; then we marched sixteen to eighteen miles. Here I omit the cause which placed my life in danger part of that day and that night, and this because it is a purely personal matter.

On the first day of this month (April) we camped in another place equally unknown, but both are encircled by the Encinal and the Carrizal. We reached it between five and six in the evening, and before giving up the march we met four countrymen leading more than three hundred head of cattle which they had picked up on the way, most of them beautiful breeding cows. We took three calves to pacify the hunger of our soldiers, who had not eaten meat since the day before we left Béjar.

On the 2nd, the Saturday before Easter, it was raining and we did not leave camp until the rain had ceased. We must have covered eight or nine miles when the president, who with his general staff had slept at a distance of six or seven miles from our rear guard, caught up with us. Since the previous day we had posted a dragoon, who was to come in all haste to notify us of his Excellency's approach; thus it was that on this occasion we saw something never

97

before seen; that is, a march stopped in order to honor the general in chief. The effort put forth made me feel that he was more a prince than a republican leader. If such action deserves to be censured, my own accomplished it at that moment, since I refused to pay tribute to his Majesty. For two hours before arriving at the Guadalupe Pass, we followed the edge of this beautiful river, whose banks have a picturesque forest; we crossed equally beautiful plains, and truly, the whole trek was pleasant. From this day, especially, some of the men confessed that the country was beautiful, although a few days before we had been condemning it, without taking into account that the increasing hardships that plagued the campaign were due to the misery and the disorderly manner in which we were led; had we been well organized, the Texas campaign would have been a delightful trek, a series of pleasant days in the country interspersed with military maneuvers. For me it was a very bitter day, because one of his Excellency's adjutants, Colonel Manuel de la Portilla, assured me that the order to shoot all the prisoners held at La Bahía had been carried out, and with compassion he told me several details that made this barbarous execution seem cruel and touching.

"Let us hope that we shall not have to pay for this," I said to Colonel de la Portilla, "for the sins and barbarity of this man!" referring to General Santa Anna.[30] Having arrived around three in the afternoon at the Guadalupe Pass, we stayed there because the water was too high to cross. I scouted the woods to find another way and spoke with my friend Colonel Francisco González Pavón, who was on the other bank, whence he sent us meat for the troops.

On the 3rd the general in chief marched in the direction of San Felipe de Austin, leaving behind the second in command, and barges were built in order to take the ammunition and other loads across at the upper crossing, since the river continued too high and the lower crossing was impassable.

The Guadalajara Battalion, however, was able to cross it at midday, with the aid of a rope and the sappers; one section crossed to the left bank and the other remained on the right at the upper pass. At night I fell into the river fully clothed and ran some risk

---

[30] Colonel Portilla must have recalled many times during his imprisonment our reflections of this day.

of being caught under one of the barges loaded with artillery and not being able to save myself, for although I am not a great swimmer, I am not the worst. Twice I crossed the river.

The 4th, although all the convoy had not yet been taken across, the greater part had been transferred to the left bank, or better yet, to the ruins of Gonzales where we remained the 5th, so that we spent two nights on one bank and two on the other. From Béjar came two eight-pounders, and they were also taken across. Reflections for the day: If the banks of the Guadalupe, going from Béjar to Austin, are extremely beautiful because the winding of the river and undulation of the woods, all of which created a beautiful contrast with its green valleys, the area in which the town of Gonzales was situated is no less pleasant. All the dwellings close to the two crossings had been burned, but those situated at some distance at both the lower and upper part of the river were still standing. In them were found pieces of furniture, not elegant but rather for daily use. There was a great abundance of pigs and chickens, which the soldiers went after hungrily.

The stock was beautiful and the meat had an exquisite taste. In Gonzales and its surroundings there were hundreds of head of cattle; nevertheless, meat was rationed to the soldier as if a purchase price had been paid for it. Some officers cried out that Colonel González Pavón had set himself up as the owner of the goods and food he had found along the way and that he would fuss and curse if he were given orders to release any of this for their sustenance. He had corralled about three hundred dairy cows and was accused of preferring to let the calves suck rather than let the officers drink the milk.[31] A few days before we arrived at Gonzales, Generals

---

[31] Those who spoke thus did not know that Colonel González Pavón had proposed the formation of a colony at Gonzales with his regiment, a proposition which, though it might have been aimed at advancing his own interests, should have been accepted because it was useful. For this reason he tried to have only those cattle which were needed slaughtered. This was the thing to do, so as not to waste them as had so frequently happened, which will be seen later. Furthermore, it was stated that the commanding general had given him between eight hundred and a thousand head, and that the greater part of these Señor Pavón brought to Béjar. It was said that General Santa Anna could hardly give away what was not his, but he did, and it was not Señor Pavón's place to advise him of it.

Ramírez y Sesma and and Tolsa had passed by, and the troops under their command had consumed and taken with them everything they could, and Señor González Pavón, who arrived afterward, found many shanks of pork and loads of corn in the neighboring dwellings.

We suppress here the narrative, found in the diary, of the misery in which the army found itself and the way it left Béjar, because this has already been mentioned. For the same reason it should be sufficient to add that as the officers arrived at Gonzales without having a bite to eat or the means with which to make a tortilla, it was ordered that they be given a few handfuls of corn, though Colonel González Pavón had some loads stored that should have been given for the sustenance of the troops, since it was obvious that on returning to Béjar he would have ample time to replenish the supply.

On the morning of the 5th a barge that had foundered between the two river passes was retrieved, fitted, and taken to the upper pass. This discovery caused a wave of general rejoicing, since it would shorten the march; had it been found a few days before, it would have eliminated much effort.

General Filisola personally worked with Lieutenant Colonel Ampudia and myself, and out of his own pocket and through me rewarded the soldiers who substituted as workers and swimmers. During the afternoon this barge transported what was left to move of the artillery equipment and the transport wagons that had arrived with it the day before, and likewise the stock of the canteen of Quartermaster General Don Ricardo Dromundo, which was being transported in two wagons, and that of a clerk to Don Antonio Tayafé, who was nicknamed "El Curro."

On the 6th, through the stupidity of the wagon bosses, which had rendered the barge useless the previous night, an early repair was necessary in order to take across the three more wagons that remained. This operation once completed and the brigade mules and the transport wagons reloaded with the ammunition, we resumed our march at ten in the morning. All along the road we found dwellings of frame construction, some well built; there were several barns full of cotton, a great deal of it already ginned and carded; spinning wheels for weaving and coffee grinders were found in most of these houses. Everything found in them was unequivocal testimony to the industry and diligence of the unfortunate families who had abandoned them. Some miles above Gonzales two sawmills were also found. The thinking and sensible man, the Mexican who loves his native land and understands its true interests, could do no less than lament and weep with heartfelt tears the destruction of developing establishments which, having in themselves the elements of progress, would have flourished in a few years into populous and wealthy cities. It is true that the circumstances of the war had brought things to this extreme, but it is also true that with a less dastardly policy this war so ruinous to the nation could have been avoided and the enemy still defeated. The construction of corrals for the stock and the fences around arable lands seemed astonishing to our eyes because they were so different from those we were used to seeing in the interior of the Republic. Some of the wood was cylindrical in shape and driven perpendicularly into the ground, but most of them were triangular or rectangular prisms placed horizontally and forming a line which in fortification construction we designate as saw tooths, an example of the union of symmetry with solidity. It is not easy to estimate during a march, so I have been unable to do it, the amounts of cotton and corn that had been harvested from the Guadalupe to the Colorado, but there is no doubt that around Gonzales it exceeded the amount of forty thousand *arrobas* [one *arroba* equals twenty-five pounds]. I must add that this estimate differs from the opinion of Colonel González Pavón, who had the advantage of having looked over the vicinity of the village, but it is in accord with that of some of the colonists. Here I must comment and at the same time elaborate on my ideas of the past days concerning military colonies and the benefits that could be derived from them by utilizing these men who have been so inhumanly ruined and whose blood, once shed, would result in nothing but evil. Gathering the goods and capitalizing on their use once the campaign is ended would amply repay its expenses. Today we camped at Tejocote Creek, having traveled fourteen miles; the pigs found at this place were as big as a five or six month's calf. All the road was woody with red and white oak trees except close to the creek, where, as it happens in extensive woods, there were other trees, about which I shall speak again because of their beauty.

On the 7th we started our march at eight o'clock in the morning, and after a small wooded area, we passed through some prairies so beautiful that I lack words to describe them. It was all a field of lilies and poppies of an exquisite and unique variety, not only in their varied colors but also because of the forms nature had given them. The soul expanded, and it is difficult to explain the joy that it felt in its enchantment. Admirer as I am of all that is beautiful, an enthusiast to such an extreme that a burning imagination and a sensitive soul live in unison in me; being at the head of a sapper unit and extraordinarily affected by what my eyes admired, and seized by an enthusiasm bordering on insanity; I called to the soldiers to shoot me, that I might be buried in this vast garden, so beautifully interrupted by woods. Aside from the house located at Tejocote, on this day we only found one that had been set on fire and another still habitable. Out of sheer pleasure I dismounted to make the trip; although toward the end I became tired, I kept on because of an agreement with one of my companions; to overcome my fatigue, General Filisola invited me to have lunch. We encamped at Vaca Creek after having traveled fifteen or sixteen miles. There were two houses standing at the banks of the creek and a beautiful hillock around which we pitched camp. A cavalry officer from Ramírez y Sesma's division brought us news of little interest.

On the 8th we left at the same hour, always traveling among flowers where there was a prairie and under a pleasant canopy where there were woods. We halted in order to organize a passage over a creek, the name of which I did not know. I was not able to prevent women and some soldiers not in the ranks from destroying some dressers and other fine pieces of furniture found in one of the houses on our path. There we were able to round up a considerable herd of tame livestock, which we added to that already in our possession. We camped on the left bank of Navidad Creek after we had traveled twelve miles. We also found houses that had been burned, and one usable but without furniture. There were also tilled fields, and in one of these we found the corpse of a man that must have belonged to Ramírez y Sesma's division.

On the 9th we left Navidad, leaving behind the wagons that had been unable to make the crossing of the creek, and marched along an ever-changing and beautiful road; but nothing was as lovely as a little wooded spot, very dense, with a tree whose leaves and color are very similar to the orange tree, which formed a narrow path so that the road seemed to have a canopy, and walking under it was so delightful and enchanting that I was sorry when it came to an end. On the road, General Filisola received the post, which informed him that the general in chief had arrived at San Felipe de Austin, and that the enemy, after having set fire to that city, had retreated to the other side of the Brazos River, where he remained. The same mail declared that a message sent by General Gaona stated that his brigade had found the dwellings on the march to Nacogdoches so well supplied that neither the officers nor the soldiers had any more space in which to carry furniture and effects and were being forced to abandon them. This day the road, though pleasant, was also difficult because of the many mudholes that slowed the march. We arrived at eight in the evening at the edge of a forest on the Colorado, and I retreated one league to where a field piece had got stuck in the mud, so that I could guide it, along with the mules that were carrying the ammunition and baggage; they had become lost in the darkness and in the extreme disorder had bogged down in the mire.

Bad luck always led to disorder, for when the road was good we made moderate marches, but the march had to be forced when the road was impassable, as happened on this day. The Sapper Battalion received orders to advance to the edge of the river. The night was dark and the forest very dense and swampy, which caused much suffering and finally the dispersal of the men. I protested on the spot an order that was against all prudence and would render the soldier useless in case of need, as actually happened, leaving him without food at the end of a long march. The order was given to arm, although according to the news received there was nothing to fear. The general passed to the other side of the river, where General Woll awaited with a cavalry unit.

On the afternoon of the 10th we got close to the lower bank of the river by a new road that we had opened along an oblique line that morning, traveling through about one mile of a most delightful forest, like the one on the Guadalupe but of greater expanse. The size of all the forests we have seen has always been in proportion to that of the rivers. The artillery and part of the sappers crossed to the left bank. The battalion from Guadalajara and the supplies and ammunition remained at the entrance of the forest. We spent the night on the left bank.

On the 11th we took all the ammunition across from the right to the left bank and with us (the main staff), the remainder of the sappers. We met several natives, a mulatto woman, two Negro women, and several Negro men, who were very useful in making the crossing and who washed our clothes. On this day one company from Guadalajara crossed and another came near the right bank for the crossing. We assembled a tent under a large shady tree and the commander of artillery did likewise under another. We set up camp in a small valley surrounded by forest.

On the 12th the crossings continued, and I met two young boys of ten or twelve years who lived in one of the dwellings on the banks of the river and who, having gone hunting, returned to find their parents gone. Looking for help where they knew people lived, they ran into the troops. They assured me that several families had fled. Through the compassion that is naturally aroused by the sad plight of orphans, I asked to take one of them and that one of my companions should take the other, but we were told that they were to leave the next day with a Frenchman, who had already taken charge of them the day before and who had himself escaped from the enemy, leaving with them his wife and six children, three of them adopted.

On the 13th the wagons that had joined us the previous day crossed, together with everything else that had remained on the right bank; the cattle were left behind because all efforts to take them across proved in vain. A message arrived from General Ramírez y Sesma which informed us that the general in chief had crossed the Brazos at Orazimbo. Reveille was sounded by the bugles because of this incident, and there were artillery salvos, as though a great victory were being celebrated.[32]

On the 14th the march was continued, the vanguard having

---

[32] The commander in chief crossed the Brazos River at Thompson's Pass and no section of the army went to Orazimbo.

begun at nine and the rear guard at ten on account of the confusion caused by transferring the loads from the mules to the wagons. At one o'clock in the afternoon we arrived at Arenoso Creek, where General Filisola was knocked to the ground by the shaft of a cart. We should have camped there, but because of the distance to the wood supply, we continued to San Felipe de Austin, where our vanguard arrived before dark. We traveled about twenty-eight to thirty miles across an immense plain that extended over the horizon. On the right bank one could barely see some woods, and during parts of the day we could see our left bank. Just before sundown we were able to see the bank of the Brazos River, but by sunset we could make out some truncated pyramids that turned out to be the chimneys of houses in what had been the township of San Felipe. Before finding them our eyes searched impatiently for those ruins, which were discovered on a small hill with a gentle incline adjoining the river at the edge of the plain we had crossed. Before we arrived all this appeared picturesque, and one could see great numbers of cattle to both right and left. Upon arrival the first sight that presented itself to my eyes was that of a fine and beautiful dog next to a cat, both with a most mournful expression; no doubt they wept for the absence of their masters and lamented their loss.

On the 15th at seven o'clock in the morning, while concluding my notes on the events of the previous day, I heard voices of alarm and left my tent hurriedly. Its cause was the passing of an enemy steamboat, which had not been even remotely anticipated.[33] The soldiers forming the advance posts on the river, who belonged to the Guadalajara Battalion, were dumbfounded by the sight of a machine so totally unfamiliar and unexpected. The other soldiers who saw it were likewise surprised. Few in the camp were acquainted with steamboats, so all was in confusion. Immediately a detachment was dispatched to that bank of the river away from the woods, which was like running after a bird; General Filisola thus showed his ignorance of the speed with which steam engines can travel, the more so as the steamboat was moving with the current.

A shot from the eight-pounder was fired, which served only to

---

[33] The steamboat was the *Yellow Stone*, heading downstream after it had been impressed by Houston to ferry his troops across the Brazos.—*Ed.*

let them know that we had artillery to fire at a target. Because we arrived at San Felipe de Austin at nightfall, I could observe nothing then. During today's morning hours and before the incident of the steamboat, I visited the ruins hurriedly; since these had been frame buildings with chimneys of brick, a few of the latter remained, the ones we had identified some distance before our arrival. I could not estimate the exact number of houses that had been there, but it was my impression that there were fifty in all. Some of these no doubt had been beautiful and comfortable, but one especially, located a hundred feet from the river, gave an idea of its magnificence; it had a cellar with brick walls of about thirty cubic feet. As in the town of Gonzales, there were numerous tools for different purposes, but principally for wagons and plows. There was also machinery, which had been destroyed, and a great assortment of nails and iron bars in the rough, so that many families might have made a fortune collecting the stuff found in Gonzales and San Felipe de Austin. In these latter ruins there were several peach orchards and vegetable gardens, some planted with sweet and Irish potatoes. In front of the pass, there was a house and evidence of a trench built by the enemy.

The great heaps of broken china indicated where its store rooms had been and also that some families must have possessed splendid table services. Let me say in conclusion, to be amplified later, that the fruits of many years of hard work had been destroyed in one moment of madness. Those who had dared to insult the nation that had taken them to its bosom forgot in their recklessness the victims that they would offer up for sacrifice.

The general had intended that we should wait in San Felipe de Austin for the wagons that had remained behind, but the incident of the steamboat made him change his mind, so we began the march hurriedly around ten o'clock in the morning. We advanced close to the course of the river through a plain surrounded by woods, which seemed more like a garden. One could see at a distance abundant cattle on the banks that we followed, and it invited compassion to see them wandering as aimlessly as their owners. About nine or ten miles from San Felipe de Austin and under the cover of a beautiful little wooded area was a lovely house with its vegetable garden and many flowers, all of which indicated that it had been occupied by industrious women. It had two barns full of cotton.

San Felipe de Austin, as we have mentioned before, is situated on a small hill covered by a forest which stretches out to its right, and at a distance of three miles there was also a well-constructed house tastefully furnished. The friend who visited it gave a glowing description of it. He said that there were many hogs and chickens and that the cattle were so domesticated that they rushed up to anyone coming near the house, thinking they were the owners. That day we camped at a burned farm called the Arroyo del Molino, a distance of twenty or twenty-one miles from San Felipe. On the road we met some cavalry of the Tampico Regiment under the command of Captain Valera, who was going at the request of General Gaona.

April 17th, in the morning, at Thompson's Pass (Old Fort) on the Brazos River. At the entrance of a forest, where my ears rejoiced with the chirping of a multitude of birds whose beautiful colors at times greatly delighted my eyes, with a tree trunk for a table and another as chair, I continued my diary. Yesterday between seven and eight in the morning we left the Arroyo del Molino in the midst of a severe storm that pursued us more than half the way, and at two in the afternoon we arrived at this spot after having marched from fourteen to fifteen miles. From the ruins of San Felipe de Austin we marched along the river, sometimes getting away as far as one, two, and even three miles, then getting so near again we could see the water's edge where there was an opening in the forest. The San Antonio River being an exception, the Guadalupe, Colorado, and Brazos rivers have no banks, but steep cliffs instead, even close to the passes, in some cases as high as thirty feet. On the road we met the officers who had come on the 10th to notify the general about the unlucky encounter with the steamboat. They brought us wine in quantity, and we learned through them that they had attributed the effects of the storm to cannon shots; that the aforementioned general had been notified that the steamboat had to pass by the place where he was; but that they were unable to do it any harm, in spite of the fact that they had prepared for it. About eight or ten miles down the road we found near an arroyo a house belonging to a widow who, according to the testimony of a prisoner, was a young woman of beautiful stature, but according to that of a woman was middle-aged. What left no doubt was that her house was beautifully situated, with a beautiful vegetable garden, a peach orchard, and

107

all its fields beautifully cultivated. I was assured that the cattle alone of this fine estate were worth between seventy and eighty thousand dollars. What we were able to see was beyond calculation, and the author writing this suffered greatly to see so many fine possessions abandoned, and was forced to reflect sadly about his country. We learned from what these officers said that the troops of Generals Ramírez y Sesma and Tolsa, consisting of over one hundred from the first Matamoros Battalion and eight selected companies from other undermanned corps, had collected some of the effects that had not been molested by the general in chief. We also knew that dwellings on the right shore of the river had wines in abundance, equipment, and furniture quaint as well as useful. On the road we met some of the soldiers who had been sent to inspect these dwellings, shamelessly inebriated, the ones under orders of the generals already mentioned. Shortly after General Filisola arrived, the brigade arrived and was ordered to camp on the bank of the river; the artillery and the sappers were transferred to the left bank; but when they gave this order, the initiators forgot that the troops were in bad shape and wet, that they needed to restore their strength and had to be fed before returning to fatigue duty, and that for all this time is needed, the lack which prevented the crossing from being made. The dwellings in the vicinity of the right bank were 450 to 500 paces distant, but before I approached them, I went to inspect a cotton gin, and there I found an infirmary, known as a hospital; it had no surgeon, no medicines, and no food for the patients, and in order to make room for these articles, part of the cotton gin had been destroyed. When we arrived the only topic of conversation was the steamboat: we discussed the surprise we had received at San Felipe de Austin and here, the firing that the rest of the battalions of Guerrero, Aldama, Toluca, and the first active of Mexico had directed at it, together with that from a six-pounder, which had jammed at the second shot. Everyone agrees that as it passed, it hoisted the flag of the United States of the North, and although this may have been more than a strategem, it would not be strange if it gave cause for protest from that country; well, there will be more than enough reasons for arguing pro or con. By the general order issued yesterday, the brigade of which I was the officer in command was dissolved, and the same orders put General Cos on notice to

108

march today (it is said that it is to be in the direction of the fort at Velasco) with the Sapper battalions from Guerrero and Aldama, and attached to the former three of the five pickets that had left with the one from Béjar. Also to march were two companies of the Guadalajara Battalion, the cavalry there from the two regiments of Dolores and Tampico, the general commander of the artillery, with two cannons, one howitzer, and their crews, as well as thirty cases of rifle cartridges and one thousand flintstones. General Filisola must remain in the new headquarters, and General Tolsa has been given command of the troops that are left there; it is ascertained that the general in chief, in the instructions he has given his second in command, advises that no authority be given to General Ramírez y Sesma, although the latter continues to give orders. Since Colonel Céspedes, who was acting as major general, was to depart, he was replaced by the first adjutant, Don Francisco Quintero, until the arrival of General Woll. My corps (that of the sappers) having camped in the vicinity of the river, we, the commanders and officers not on duty, went at night to headquarters to find out what had happened during the day. Among one of the officer groups, General Ramírez y Sesma was enraged over the criticisms made in the camp against his conduct, as well as over the fact that although the steamboat had remained anchored for several hours to take on wood at a short distance upriver from his camp, he had not known it. This general was saying that the gossip being bantered about by the whores that followed the army (as though you could accuse the chiefs and officers of such) hurt his military reputation and put him in bad with the general in chief. Colonel Céspedes was of the opinion that they should have gone aboard the steamboat with troops from the barge, and other similar absurd statements were made; but there is no doubt that it could have been taken by placing strong obstacles in the river that would have prevented its passage; this could have been done with small effort by throwing from both banks of the river thick trees held together with chains. General Ramírez y Sesma had had enough time in which to do it, by selecting the narrowest part of the river, since big trees are to be found over an extensive area of its banks and he had plenty of warning that the steamboat was coming. Without this maneuver, nothing could be done. We, the chiefs and officers of the sappers,

109

went to General Cos to receive our orders, *but because he had already retired, he did not deign to receive us,* and from inside his tent he ordered that at dawn the next day the battalion should cross the river. We then went to the tent of Colonel Céspedes, and at ten that night returned to our camp.

# ≈§ 9 §≈

On the 17th from inside my tent I overheard them calling from the opposite bank for the barge, which was on our side, so that the courier could cross over. It was Captain Miguel Bachiller, who was bringing sealed documents for the second in command, which suspended the march of the Sapper Battalion, reference being made only to the Guerrero and Aldama battalions, to two companies from Guadalajara, and to two cannon and one eight-pounder, as the howitzer piece had already passed the previous day. The two companies of the Guadalajara Battalion passed, since those of Guerrero and Aldama were already on the other bank, and I, who had already crossed the river with two companies of sappers, received orders to recross the river. During an observation I made on the left bank, I found one house still standing and others that had been burned, among which there were indications that one had been a large one and that another cotton gin had been lost during the fire. There was also a medium-sized barn full of cotton bales, many of which had apparently been used for a trench, all scattered along the bank of the river, some on this side. Because the cotton had been pressed and processed, each one of these was valued at around two hundred pesos; they were all the same size and bulky, but I never did know how many *arrobas* each one weighed. It was really sickening to see so many of these destroyed. Our soldiers, like any others in the world, are destructive; some make their thick beds out of cotton, which the next day are renewed, and the women followers are even worse. I have seen some of these monsters spread out the cotton on the banks of the river, in the fashion of delicate females, so as not to dirty their monstrous feet as they emerge from their bath. No one in command tried to put a stop to this unnecessary destruction, and it is not up to us who lament it to do so. It is impossible to estimate the value of the cotton that we have seen between Gonzales

111

and here, both baled and stored unginned, but even less that still found in the fields and in distant houses that we have not been able to visit but that others have seen. A young Béjar woman whom I met on the other side, Doña María Francisca de los Reyes, member of a family which for six years has resided among the colonists, told me that according to their calculations, the losses around San Felipe de Austin passed a half-million pesos total, and that they further estimate that their losses around the Brazos are ten million. However, this seems to be exaggerated, and it could be that it represents the figure for all the colonies.[34] She has also assured me, as have many other people, that some of the families who did not participate in the war had resolved to wait for us so that they could salvage their possessions, but that they could not do so, because armed men set fire to their dwellings, by this barbarous method forcing them to flee from us, or, when this method failed, by telling of the death scenes at the Alamo and at Goliad, which they narrated with all the vehemence of which they are capable. So it was that the owners who did not themselves set fire to their homes saw them go up in smoke by other hands, principally by the volunteers who had come from the north and had nothing to lose. This same person has told me that in San Felipe de Austin there were more than fifty factories, full of objects of great value that were all lost because the warehouses were locked and set on fire. Much food for thought do facts like these create. What sensitive soul could observe with indifference a war that is so disastrous and injurious to both sides? The truth is that there are some who can, and that men who pretend to be civilized but in fact are nothing but idiots seemed highly pleased with the misfortunes of their fellow man, and even tried to augment them.

The 18th.—Yesterday, in a hammock in the woods, I had to lay aside my pen repeatedly in order to delight myself with the harmonious song of the birds and to feast my eyes upon their beautiful

---

[34] The person I mentioned was related to others and could speak from fact about this matter, but when I spoke to the colonists who were in our midst after San Jacinto, they assured me that they still had not been able to estimate their losses, but that they could possibly amount to eighteen or twenty million *pesos fuertes*.

colors and the agile antics of the squirrels. So close to men who go around seeking destruction, anxious to give death or to receive it, I took pleasure in my moments of solitude in imagining myself alone with nature. At sundown, as I left the woods and went toward the camp, I met a group of Indians who had been found pillaging some of the houses. I was surprised, because they were different from those we had seen up to now, most of whom had been naked, some covered with animal skins. These wear a turban, an earring, and a decent costume, although not the same among all. They are well built, speak English in addition to their own language, and one of them some Spanish. Among the women with them were two young girls aged thirteen or fourteen, fair-skinned, with nice features, and one of them with beautiful eyes. They call themselves "Conchatis."[35]

This morning Lieutenant Colonel José M. Castillo Iberry, aide-de-camp of the commanding general, has returned from the vanguard with an order that General Cos initiate a march with five hundred infantrymen and no artillery to rejoin his Excellency. Since this river is wider and swifter than the Colorado and Guadalupe, it has been more difficult to get the herd of mules across, and it has required more time for the equipment. Because there was no barge available and no rowers or boatmen other than the few prisoners taken here and at the Colorado River, some mules and horses drowned; if we have seen many pitiful sights with these beasts before, here it was even worse. Also, we saw the women, who up to now had shared hardships with the soldiers, suffering today the pain of having to separate from them, a measure already taken by the general in command, which, though apparently harsh, was nevertheless expedient for the success and speed of the operations. General Cos marched this afternoon with the Guerrero Battalion, the remnants from the Aldama and the Toluca, and two companies from the Guadalajara, and although I have not been able to obtain an accurate estimate of this force, I have been assured that it is somewhat over five hundred men. It will carry the ammunition, leaving behind the rest of the equipment. I returned to the other side and confirmed with the mother of the young girl the news that she had

---

[35] Probably Coushattas. De la Peña rendered the name as he heard it.—*Ed.*

given me, and this same lady told me that besides the cotton gin, there was also a corn-grinding machine.

The 19th.—Yesterday Castillo Iberry also marched, having stated that the commander in chief, greatly annoyed at having failed in the plan he had prepared against the revolutionary heads congregated at Harrisburg, among them Lorenzo de Zavala, ordered him [Iberry] to set fire to this township, and that his Excellency personally lent a hand in its destruction; also stating that Colonel Almonte, in the vicinity of New Washington, had caught up with a group of families who were fleeing with the colonists. In time we shall know what sort of treatment they received.[36]

My daily occupations have prevented me from noting the pitiful state of the army. We have given an idea during the course of this diary of the happenings up to the departure from Béjar, and in part up to Gonzales, but we should record for the history of this campaign that at the Colorado the soldier's half-rations of corn tortilla terminated, and his total diet was reduced to one pound of meat and a half-ration of beans. Think of the soldier so poorly fed, clothed and shod even worse, sleeping always in the open, crossing rivers and swamps, exposed to hours of burning sun, at other times to heavy downpours, and even during hours of rest having to protect his firearms from the rain, as he had no protective covers for them, though the campaign required crossing wilderness. No one would object if these sufferings were all the results of circumstances and not of the disregard and neglect with which the poor soldier has been treated up to now; yet despite these conditions, this half-starved soldier guarded loads of corn and strictly followed the orders of the general in chief that no one should make use of it. When by

---

[36] I have not been able to get any other news, except that provided by the enemy, and it is greatly exaggerated, because the Texans are being prejudiced against Señor Almonte, whom they know well. They have attributed to him crimes he is incapable of committing. He has been one of those most opposed to bloodshed, and it is incredible that he would execute women. It has been, therefore, an infamous lie to accuse him of this. Later, when editing this, I have formed a less favorable opinion of this gentleman, due to his changeable and inconsistent conduct when he served so poorly as secretary in the War Ministry, fighting the very principles he had professed.

accident a sack would tear, we have had the unpleasant experience of seeing the soldiers and the women who accompanied them gather around like chickens in order to pick up the last grain, and further, with their bare hands making certain that no single grain was left. In these cultivated lands around the houses, we have seen them dig up and expose seeds of sweet potatoes and Irish potatoes that had not yet had a chance to germinate.

If the fate of the soldier is pitiful, that of the officer is no less so. Few of them are fed any less poorly than the soldier, and frequently they are seen begging for a tortilla from the muledrivers. There are many here on the Brazos River who have often begged to buy one for eight or ten reales. Shocked, we have seen a muledriver make as much as fifty pesos and four reales for a single liter of corn. In this sad situation the soldier has suffered without complaint, and no one has seen him mutiny for the sake of food, as any but a Mexican soldier would have done. This suffering among our soldiers is not necessarily because they are stupid, but only because the Mexican soldier is the most long-suffering in the universe. If they do not complain, this does not mean that they are not ready to criticize among themselves. Their criticism is as just as it is cutting and sometimes so sharp and amusing that one is compelled to laughter, even in the midst of the compassion that it inspires. Occasionally during the march these complaints are made loudly, intended to be heard by their immediate superiors, but even the most severe among these are compelled to overlook it, for no one dares to reprimand a soldier who is disgruntled because he is not given the rations that have been charged against his pay in advance. The insulting reprimands that some thoughtless officers have made at times have been the more unjust, for the officers themselves have also complained.[37]

It has become a byword in this camp to call the house occupied by General Ramírez y Sesma the "Customs House," for it is there that the greater part of the goods and foodstuffs gathered from the neighboring houses have been kept. These seemed to be mostly

---

[37] Nevertheless, discipline demands this type of strictness. No one is more convinced than I of the justice of the criticisms expressed by the soldiers, but ultimately I was forced to commit the misdeed which I condemn, though I agonized in doing it.

deposits of liquor and hardware, according to the tales of the luckier ones who had been there. Up to now we have seen those men who have worked the least profit the most, men who occupy themselves with pilfering and neglect their duties, which is not strange, for it always happens thus. The booty, which should be distributed impartially, at least the most essential items, has remained as in Béjar among favorites and some chiefs with rank but devoid of honor.[38]

If one judges by the number of gilded pitchers of different sizes, the pieces of shining crystal, and other articles in fine taste that we have seen in the hands of the soldiers and their women, there must have been a great abundance of these in the houses from which they were taken. Elegant clocks and large mirrors we have seen only in the so-called Customs House and in a few other places. Good wines and brandies are found in abundance among certain persons. It seems that the effect of these liquors was responsible for the disorders in one of the forays, when the troops became insubordinate against the captain of the presidial soldiers, [Don Marcos] Barragán, and another cavalry officer. It is unquestionable that the day we arrived at this point we found along the road some soldiers fallen by the wayside, overcome by drunkenness, and one of the sappers who left his ranks and was killed by a soldier from the first active battalion from Mexico City, who in turn was wounded.

Old Fort, April 22nd. On the afternoon of the 19th the camp was moved from the riverbank to a line that had been drawn in front of the houses, a day on which I thoroughly convinced myself of the servile character of a military career, which no sensitive or thinking being should pursue. We had just finished establishing the new camp when we received orders to march with 150 sappers, a six-pounder, and fifty horses. Between eleven and twelve at night we initiated the march, guided by a relatively civilized Conchati who spoke Spanish poorly, but English well, so we had an interpreter for this language. We marched until one or two o'clock in the afternoon of the 21st, but since the commander of this section, Don Agustín Amat, thought that we had gone further than planned, he

---

[38] I have the satisfaction of not having taken even a pin, nor having asked for the least thing, although, like many others, I lost several things belonging to me during the campaign. I have such horror of booty that I deprived myself of firearms very much to my liking.

ordered a countermarch, during which we recrossed a very swampy, wooded creek that lost us much time both going and coming. We camped when we left the woods, and the troops, who had had no food since the day before because we had marched without rations, now ate barbecue meat, and the next day between six and seven in the morning we continued our countermarch toward this camp, where we arrived at noon. It is estimated, judging by the time, that we had detoured about thirty miles, although some were convinced that the distance was longer, for it always seems greater when one marches hungry and sleepy. Others believed that the guide and the interpreter had acted in bad faith, and there was even some talk of executing them. As the latter had left his companions and all his family in our camp, it is scarcely credible that he would have acted in bad faith, since it would have compromised both his family and friends.

The object of this expedition had been to take Columbia by surprise, where the Conchati who guided us gave us the assurance that there was a rich load guarded by only seventy of the enemy, but it is probable that there was no force present, since our vanguard had arrived there ten days before and it is not likely that an enemy in retreat would leave a detachment on this side of the river so close to us. The expedition should have been carried out and we should not have countermarched except for very weighty reasons, more especially since the guide assured us that Columbia was hardly six or eight miles from where the countermarch was executed. Yet even if the distance had been doubled, it would have been the lesser evil, in my estimate, to have gone ahead rather than return to camp ignominiously. There was the added circumstance that Colonel Amat[39] was ill when he was designated to carry out this commission,

---

[39] This commander assured me later that he had received orders from General Filisola not to wander further from headquarters than ten leagues. Had he arrived at Columbia and had the misfortune of the 21st not occurred, his decision would have been approved, because results generally decide whether one has acted well or otherwise. Wishing to distinguish myself in a campaign for which I had volunteered just as I was scheduled to leave for Europe and having wanted to undertake the expedition to Columbia before it was planned, I solicited the influence of the commanding general of the artillery, so as to obtain command of it. But General

and he conceded only as a point of honor. The lack of understanding of the English language influenced the lack of success and was the cause also of the many errors and contradictions.

On the night of the 9th we noticed many cattle, but on the mornings of the 20th and 21st, we saw them in such abundance that doubtless these are the days on which we saw the greatest number. We observed that besides being very fat, most of them had light-colored spots, and from a distance it was a beautiful sight, as they looked completely white. They are numerous, and the hornless variety is abundant, these cows producing three times as much milk as the others. On the edge of the woods and a few miles from the river one could see many houses and extensive fields. Among the ones we visited there were some still under construction, but in a group already finished, which seemed to belong to the same family, there was one that deserved to be called beautiful for its architecture and its comforts, as well as the beauty of its location. Its principal view is toward the south, in which direction runs a beautiful hall and another toward the east. The main entrance to the house is on the north side, where there is another very wide hall, and behind a peach orchard is the forest. On the left of the principal façade there was an extensive field of corn, each plant being a *vara* [a little less than a yard] in height, and another peach orchard. On the eastern side and from north and south there was a garden enclosed by a fine picket fence, in which vegetables grew in abundance and from which we gathered quite a lot of onions. This is a frame house, as they all are in Texas, and if its exterior was enchanting to the eyes of him who is writing this, at the same time how sad were the inevitable reflections once inside, which made the heart quiver with

---

Ampudia, despite the extreme affection he had displayed toward me and his insistence that I address him in the familiar form to make our friendship a closer one, displayed little interest in this request, and I, confident in his promises, did not solicit it directly from the commission, which might have granted it. Señor Filisola made public the good opinion he had of me. Since I had opposed the countermarch, I requested charge of the cavalry on the day we began it in order to proceed ahead, but Señor Amat denied my request and misinterpreted it, thinking that I attributed his not wanting to proceed to his weakness. The same day that we would have entered Columbia, part of Urrea's division entered and in fact found much food, goods, and liquor in abundance, but no enemy force.

tenderness. Mantle clocks, large mirrors all broken, beds not luxurious but decent, ladies' and children's curlers on the tables, spinning wheels and small weaving equipment, fine chinaware, crystal, scattered books, iron pots, and a multitude of useful furnishings and necessary domestic objects, all testified that the family using them was happy and industrious and had good taste. All these objects revealed that this family had been a large one, and nothing touched me more than the curlers, in spite of the fact that I am not yet a father. Upon the New Testament, the only thing I dared touch, I now write.

Between the north and west of this house are all the others, and almost in the center of them is a well surrounded by buckets perfectly made, with one at the end of a chain and the other joined by a cylinder placed horizontally, so that as they turned on this cylinder water could be drawn quickly and easily. All the wells that we have seen are modeled in this fashion, and some of them are reinforced at a certain distance from the curbstone to a depth of as much as fifty to sixty or more *varas*.

Since the colonists' dwellings are scattered along the banks of the rivers, sometimes miles apart from each other, it was impossible during our march to visit all those that were left standing, but according to the narratives of those who have seen them, we can be certain that there are many more similar to or better than those we have just described, according to the good taste or the good fortune of those who built them. The cattle around these houses were so domesticated that they ran in herds after the soldiers when they saw them approaching. In the midst of these we found pigs of unusual size and some hens and ducks. In all the houses, even the poorer ones, were machines for grinding corn and coffee and many implements for carpentry and tilling the soil; the ploughs are of an unusual and ingenious design, and one can see at a glance that they are more efficient than those used by our own farmers. Some of these houses were still watched by dogs so loyal that they tried to keep us away from them, while others fled, perhaps hating us as much as their masters do.

Let us look for a moment at these families forsaking their easy life, their labors, their herds, and all their other goods; in flight through the woods, having left everything behind in their hurried get-away, with nothing but the most essential items, not knowing where to go. Think of them as they destroy and set fire with their own hands; give thought to the fact that the fortunes of war forced many of these families to act in this way against their wishes, that they were dragged into the war by those who promoted it, who painted us in the blackest colors, describing us to them as savages, as men more ferocious than beasts, to which belief the events of the Alamo, La Bahía, and the mission at Refugio unfortunately contributed. Reflect also that among the victims of the revolution were many innocent ones who had been born within our borders. No one would disagree with me that provisions should have been made to prevent the war, or that, once begun in order to vindicate an injured nation, it should have been carried out in a less disastrous fashion. It will be demonstrated in time that both parties were guilty, and mention will be made of the generous conduct of the colonists toward our wounded when Béjar was taken, which we in turn followed and later they adopted as a consequence of ours.[40]

After our arrival at Gonzales we started drinking milk and we have been leading cows with us; up to now we have had a supply, but the order of the 19th forbade the tying of calves for this purpose, because the bleating of those animals is alleged to disturb the sleep during the hours of rest, though no one reflects that the cry of the sentinels is worse and keeps us from sleeping.[41] However, until now this order has not been carried out, because our current needs are far greater than the duties and oblige the commanders and officers to pretend not to notice. Certainly there is a contrast between an order intended to deprive us of one of our chief sources of food, and the tolerance shown those usurers, the sutlers, who are in no way required to moderate their greed.[42]

---

[40] Regarding this indication in the diary, we believe that what has been mentioned on page 83 of this volume has been sufficient.

[41] Perhaps because we were not face to face with the enemy.

[42] At the Brazos River, a bar of poor chocolate was worth five or six reales, and sometimes one paid as much as twelve if one wanted to satisfy one's appetite. The *piloncillo* which sold in Monterrey for three *granos* [.0648 grams] was sold at the canteen run by the brother-in-law of the general in chief for twenty reales to three pesos. Corn, which cost the sutlers only the trouble of gathering it with the aid of mules, for the use

Yesterday's order of the day (the 21st) prohibits, under the responsibility of the corps chiefs, the continued destruction of cotton bales, but this provision was belatedly given, since most of these have already been destroyed for the wretched purpose of using the rough material in which they were packed. As we noted before, many of these bales had been destroyed to make beds for the soldiers, and others in order to condition the crossings at the river so that the women who accompanied the soldiers would not soil their feet on coming out of the water.

General Gaona likewise arrived yesterday with his brigade at this general headquarters, and he has been reinforced with the rest of the Guadalajara Battalion. He has made efforts, as he did in Béjar, to take away the sappers. This commander, as we have seen, left the city on the 24th of March in the direction of Nacogdoches. He arrived on the 1st of this month at the village of Bastrop, situated on the east bank of the Colorado, which he found deserted, although some goods, furniture, and provisions had been left behind. He countermarched to this point, following orders he received to that effect. Today his brigade began to cross to the other side in order to continue his march toward Nacogdoches, and when I emerged from the woods between two and three in the afternoon, I came close to the river crossing and found that the part of the brigade that had already crossed was crossing back again. Everyone was asking the cause of this countermovement, and no one could give a reason, but at five in the afternoon rumors are circulating that the commander in chief was defeated yesterday. This seems to be true, as several individuals have arrived who confirm this; I have spoken to one of them, and, if the rumor is confirmed, the only surprise to me would be that it had not happened before, given the disorder with which the commander in chief has led us, with his errors and aberrations. The different things said about this campaign can be stated only at the conclusion or suspension of it, because there is so

---

of which the nation paid five and six pesos per day, would be sold to us at three or four pesos for a little over a bushel, sometimes at five or six pesos; at times during the retreat, we were obliged to pay as much as eight. Some of these sutlers were themselves the owners of these herds. At the camp at the Brazos, messages were not passed on, as one expects them to be during a campaign.

much to say about the diversity of opinions and fears. Up to now the enemy has not known how to conduct the war, and this has saved us; who knows, yesterday may have been the beginning. Some confusion and lack of enthusiasm has been noticed among the generals and some of the commanders, but I have observed with satisfaction the excellent spirit of the soldier, who speaks of nothing but going and avenging our leader and companion—let us march.

## ❧ 10 ❧

I have inserted my diary uninterrupted since the departure from
Béjar, and I have left it as is, although it may be annoying that
episodes are not narrated in the present tense, because I have considered this incoherence less irritating than any substantial altera-
tion would be. From now on without altering time or concepts,
I shall be obliged to interrupt it many times, using phrases not
necessarily in pure Castilian, to make those reflections only noted
in the diary; for as I have said in the letter that has served as a
prologue, I could only make notes during the march and this only
by using the hours that the others devoted to rest. The diary will
continue as heretofore, in order to differentiate from the additions
that I am going to make. With this admonition, I continue.

Sunday the 24th of April. This is an unknown plain where we
arrived between two and three o'clock in the morning. The captain
of the Tampico Regiment, Don Miguel Aguirre, who commanded
the general in chief's guard and who returned on the 22nd, is, among
others, one of those who affirmed the total destruction of the forces
under his own immediate and personal command, together with
those which General Cos commanded. According to what this officer
says, it is known that the action during which this catastrophe occurred took place on the 21st at four o'clock in the afternoon on the
near bank of the San Jacinto, and that there perished in it, by surprise (a surprise at four o'clock in the afternoon!), the Guerrero
Battalion [under command of Colonel Manuel Céspedes], the
Aldama under the command of First Adjutant Felipe Romero, the
Matamoros under the command of Colonel Manuel Romero, and the
Toluca: almost all in the formation, especially the second and the
last, which had suffered considerable casualties in the Alamo assault.
Other victims also were two companies from the Guadalajara Battal-
ion under the command of Captains Rocha and Lisola, and the select
ones from the first active of Mexico City under the command of

Captains [José María] Avila and————[sic]. The artillery has lost only one six-pounder, under the command of Lieutenant [Ignacio] Arenal. Aguirre declares that the commander in chief, unable to negotiate a bayou,[43] remained on foot in the midst of a wooded area; that General Castrillón and Colonels Almonte, Batres, and Mora had perished, as well as Colonels Castillo Iberry, Aguirre (Don Marcial), and all the rest of the commanders and officers of the general staff and the rest of the corps; but nothing is definitely known because none of those actively engaged in the affray has arrived except Aguirre, who is wounded, and a few soldiers and domestics.

The night of the 22nd the Sapper Battalion received orders to approach the banks of the river, and we commanders and officers were under the impression that we were going on the offensive to hold the crossing while the rest of the army went over it, a natural assumption; but we occupied the whole bank, not without some surprise and indignation at the recrossing of the loads of ammunition and supplies that had already crossed to the other side during the march under General Gaona. Yesterday morning as we retreated toward the camp we found our tents down, but we did not begin the countermarch until sundown, leaving the aforementioned general to look out for the recrossing of the loads that still remained on the opposite side. On the same night of the 22nd we noticed a sort of aurora borealis on the side where the encounter had been; under the circumstances, some of us attributed this brilliant reflection to the cremation of our dead. We had already marched a few hours and darkness had obscured some objects when we noticed that the houses we had left were on fire.

Thoughts and sensations of this day. This countermarch is really cruel and harsh to me, for, in my opinion, after effecting a reunion with General Urrea, we should have marched to vindicate the honor of our arms, to avenge our companions, and to save those who might still be alive, but unfortunately only some of the commanders and the majority of the subalterns share this view, for the generals have not even wanted to wait for the stragglers who might rejoin us, when General Santa Anna might perhaps be one of them. Whoever is courageous enough, let him imagine a multitude of our comrades

---

[43] In Texas they call a short and usually muddy stream a *bayuco*.

wandering through the woods, half-starved, surrounded by enemies, and not knowing where to go, for those able to reach headquarters have nothing with which to cross the Brazos, since the only available barge was ordered destroyed. Some of these in their desperation plunged into the river and perished, even though they had escaped the enemy's fury . . . [*sic*]. Consider our wounded, without anyone to care for them, and our prisoners, sacrificed in a barbarous rite, and one will curse this retreat with greater vigor, there being only a remote hope, based on the enemy's generosity, of which proof has already been given, and, no less, the justice on our side in fighting this war, which lets me believe that they might be saved. Until now hunger, the distances, and the disorder in which we have been led have been the principal enemy we have had to fight, for the colonists, although exceedingly courageous, have neither discipline nor rules. They have been able to conquer only General Santa Anna, who himself does everything without rules; General Urrea has fought them with inferior forces. Last night we found out that this general is in Brazoria, that he has received executive orders to join us with his division, and we went to meet him, because our old generals do not feel very safe without him. Reflections we should make concerning our retreat at the first blow we have suffered, and the consequences that will follow: The campaign was about to conclude, but through an idiotic act everything has been lost. Everyone is concerned about what might happen in the interior of the Republic; they fear political changes, and some the loss of their employment; as for me, nothing affects me more than seeing the national honor compromised and us on the threshold of losing the most precious part of our territory. An evaluation of the following campaign based on the failure of this one. Reasons upon which I base my belief that General Santa Anna's errors might still be corrected. Putting an end to the issue once and for all, by risking all or by remaining buried in Texas before thinking in terms of retreat. In due time I will clarify these ideas, for the brevity of time and the inconvenience under which I am writing do not permit me to do more than to set down these reminders.

Lieutenant Colonel Nicolás de la Portilla has told me that he requested some cavalry in order to search for the stragglers and also to see if he could locate his brother, Don Manuel, aide to the commander in chief, and that this had been denied him; but on the 22nd a cavalry patrol and some infantry were sent as far as the exit from the woods. No doubt our general has remained very proud in the thought that he has exhausted every means of reuniting the scattered troops, but he has misled himself miserably, and I am forced to conclude that because he is a foreigner, he is not interested in the fate of Mexicans. On this day (the 24th), he has issued a valiant proclamation, which I hope he will carry out as promised, but I doubt it, because his actions contradict his words. (Check the general order of the 24th of April.)[44]

The 25th. Yesterday between two and three o'clock in the afternoon we broke up camp and traveled toward another in the vicinity, where we found houses and the Jiménez Battalion, which belonged to Urrea's division, in possession of rich booty taken at Columbia. During the march we learned that there were some of the dispersed men on the other side of the river and that they had no way of crossing, which assures me more and more in my thinking that we should not have abandoned Thompson's Pass, or at least not in such haste. Before this was done, some barrels of brandy were destroyed, when some days before, only a miserable ration of a *cuartillo* [0.482 liquid qt.] had been given for each sixteen men among the troops; provisions were thrown into the river for lack of transportation, provisions which up to now had been economized to the extreme of depriving the soldier of his needs. Some equipment was set on fire, principally that belonging to officers who had fallen at San Jacinto, and also knapsacks, which could have been distributed among the battalions of Guadalajara and the auxiliaries from Guanajuato, which had none. Last night at twelve the undefeated General Urrea arrived with the rest of his triumphant division. There is no time to listen to all the individuals who were a part of it tell of the abundance in which they had lived while we were marching in the most horrible misery. In Matagorda, Brazoria, and in Columbia particularly, they found an abundance of food and supplies of all descriptions, of fine furniture, and of liquor. Today Señor Urrea's camp

---

[44] Filisola's proclamation to his division denounced the "treacherous enemy" and called for avenging "our most illustrious son, General Santa Anna." De la Peña quotes the entire proclamation in chapter 11 (see also *La Rebelión de Texas*, appendix 18).—Ed.

looked like a marketplace, and they have come to ours to sell various things, such as candle wax, very white sugar, bitter chocolate, cigars at a peso a box, crystal, fine hats, tailored clothes, etc. Yesterday during the march I noticed thick clouds of smoke on our left flank from the burning houses we had seen before beginning the march. About seven o'clock this morning, Captain Don Marcos Barragán, aide to General Santa Anna, Somosa, an officer from Matamoros, and a presidial soldier from those dispersed at San Jacinto joined us. Since they found nothing at Thompson's Pass with which to cross the Brazos, they had to build a barge, tying the logs with their sashes. Afterward, there arrived an artilleryman and Luis Espinosa, fifer of the Guerrero Battalion, a young man twelve years old and extraordinarily alert, who has given me a detailed narrative of the happenings at San Jacinto and who confirms, as the others have, that the defeat was by surprise and that the greater part of our forces perished. He left the battlefield the following day, and he assures me that it had not lasted even half an hour, that the troops hardly had time to fall into ranks, and that a very few of the select companies were the only ones to give battle. He states that the division of the president-general, in the position it occupied, had a wooded area to its right and a lake at its rear, leaving the left as its only avenue of retreat; that the enemy advanced frontally with a body of infantry, two artillery pieces, and its cavalry to the left, in order to attract attention while the main body of the troops marched hidden behind tall grass in order to flank our right, which they managed to do; that our troops were surrounded in a few moments, and since all was confusion and disorder, most of them were pushed into the lagoon; and that those who could escape fled toward the position we occupied on the Brazos, but, finding the bridge burned at Buffalo Bayou and unable to cross it, our soldiers were overtaken by the enemy, who wreaked on them a horrible carnage to avenge themselves for those we had executed. It is for that reason that Espinosa believes that General Santa Anna and his general staff, who had been able to save themselves as far as Buffalo Bayou, have perished. He has also told me that he thinks there were Conchati and Cheroquis Indians among the enemy, judging by the yells that were heard during the battle. But such rumor is not credible for a

127

variety of reasons, among them the many disagreements about it among the stragglers and also about the number of the enemy's force, some being of the opinion that there were as many as 1,500 men. Our force was made up of 1,100 infantrymen, one six-pounder, and 70 cavalrymen, who, under any other than General Santa Anna, would have never been caught by surprise. The fact that he himself perished, being the commander in chief, is the best proof of his negligence. It is also said that the enemy greatly fears that we will attack him, as we should have done, the more so when he knows that our forces are superior, since he does not operate blindly, as we do, for up to now we have not had a single spy in his camp.[45] Six, eight, or ten thousand pesos given to one of our prisoners would have given us victory; but no one in the army is ignorant of the ridiculous economy General Santa Anna has practiced regarding this in all his campaigns, an economy that has been detrimental and the cause of so much suffering. I have a feeling that the enemy disguises himself in the uniform of our soldiers and that he adds to his ranks those prisoners not executed; it is rumored that this is done only in the case of officers. The aforementioned Espinosa assures us that many of the stragglers who did not dare to cross the river have returned and delivered themselves to the enemy so as not to die of starvation. Though we know nothing positively, it is nevertheless certain that we have been more cruel with ourselves than the enemy has been, retreating precipitately and blocking our own retreat. This will continue tomorrow toward Guadalupe Victoria, this plan having been definitely agreed upon at a meeting of Generals Vicente Filisola, José Urrea, Don Antonio Gaona, Don Eugenio Tolsa, Don Adrián Woll, Don Joaquín Ramírez y Sesma, and Lieutenant Colonel Pedro Ampudia, commandant general of artillery. If these commanders had wished to sound the opinion of their subordinates, if they had not purposely avoided listening to their voice, they would have blushed at being convinced that among these there was greater willingness, patriotism, and courage. At every moment I become more convinced that we should have died and died honorably before abandoning the camp to the enemy, burdened with ignominy.

---

[45] Through hearsay from some of the enemy I learned that after our invasion they organized a company of spies who kept them informed of all our movements.

It is impossible for me to proceed further without stopping here to reflect on the sad but serious thoughts that run wild, invading the imagination, and that will no doubt weigh heavily in the thoughts of any Mexican zealous of his country's honor and the good name of its military.

We should note above all that the enemy, disconcerted by the successive victories of our army, terrified by the fall of the Alamo, by Fannin's defeat and the accelerated movements of General Urrea, was seeking safety in retreat, and a well-ordered march would have been the only thing necessary to end the campaign without having to fire another single shot. Were I the most devoted admirer of General Santa Anna, I would not dare to excuse him of the great error committed in venturing to cross to the other side of the Brazos with only 700 men when he could have had General Ramírez y Sesma's full division made up of over 1,400 men, for by delaying the march ten days he could have had with him over 2,000. But the assurances given him by some of the prisoners that the families fleeing from us carried with them valuable assets, and the avarice that has characterized all his actions; the desire to make the campaign as horrible as possible and to end it quickly, so that he could return to the interior to receive homage and to consolidate his power, perhaps for life, according to the news that had leaked out and which I have referred to previously; all these things drove him to act precipitately. This is the more believable as one sees that his advance was by a route where no enemy was to be found, leaving him to the left, although the ostensible object for which he abandoned the general headquarters at Thompson's on the 14th of April was to seize the men who made up the so-called government of Texas, who at that moment were at the town of Harrisburg. It is not credible that this could have been the sole object of his march, because apprehending a handful of men who had no force on hand to defend them would have been an easy task for a cavalry patrol to carry out, since they have fast mobility and would not attract attention, circumstances which would not be as favorable were a division to execute it, no matter how mobile. It would have been more worthy for our commander in chief to advance to meet the enemy than to apprehend those judged to be the leaders of the revolution, something the most insignificant army member could have done.

129

Battles, says one of the masters of war, that compromise the reputation of the leader and the honor and security of the nation being served should not be initiated in the absence of absolute necessity, a necessity rarely verified and nearly always bearing fatal results. There are cases, however, where it becomes inevitable to give battle; for, since there is no means by which it may be prevented, it is expedient to accept it; the general who, without any advantages, finds himself compromised and forced into battle has unquestionably committed errors of strategy that impose on him this harsh and terrible law. These truths apply to General Santa Anna, not only because of the harsh lesson received at San Jacinto, but also because of those received at Tolomé on the 3rd of March 1832, and in other encounters in which he was vanquished, for it is always an adage among Mexicans that *he loses battles and wins the wars with words.*[46]

There is no doubt that we were about to end the campaign without having to sacrifice a single soldier, so why gamble with its success and why render useless the immense sacrifices we had made until then, when a little caution would have been sufficient to crown the heroic efforts of the army?

The enemy was without question in full retreat, but when he was cut off, necessity compelled him to advance. His whole object was to maneuver in such a way as to give ample time for the families of the colonists to retreat and to save as much as possible of their possessions. If he could have counted on the humanity of our leader, if he had not feared the bloodthirsty nature of the one who had subjected him to such terrible ordeals, he might have tried to capitulate before risking all, where instead he gained all, thanks to a criminal abandon unforgivable in a general.

"Beware," said Turenne, "of underestimating your adversary, for surely this is one of the greatest risks in war"; but General Santa Anna greatly deprecated an enemy whom heretofore he had vanquished in every encounter when he had dared to show his face. He was over-confident, and he communicated this feeling to those under

---

[46] The adage refers specifically to the many *pronunciamientos*, or proclamations, issued by Santa Anna to foment political revolts.—*Ed.*

130

him, giving the enemy an advantage that he could not have had otherwise.

A slave appeared before Houston at three o'clock the afternoon of the 21st, informing him that General Santa Anna was sleeping and that his camp had delivered itself over to a feeling of confidence and great abandon. Houston hurried to take advantage of the beautiful opportunity that presented itself to him, to be freed of a critical and anxious situation, mobilizing his force immediately with the greatest caution, then giving the sign for the attack. This circumstance explains why he decided to battle an enemy who had just received reinforcements of four hundred men when the previous day he had not accepted combat offered to him with inferior numbers. For men who had been placed in the cruel dilemma of either vanquishing or dying, who knew by past experience that no quarter would be given, it was not difficult to overcome an enemy that slept and was unprepared to resist. So, to advance, to surprise our advance posts, to introduce confusion and disorder, and to spread terror and death in our camp was the work of a few moments. The cry *Remember the Alamo!* that the enemy shouted as he dealt his blows served to increase his fury during that terrible moment, to make the conflict more bitter for our men, and to avenge twice over their comrades who had fallen at the place of that name. The thirst for vengeance that dominated them when they recalled the scenes at the Alamo and Goliad, so fresh in their memory, was so strong that they became intoxicated with the carnage and could not be controlled in their devastating fury by those of their leaders and companions who, though justly indignant at the inhumanity with which our own leader had conducted himself with their men, did not wish to stain their victory with the same excesses that had blotted our own.

Nothing speaks more convincingly for the instantaneous surprise registered in our camp and the fact that it was carried out with a horrible carnage of men who showed no resistance than Houston's dispatch, in which he reveals that he had only 2 dead and 23 wounded.[47] Although it is stated there that our dead numbered 600,

---

[47] Samuel Houston, commander in chief, to David G. Burnet, president of the Republic of Texas, San Jacinto, April 25, 1836.—*Ed.*

one can say without qualms that it was less by 100, for as stated before our force consisted of slightly over 1,170 men, but though 100 were added to this figure by the number of officers not included in reports, by the artillerymen, muledrivers, domestics, and a sutler or two, some were dispersed, and only 730 were taken prisoner, according to the aforesaid dispatch; it has not been possible for me to investigate the truth, because the statements of those mentioned above and those of the enemy are in disagreement, as one might observe in the course of my diary.

Among the victims immolated by the criminal and unforgivable carelessness that has been occupying our attention we find General Manuel Fernández Castrillón, who perished while bravely trying to restore order in our ranks; Colonel Don José Batres, our aide to the commander in chief, who was overtaken in flight and cut down without offering any resistance; the courageous Lieutenant Colonel Esteban Mora and the amiable Don Marcial Peralta Aguirre, of the same rank; and many other meritorious officers, among them Don Santiago Luelmo, Don Néstor Guzmán Larumbe, Vallejo Rocha, and others whom I do not recall at the moment. Among the 730 prisoners whose lives were spared, perhaps to suffer greater tortures than death itself, were 50 leaders and officers, including the commander in chief, his secretary, and his chaplain, whose names are found in the accompanying narrative.[48]

Houston has purposely withheld from his dispatch the circumstance to which he owed his victory, in order not to diminish the renown it has bestowed on him, for certainly without such a complete surprise, the more reprehensible because it was at midday, he never could have obtained it. General Santa Anna had under his command forces superior in both number and discipline; he had excellent officers, and though there were some recruits in his ranks, these were the lesser number; of choice companies he had ten, and among the fusiliers of the other contingents there were veteran soldiers, soldiers who on more than one occasion had decked their foreheads with the laurels of victory. Houston, on the contrary, had

---

[48] The document referred to is a list, dated July 1, 1836, in Matamoros, of the chiefs and officers taken prisoner at San Jacinto, including Santa Anna and twenty officers, and fifty wounded. A facsimile of the manuscript is reproduced in *La Rebelión de Texas*, appendix 20.—*Ed.*

forces inferior in number which, though composed of men of courage, were not subject to the discipline that makes the soldier; they did not follow any specific tactics nor had they mastered the fundamentals of war. It can be said of them that they were all recruits, courageous men, who tried only to save or to sell their lives dearly, for which reason the defeat at San Jacinto appears the more humiliating, for in defeat disgrace is quite possible, just as one can be vanquished without necessarily losing honor; but on the 21st of April everything was lost, men, arms, and reputation.

But let us leave this scene, in order to turn our sight to the one enacted at Thompson's Pass when the news of this disaster was received, and that enacted three days later at Madam Powell's.

## ⊷§ 11 §⊷

The first impression the events at San Jacinto produced in the camp at Thompson's has already been observed in my diary, but allow me to amplify here the observations recorded there only as notes. Our chieftain had been surprised and consequently the rest of the army was routed in a shameful retreat as precipitate as it was unnecessary, carried out against all military principles. On the 23rd we abandoned our position on the Brazos, and our countermarch was hushed and taciturn in the midst of the haste and confusion with which it was executed. Aware that our departure would leave our unfortunate comrades to the mercy of the victor, cut off from any possible means of rescue, many were greatly upset; as on the previous day, they were beside themselves with anger, outraged and furious to see that our retreat greatly compromised the national honor and the self-esteem of the army, when they thought that we should avenge the recent insult we had suffered. These were the general sentiments among the army, more particularly among Urrea's division, whose actions until then had been glorious. Few were seen to have been overcome by fear, but in this insignificant number there were some who should have shown greater serenity and who should have set the example and encouraged the rest. Who among those of us who were present there could be unaware of those who were overcome by terror, upon learning of the catastrophe of the 21st?

The confusion with which we executed our reverse maneuver was so great that the order for the day on the 24th stated: "It having come to the knowledge of his Excellency, acting as second to the commander in chief, that, owing to the darkness of the previous night, some mules have left their herds, thus causing a loss of some of the cargo, which does not appear to be in the possession of its legitimate owners, he stipulates that any cargo not being in the hands of the owners should be delivered today to the guards of the

134

Morelos Battalion. His Excellency cannot believe that there could be in the division under his command persons capable of perpetrating the infamous crime of theft, so it is stipulated by his order that after today the punishments indicated in articles 70, 71, and 72, eighth treatise, title one of the Military Code should be applied to any person found with trunks, goods, horses, or mules that might not belong to him and failing to deliver them in conformity with the present order." It would have been more sensible to prevent those crimes by maintaining order than to dictate punishment to correct them. According to this order, a battalion made up of all infantry pickets under the command of the first adjutant, Don Mariano García, was to be organized, and a cavalry squadron under orders of Captain Don Mariano Valera; but this organization, like all the other good ideas, came to nothing.

The disorganization that had reigned in the army from the very beginning increased after the defeat at San Jacinto, turning the troops into a formless mass, which made it impossible for me to ascertain the numbers of the effective force remaining after this event, but without exaggerating, I think it was over 4,000 men. On the 1st of July, after suffering a considerable loss, the Matamoros Battalion had 3,080 infantry, including 168 sappers, 166 artillerymen, and 746 cavalry, as is testified to by the accompanying statement which was gathered during those days.[49] It takes no special effort to believe that its numbers were greater at the theater of war, where desertions, so common in our army because of its poor organization and worse maintenance, could not be contained, for the same reason that we found ourselves in a desert. Of these 4,000 or more men, 1,000 were at Béjar under the command of General Andrade, most of them from the cavalry, which had remained there because the horses could not be used; 300 of these men were either wounded or ill. Fifteen hundred were at Thompson's with four artillery pieces, under General Filisola's command; General Gaona's brigade alone, made up of the Morelos battalions and the auxiliaries from Guanajuato, had been reinforced with the remainder of the Guadalajara

---

[49] The document referred to is a chart of the total forces remaining to the army of operations, broken down by brigades, cavalry, and infantry, dated July 1, 1836, at Matamoros. A facsimile of the manuscript is reproduced in *La Rebelión de Texas*, appendix 20.—*Ed.*

Battalion in order to continue its march to Nacogdoches with 900 men; furthermore, the Sapper Battalion, the first active of Mexico City, several isolated pickets, and about 60 to 80 horses were also there. General Urrea had 200 infantrymen from the Jiménez, San Luis Potosí, and Querétaro battalions, with four artillery pieces and 150 horses at Columbia and Brazoria. The Tres Villas Battalion had been detached and stationed at Matagorda, and the one from Yucatán, at Goliad, Cópano, and Victoria.

The force under the command of General Filisola should be considered as a reserve to that under the immediate orders of General Santa Anna, as these were hardly more than two days' journey apart.

From confirmed depositions taken of various prisoners during the march, it was known that Houston had no more than 800 men and that, including the detachment he held at Velasco and another party that was scouting the country, the total force left in Texas did not amount to 1,200 men.

Once our advance guard was defeated, it was to be supposed that it was either by surprise or by force of arms. If the former, the victory was insignificant; if the latter, the enemy would have then been weak and easy to vanquish. All troops, whatever the number, are in such disorder after combat that the slightest incident can bring defeat—a military axiom that should not have been ignored by the second in command and the other generals. Napoleon had lost the Battle of Marengo and the Austrians were scattered everywhere, intoxicated with their victory, when General Desaix appeared with a reserve column, fewer in number than the forces that had succumbed, re-initiated the combat, and obtained a victory that was among those giving most fame to that illustrious warrior, though at the expense of a glorious death for him. The faithful companions of the captive of Santa Elena were greatly moved and did him great honor, burying his body in the cape that he was wearing on the day of that battle.

"If misfortune dogs a battle and it is lost, that is no reason for the general to become discouraged; on the contrary, the superiority of his talent should inspire others and bring forth those energetic plans already mapped out in his mind." But we had received the death blow and the successor to the command became paralyzed;

General Filisola proved himself an insignificant being, unworthy of the military rank to which the nation had elevated him, throwing that nation into abysmal calamities, present and future, and casting on the whole Republic and on the army a shameful blot, a mark of ignominy.

When the news of the adverse blow sustained reached Old Fort, or Thompson's Pass, we had, as I have mentioned before, around 1,500 men. General Gaona's brigade with its train was all along the left bank; it would have taken but a few hours to transfer the rest of the existing force to join it there, for officer and soldier would have worked with zeal in order to advance against the enemy, as they did with indifference to escape him. That same day, the 23rd, we could have moved, and without forcing the march too much we would have been within sight of the victor by the 25th. Our sudden appearance would have transformed into confusion and dismay the pride that possessed him after a victory owed simply to an accident and to a punishable carelessness. A short, strong warning made with courage, to let him feel our strength, would have been enough to have saved the lives of our prisoners, for it is more rational to believe that they would have been spared by this means than by our running away and abandoning them to the discretion of the victor. There is no doubt that we should have returned to restore the honor of our arms and to avenge the blood of our comrades; we were in a better position than ever to give battle and to end the campaign with a glorious and decisive action. All prospects favored us: number and discipline, but above all, justice. Before retreating we should at least have tried to find our commander in chief; an effort should have been made to rescue him if he were still alive, even if only for the honor of the nation, for he was after all its first magistrate. Had General Santa Anna succeeded in rejoining us after the defeat, doubtless he would have led us to revenge. Had he, as commander in chief, not been so imprudent as to compromise both himself and the success of the campaign, had the misfortune that befell him fallen on, let us say, General Filisola, it is certain that he would have followed a course of action contrary to what the latter did.

But since the second in command did not consider himself strong enough to pursue the enemy immediately, fearing to meet the fate of the commander in chief, he could and should have done it jointly with General Urrea, for although any one of these divisions was sufficient by itself to have snatched the victor's laurels, combined or united they were even more likely to have obtained complete victory, as is borne out by the fears which we later discovered the enemy to have entertained and the small force with which he had surprised the camp at San Jacinto, which could not even have held our prisoners had they had any sort of help. General Urrea was at Brazoria on the 21st of April, part of his division had crossed to the other bank of the Brazos, and two days would have sufficed to bring him within reach, for he had joined us in less than two. In this case, victory would have been delayed about two days, but it would have been certain.

If one should protest that the enemy could have retreated and evaded our march, this being the only recourse left him, the objection would not be in order, because our prisoners encumbered him and so would have prevented his doing this with the necessary speed, and our maneuver would have been accomplished to impede it, as General Santa Anna had already done. But, even if he had escaped through our lack of foresight, our march in pursuit would have yielded great results, one being that of providing us with foodstuffs; the honor of our arms would have remained unsullied, and the campaign would have come to an end.

It has been said, and believed by some, that our first reverse maneuver was intended to disengage us from what was useless and to reunite with General Urrea in order to pursue the enemy, and General Filisola has so stated in some of his dispatches, but the destruction of the meager means at our disposal for crossing the Brazos indicated that the sole object was to consolidate his victory. A courageous proclamation addressed to the army on the 24th was a further move to nourish the hopes of the many who wished far more to advance, since retreat was so distasteful. What honor, what glory, would have been General Filisola's had he carried out in deeds what he offered in his speech, as the country and duty categorically demanded! "Soldiers," he said on this day, "a cowardly and treacherous enemy has by accident gained the advantage over that section personally commanded by the president-general because of the very disdain with which he looked upon them, for in no other way could the courage of the valorous ones accompanying him have been stopped even momentarily. This small but significant episode excites to vengeance, and should increase the indignation of the Mexican Army against the vile enemy it is fighting. Soldiers, we are strong, and the honor of the nation has been entrusted to us, as well as the revenge for its illustrious son, General Santa Anna. Should we leave him unavenged? No! Rather die than commit such infamy. Let us therefore prepare for the fight, certain of victory, and let the evil ones who have sought to steal a part of our country regret most strongly their accidental victory. Your leader has no doubts of the sentiments of the brave ones he commands, and he will always accompany them in their privations, their labors, and their danger."

In undertaking the narrative of the events in Texas, I am also compelled to assume the role of accuser, as I have already done in my diary, though I greatly regret having to do so against a general who merits personal consideration and whose private virtues command my esteem. Were General Filisola as well trained and courageous as he is honest, he would be among the first commanders of the Republic.

Frankness and sincerity are qualities that speak highly for men, but they should particularly characterize a soldier. To say what one does not feel for personal considerations or because of fear, is, to say the least, a base act.

Having declared this, I shall make some minor observations about a proclamation that misled the hopes of the army, the contents of which was contradicted by the facts and by subsequent dispatches. If General Filisola was convinced on the 24th of April that the victory obtained by the enemy was purely accidental and caused by the disdain with which General Santa Anna regarded the enemy; if he judged the enemy perfidious and cowardly and incapable of vanquishing us, and considered us strong; if it is true that the honor of the nation and the avenging of its first magistrate and also our comrades had been entrusted to us; then why abandon the field to the enemy? Why consolidate his own temporary victory, why sacrifice so shamelessly the honor of the nation and abandon so pitilessly our unfortunate compatriots? Should they be left unavenged? General Filisola asked himself, restricting this question to General Santa Anna. No! *Rather die than commit such infamy.* If, therefore, he could describe as infamous the failure to avenge this commander, how much greater infamy to have sacrificed the national honor, to have departed without avenging the insult our arms had received. If General Filisola has judged himself as he deserves, why should he take offence when I reiterate what I have said? Not having fulfilled what he offered the army, that to which he invited it, that to which he had excited its indignation and provoked its fury, he appeared as a despicable buffoon and gave the enemy cause for laughter.

As a contrast to General Filisola's proclamation, one could present almost all the communications he subsequently addressed to the government, but especially the one dated May 14th at Victoria.[50] This not only contradicts the reports of others, but his own as well, and proves without any shadow of a doubt that Señor Filisola is a man without memory, for at times he anticipates and at others retards events. Although the picture he paints of our sufferings during the retreat is truthful, there are, nevertheless, serious mistakes.

In this communication, Señor Filisola stated: "Alarm and dismay were general among all ranks after the news of the events at San Jacinto, for it was thought that all prisoners, including the president, would be executed in reprisal for our conduct toward theirs at Béjar and Goliad, that is to say, those of the enemy." Such an assertion was an injurious falsehood about the army, which as a whole had opposed the retreat, since they would have been shamed at being stopped within sight of the enemy's weakness when heretofore not even the enemy's entrenchments nor the thought of his substantial numbers or the superior quality of his force had detained them. They became indignant against those who held them back and outraged to see honor debased and a country sacrificed, which they had been charged to defend; they showed resentment and pain upon seeing that through folly and weakness without parallel, their cruel sufferings, their sacrifices, so numerous and great, had been rendered fruitless. Only weak souls are crushed in the presence of adversity; the strong, on the contrary, are stirred by fortune's blows; they grow

---

[50] Official report of General Vicente Filisola to the secretary of war and the navy, Guadalupe Victoria, May 14, 1836. It was published by José Urrea in his *Diario* in 1838, and is included as appendix 22 in *La Rebelión de Texas.*—Ed.

in stature and rise above the whims of this fickle deity. General Filisola measured the sentiments of the army by his own, so it is pleasing to me and very satisfying to affirm for the sake of truth and the honor of my comrades-in-arms, and for my own sake as a Mexican and a soldier, that his judgment was in error. This dismay to which General Filisola refers was not evident at Thompson's, except among certain persons he had taken as counselors, who did not counsel him well and who compromised his reputation and that of all the army. Generals Gaona and Woll were there, but neither they nor the commander of artillery showed any noticeable dismay, nor did any in the lower ranks of the army. In the Sapper Battalion, with which I made the campaign, there was, except for its commander, not a single individual who did not raise his voice against the retreat from the very moment he was ordered to retrieve everything that had been transported to the left bank of the Brazos, General Woll, under whose orders this operation was carried out, being a witness to these sentiments, and General Ampudia also, as well as many persons in the army. It is true that some, who thought we were taking too much time to get away from the enemy, loudly protested against the retreat when they saw that we were already incapable of taking the offensive, but, as I have said, they were a numbered few, whose names I omit not out of fear or consideration for the friendship with which some have honored me, but because they are well known and it is useless to name them. All of them have been pointed out.

It was also a deception to say that we were lacking supplies; this was nothing but a pretext to justify the necessity and expedience of retreat. At Matagorda, Columbia, and Brazoria, flour, rice, sugar, and potatoes were plentiful. Cattle and pork were to be found in all directions, the former seeming to flow forth from the woods, the latter to be found in the corrals of many homes along the Colorado and Brazos. Between the Brazos and the San Jacinto there were also great quantities of supplies. Although the army needed no more than a months' supply to end the campaign and hoist its eagles on the banks of the Sabine, it would have had supplies for more than six months had it been ordered to remain in Texas; during that time it could have received, in spite of any possible delays, those supplies so frequently offered, part of which later fell in the hands of the enemy because of the retreat. The sloop *Watchman* arrived at Cópano loaded with supplies for the army, when it was on the side of the Nueces River and a prey of the enemy. Between Río Grande and Laredo, the best part of the depots were abandoned, and even at Béjar some were left.[51] Therefore, we repeat, there was no lack of supplies; what was lacking was foresight, common sense, and an organizing genius, industrious and alert, who could have replaced the cold indifference with which the soldier was seen to suffer and the neglect of his sustenance; supplies there were in abundance, we repeat a hundred times, and, as we have seen in my diary, some were thrown into the water at Thompson's for lack of adequate transportation. I believe I have already said that if the government and the commander in chief had realized what Texas was worth, they would have also known that from this source the expense of the war could have been paid, and would have seen it as a source of increasing the public wealth, in the manner that Napoleon did in Italy. However, the country and the budding townships of Texas were unknown to them, because of immense distances that sometimes alter or distort the facts.

When we rejoined General Urrea, we saw that he was not greedy, and that, having traveled in the midst of abundance, not only of the useful things, but of the superfluous as well, he nevertheless had shown himself to be magnanimous. Taking for himself only what he needed, he would distribute among his chief officers and soldiers whatever they could carry; these, in turn, believed they had purchased what they were given by their exposure to danger and their fatigue. In all of this, General Urrea was only carrying out orders he had received from the commander in chief. What to do with so many goods of all descriptions, with such beautiful furnishings that no one could use, transport, or keep? Upon entering houses so magnificently furnished, our soldiers would be awestruck and would destroy without any mercy whatever happened to come

---

[51] I came in possession of a list of its number and quality made available to me by Lieutenant Colonel Machado, who discharged the office of provisioner at that post. But his document, as well as the report of the supplies which we had at Thompson's Pass, recorded by Manuel Villalba, the purveyor, has disappeared with other papers. Fortunately the two persons are living and they will not countenance a lie.

within sight, as a sign of regret, perhaps, at not being able to use them. On entering warehouses, they would throw away what had already been loaded in order to take away other things, ultimately not using anything.

The rumor spread by General Filisola, as well as by those who repeat without verifying rumors, to the effect that General Urrea enriched himself with the spoils of the enemy, has been as unjust as it is contemptible. How would it have been possible to transport them, when it was well known that he lacked transportation for supplies and ammunition? But, even had it been so, who could complain, to whom was all this harmful but to him who had forced us to carry on the war and to make so many sacrifices? But, I repeat, this is only one of the many groundless accusations that have been directed at this Mexican.

## ↝§ 12 §↜

THE first disposition made by General Filisola because of the terror produced in his mind by the news of the misfortune at San Jacinto was to order General Urrea to rejoin him with his division; at the very moment that he was receiving the news of this event (San Jacinto), he actually addressed to Urrea, in duplicate, an executive order urging him to do this without delay. He addressed a similar order to Colonel Salas, stationed at Columbia, commanding him to join him without awaiting orders from the general who was his immediate superior, and making him responsible for any possible delay.[52] The confusion did not allow General Filisola to reflect upon the error he was committing in leaving General Urrea's rear guard unprotected, without the supporting force necessary for his operations. For had this general proceeded to Velasco, as he had planned to do before receiving the order to countermarch, he would have found himself in a very precarious situation.

Great anxiety and much interest was manifested for joining with General Urrea, for he was looked upon as an anchor of salvation, so great was the reputation he had established during the campaign. Such is the condition of the human species and such the follies to which we are driven by passions that the very ones who were now praising him and rendering him tribute later censured him and painted him in the blackest colors. As has been noted in the diary, this reunion was accomplished on the afternoon and night of the 24th.

The 25th dawned, and with it hopes were born, yearnings were stirred, and new controversies arose. No one cared to approve the

---

[52] Vicente Filisola to José Urrea, April 23, 1836; José Mariano Salas to the general in chief of the division of operations at Brazoria, Columbia, April 27, 1836. Salas reports that he is marching in compliance with Filisola's order (see *La Rebelión de Texas*, appendix 24).—*Ed.*

retreat, and it was taken for granted that we would again descend upon the enemy, because many wished it. Our generals, it was said, would never consent to their own shame and that of the whole nation, nor would they lightly sacrifice their own interests; General Urrea, who has proved his courage and patriotism, will oppose it, and he has only to wish it for us to follow him; all those who do not will remain among the women and will appear as weak as these. But our star, eclipsed on the 21st, was not destined to shine brilliantly again. The first link of our ignominy had been forged, and the chain was to continue to the end, which no one could foresee. Our ranks had no Epaminondas, no Leonidas, none of the many heroes that abounded in ancient Greece. Pure patriotism, which casts aside all other interests, is the most sublime and heroic passion of the human heart, but unfortunately it is the rarest, the most easily confused with ambition, the one that brings on greater cares and attracts more enemies, because the sect of evil is and always will be the most numerous among men. This sacred love of country finds an easier dwelling place within the breasts of the young than in those of the old, whose hearts seem dead to all noble passions, susceptible only to those which degrade.

Assembled at General Filisola's tent were Generals Urrea, Ramírez y Sesma, Tolsa, Gaona, and Woll, and Lieutenant Colonel Ampudia of the artillery, all firmly agreed to continue the retreat. The mystery with which this meeting was held, with no one allowed to come close enough to hear the discussion, augured ill and prevented my knowing the reasons that inspired this resolution, but doubtless they did not differ from those made public. The seven persons who of their own accord decreed in a few moments the loss of the most valuable and interesting part of our territory, they who with little thought resolved to sacrifice the national honor, the army's, and their own, they who in a weak moment contributed with General Filisola in thrusting the nation into a bottomless sea of misfortunes, these men, to say the least, share in the opprobium of that general, although the responsibility is his alone. In taking a resolution so difficult, so delicate, and of such vast import and such far-reaching consequences, they forgot the extreme sacrifices the nation had made and the great difficulties it had overcome to organize the expedition even halfway; they never thought of the greater difficul-

145

ties a second expedition would encounter after they had allowed the enemy to take heart and to gain strength; they never gave a thought to the effect a retreat has on the morale of the soldier; the abundance of blood already shed carried no weight in their thoughts, nor did the fact that many more victims and sacrifices of all kinds would be required to reconquer the abandoned territory and to repair the losses that a retreat always incurs; when all that was needed to dam up the torrent of calamities that the retreat was bringing upon us and to restore the good name of our arms and change into glory the face of the Republic was to take the one step that patriotism, honor, and duty urgently demanded; but in all this they childishly and shamefully failed.

The great man of the century, who the illustrious Volney has said bore the head of Caesar on the shoulders of Alexander, says of retreats: "At the beginning of a campaign one must consider carefully whether to advance or not, but once offensive war is initiated *it is appropriate to sustain it to the ultimate extreme*. No matter how wise the maneuvers of a retreat may be, the morale of the army is always undermined, for as the prospects of victory are lost, the advantage passes to the enemy. On the other hand, even if one puts aside the losses of men and army matériel, retreats are far more costly than the bloodiest engagements, the difference being that in battle our losses and the enemy's are more or less the same, whereas in a retreat we take losses and he does not." Elsewhere he states: "The glory and honor of an army is the prime duty to be borne in mind by a general who initiates or accepts a battle; the conservation of men is a secondary duty, but at the same time it is through courage, daring, and perseverance that the saving of men is accomplished. In a retreat, discounting the honor of arms, frequently more men are lost than during two battles; for this reason one should never despair as long as there are a few brave ones standing firm by the flags. With such conduct victory is, or deserves to be, obtained." Doubtless we would have achieved it, had there only been a commander who would have led us into it and who could have appraised the advantages to be gained by not showing the enemy our backs; we would have conquered had there been among those in charge a single one desiring glory, who could have foreseen the renown that would have been his if he had taken that resolution, for which no great heroism was necessary. General Urrea seemed destined to play this brilliant role and everyone pointed to him as the best suited to carry it out, but he let himself be influenced by the ideas of his comrades. He was disgusted by the retreat from the moment he knew that it had been initiated, even more by the haste with which it was executed; the language he used with Generals Filisola and Ramírez y Sesma during some moments of conflict will always do him honor, but he did not oppose it openly, as he did later,[53] and on the 25th of April his energetic opposition would have been enough to have exchanged our shame for laurels.

Most of the army would have followed him gladly to rectify the disaster at San Jacinto, had he wanted to place himself at their head. Several of us officers, indignant to learn that our disgrace was to be consummated, invited him to do so; but a misguided principle of delicacy made him gently reject our invitation, expressing his appreciation for our good intentions. I believe that an act of indiscipline is permissible if it is for the salvation of the country. I have no doubt that my opinion will scandalize some and will bring anathema upon me from those who preach passive obedience, even against their own interests. They fail to recognize that in the military there are many occasions when it is indispensable.

If fortune had placed me in General Urrea's advantageous position, I would not have hesitated to take a step which success would have justified, and by which that leader could have completed that crown of glory in which he had already woven many laurels.

I would have to quote many other facts to prove that the army was not in favor of retreat and that everything said about its loss of morale was merely a misrepresentation to justify this measure, but nothing belies this report or proves that the retreat was carried out in this fashion because of bewilderment or caprice so much as the following, which none will dare to deny. On the memorable day of the 25th, when the generals were summoned for a council of war, the corps commanders were also summoned, but, since their opinion

---

[53] From Matamoros on June 1, 1836, Urrea wrote to Filisola, commanding general of the army of operations, expressing his deep resentment against the retreat, which he considered shameful and against all military principles, and informing Filisola that he has advised the supreme government of his protest (see *La Rebelión de Texas*, appendix 25).—*Ed.*

had been previously sounded and their opposition to the retreat was known, they were ordered to withdraw under the flimsy pretext that they had been called so that they might be charged with guarding the camp while this meeting was taking place in its very center. No one should have been listened to more than the corps commanders on this occasion, for, being so close to the troops, they could accurately assess the real attitude among the soldiers, and no one would have responded more favorably than they to an advance toward the enemy. Colonels Morales and Montoya y Salas and the battalions under their command, which belonged to Urrea's division, were foremost in their repugnance for retreat. The intimacy I have had with the first of these commanders since I was his subaltern gave me sufficient confidence to urge him strongly to use the influence of his rank and recognized courage to oppose the idea of a retreat, and I have not forgotten the reply he gave me, expressing his indignation at the conduct of the generals and his conviction that nothing could alter a resolution taken by men overcome by fear, which was strengthened by the detailed and perhaps exaggerated account of the surprise at San Jacinto given to him by Captain Marcos Barragán. Nor will Señor Ampudia (a friend, now become an adversary) be able to deny that I presented sound reasons for his opposing a retreat, and that he had accompanied me to General Urrea's tent for that purpose, but the general was not there at the time. The Sapper Battalion, the one from Guadalajara, and a considerable portion of the other corps who were not in favor of the retreat are witnesses that I did all within my modest sphere to oppose it, a weak effort on the part of an officer without representation and without influence, when the military laws are so well *formulated that by virtue of them there is more patriotism, more wisdom, and greater understanding in one who commands!* The few who on the 25th favored retreat could be easily recognized either by the silence they kept or by the tenor of their conversation.

It is truly noteworthy that they should have refused to listen to the opinion of the corps commanders and that they accepted only that of those invested with the rank of general and of Señor Ampudia in order to resolve such an important question, the enormous consequences of which were difficult to foresee. Were these the only

148

gentlemen of honor, the only men who loved their native land, the only ones interested in saving the Republic? If the first in command was solely responsible, why then were his comrades consulted? And why not with the other commanders? It has already been stated, but it is necessary to repeat it: because these opposed retreat and because it would not have been as easy to convince them of its necessity as it was to convince Señores Urrea and Ampudia, who had opposed it.

Although I may appear discourteous and may be judged falsely to be a man preoccupied with selfish ideas, I must call to the attention of whosoever may read this, that in an assemblage of three thousand Mexicans, of those seven leaders who, without judgment and consideration, resolved to seal the disgrace of all, only three were Mexican by birth, who naturally should have greater interest in the good name and prosperity of their homeland than those who had abandoned their country to adopt ours, although there are honorable exceptions. The four remaining were: the commander in chief, Italian; the major general, French; and the commander of the First Brigade (according to the new organization of the army, in effect from the very beginning of the campaign), from Havana; the commander of artillery, who passes for a Cuban, is thought by some to be Andalucian, which his character verifies.[54] It is most painful and degrading for Mexicans, but this is the sad condition to which we have been condemned, for our release from the Spanish yoke has been followed by a series of foreign commanders, many of them unworthy of the honor. I would have liked to have seen men from everywhere in the world enjoying in my country the same guarantees and distinctions as those of its own sons, but not in the ranks of the army, and least of all given preference through a spirit of innovation, frequently to our own detriment. However, this does not hold true for the few who made a genuine contribution when they chose a new country.

After the army had crossed a desert of hundreds of leagues, after

---

[54] De la Peña refers to Filisola, Woll, Tolsa, and Ampudia, respectively. Sánchez Garza notes that de la Peña did not know that Gaona was Cuban. Only Ramírez y Sesma and Urrea were Mexican by birth.—*Ed.*

it had overcome great obstacles and had suffered with much patience all kinds of privations, it had more reasons to advance than to retreat. General Filisola publicly confessed this in the aforementioned communication of the 14th of May, in which, addressing himself exclusively to the commander in chief, he stated: "Your Excellency was about to give the last touch to your enterprise, for the occupation of Texas seemed to have been brought already to its sole and intended conclusion. The army had already taken the fort at the Alamo, had already fought and destroyed the greater part of the enemy's regular forces, had taken considerable amounts of artillery, rifles, and munitions, had crossed three wide rivers, and, with a determined attitude in the midst of hunger and their poorly clad condition, had ardently favored the upholding of the integrity of their native soil. Doubtless, a calmer attitude would have rewarded its heroic efforts and sufferings." A little civic pride, a sense of shame, and less fear on his part, his Excellency [Filisola] should have said, would have sufficed to have kept the nation from plunging into an abyss of misfortunes, to have rewarded the commendable efforts of the army, and to have freed it of the many deprivations that had burdened its tragic retreat. Anyone, without being a soldier, will understand that an army that had overcome all obstacles, that had crushed the enemy as often as he had dared to show his face, and that was lacking only the final touch to its undertaking, was not, as General Filisola knew and confessed, exactly in the position to retreat at the first sight of adversity, or because a division of the advance guard had been defeated. This general alone was seized by the singular idea of yielding the camp to the enemy without even facing him, on the first occasion that luck had favored that enemy; the chain of evils, the great dishonor and the humiliation that awaited him if he retreated were certainly obvious to him, as were the grave new sacrifices that the nation would have to undergo in order to reconquer Texas.

General Filisola, who from Monclova on had marched with the rear guard of the army, arrived at Béjar ten days after the Alamo assault and continued to the Brazos River, retreating without participating in any of the *skirmishes*, without seeing any of the enemy other than those who came later to witness our shame and the disgrace of our commander.

In a *Manifesto* that this general has made public,[55] with the apparent (and futile) purpose of justifying his acts, but in which the real purpose of satisfying a low passion for vengeance, the burning passion that dominates his soul, can be identified, he has distorted the facts and has fallen into many grave contradictions, for an evil cause can be made worse in being defended. In this poisonous "masterpiece," in which a dictionary of insults has been exhausted, in which there is a mixture of invectives and sarcasms, in which ridicule is employed to no purpose, and in which a bitter irony is appealed to, to make the offense greater; this pamphlet, I repeat, written in the language of the passions, in which hypocrisy abounds, is no less full of calumnies and lies; General Filisola's sole purpose being to offend and censure the very one he had warmly congratulated during the conflict *for the brilliancy of his glorious operations* which, in the opinion of his Excellency, had left nothing to be desired; to humiliate the very one whom, during days of consternation and conflict, he had showered with flatteries, reiterating that *he* [Urrea] *was the only general of any account*; to defame and scorn the very one who had been given so much prominence, having been suddenly called when terror caused them to see in him the greater strength of the army, the one who had been placed at the head of the reserves, an honor generally given to the most courageous, who had been entrusted with guarding the pass at the Colorado, when images of death tormented General Filisola's fantasy and kept him in a continuous state of alarm, causing him to search in all directions, interrupting our retreat from an enemy that did not exist. Fortunately for General Urrea, his adversary, wishing to unburden his ire with great effect, letting himself be pushed by an unbounded pride, and amassing sarcasm and effrontery, becomes disconcerted and warns the reader how suspicious a document becomes when it reveals itself to be so impassioned. Whoever examines the manifesto circumspectly will look upon it as worthy of little credence because of the frequent and stupid contradictions it contains; for those acquainted

---

[55] Author gives date as August 1837. Sánchez Garza asserts that the author refers to the *Representación dirigida al Supremo Gobierno* (report addressed to the Supreme Government) by General Vicente Filisola, concerning the Texas campaign in the year 1836. The object of Filisola's spleen was Urrea.—*Ed.*

151

with the facts will see that statement as nothing more than a pestilent rhapsody. It looks like something put together by a person to whom the wrong information and false tales were given rather than by an eyewitness, written to defame rather than to defend its author. General Filisola has used the weapons of reason in a sinister fashion; blind with the pride of having been born over there in old Europe, though he has not studied the sciences in its great armies, as he boasts, he is determined to belittle and humiliate to the extreme a Mexican general who has given us lessons in honor, one who, though less learned than his Excellency, has fulfilled his duties as a soldier more creditably. Instead of unbecoming arrogance, instead of hypocritical and vile language, he should have used frankness and sincerity; he should have admitted his errors, for in this way he might have gained indulgence, convincing the mind and, at the same time, winning the heart. How despicable does General Filisola appear, at times praising General Urrea and rendering him honors, at others censuring him, according to the passion dominating his soul. Some may see me as an enemy of that general, as one who bears a grudge, but I am nothing of the sort; on the contrary, I must repeat, I have not the slightest wrong to avenge; indeed, I am personally obligated to him. But his entire conduct in Texas caused me profound indignation; his errors, his stupidity and contemptible deeds, to which I will refer later, arouse my soul, and expressions of pain slip out, many of them caustic, no doubt, though General Filisola is more to be pitied than hated.

Since my chief purpose is to relate facts, I must be brief in the accusations that necessity requires me to make. It would be very easy for me to demolish General Filisola's manifesto, did I not know that all his assertions contradict each other, and were I not certain that General Urrea, in a just defense of his injured honor, will challenge him and will do so triumphantly. I will therefore not speak of it other than in general terms and will dwell more particularly on the dispatch of the 14th of May, already referred to.

"Convinced therefore," says General Filisola in that dispatch, "of the situation in which I found myself, I wanted to hear the opinion of the generals, my comrades-in-arms; I summoned them, and they unanimously agreed that it was necessary to recross the

Colorado, to re-establish our communications with the interior of the Republic, and to await help from the government, etc."

In this, as in other official communications and in his manifesto, General Filisola has painted a sad and pathetic picture of the physical and moral condition of the army. It was, he reports, in a most wretched state, because of the long march made without clothing, without food supplies, without reserves, practically wiped out by the plague, without hospitals, without surgeons, without supplies to the rear, forced to travel back along the same road for more than two hundred leagues when the hot season was upon them, when floods might take them by surprise, compelled to cross many torrential streams without the means to do so, and exposed to the enemy's harassment from the rear, in a march that by necessity was slow and cumbersome because of the great quantities of equipment and inadequate transport. General Filisola has repeated all this ad nauseam, as well as saying that for these same reasons he was going to establish a campsite on the right bank of the Colorado; this in spite of the miserable situation, and after we had withdrawn and abandoned the cattle and provisions already in our possession when we were in the center of the colonies. How could General Filisola have persuaded himself even for a fleeting moment that he could remain on the right bank of the Colorado awaiting orders and the help which he knew had to reach him from a distance of more than 450 leagues? How could he have assured himself that they would be sent him, when he knew the plight of the public treasury and the many difficult sacrifices that had already been made in order to field this army which he has pictured as a skeleton, incapable of dealing even with a ghost? With an army thought to be in no condition to advance against the enemy only fifteen leagues away, for fear that it might be surprised by the rainy season, or that it might evaporate in the heat, how, we repeat, could anyone then believe that he could hold his position at the Colorado with equal or greater obstacles? However, this was only a pretext, the first that entered General Filisola's mind, which he offered the government in his communication of April 25th. Thus, once he had taken the first step backward, he was forced to continue retreating, for reasons he should have foreseen; he abandoned the line at the

Colorado and those at the San Antonio River and the Nueces in turn.

To try to justify the retreat by saying that it was made in order to save the life of the president-general and the other prisoners is a contemptible deceit, because when General Filisola undertook it, he did so believing that they had all been executed in reprisal for the bloody scenes we had enacted with the enemy. Not until the 27th of April did we learn that our leader and his companions in misfortune still lived. Moreover, this is a futile excuse for the great error committed, because the honor of the nation, its justice, its welfare, its integrity and that of its army weighed more heavily than the life of our compatriots, and because it would have been more natural to have saved them, as has been said, by advancing and dominating the enemy than by leaving them at the mercy of his fury. We will amplify on the opinions that were expressed regarding the acquiescence to the orders from the prisoner [Santa Anna] at the very scene, the very moment of weak and shameful concessions.

Bent on the difficult task of justifying his reproachful conduct, General Filisola only made flagrant contradictions, sometimes in the same document. Thus at times he pictures the army deprived of everything, as naked as the man in the jungle, without will, half dead, overcome with terror, incapable of fighting a handful of adventurers; at others, he depicts it as if by magic capable of everything, saying that it has overcome and destroyed the greater part of the enemy's regular forces and has surmounted all obstacles, adding that it was made up of courageous Mexicans who never knew fear during the whole campaign. This being an incontestable truth, he paints the former picture to justify himself and admits to the latter in order to blame others.

For General Filisola to try to exonerate himself by stating that the commander in chief had not acquainted him with his plan of operations, though he was second in command, is such a miserable excuse that it hardly merits mention. After the victory of March 19th no one in the army was ignorant of the plan that General Santa Anna had adopted and had ordered Generals Ramírez y Sesma, Urrea, and Gaona to carry out. If General Filisola had said that the plan as conceived by the commander in chief was a poor one, many of us would agree with him. It is true that we lacked a firm base of operations, and it was up to Señor Filisola to establish one when, after the

154

catastrophe at San Jacinto, the nation's honor was entrusted to him; but to give the bugle call for quick marches and to issue impulsive orders was not the way to undo what had already been done; committing even greater errors was a poor way of correcting those already made. And under these circumstances he has had the courage to criticize others? It is true that he took command in a time of conflict, but for that very reason he should have shown greatness of soul and a display of military genius rather than falling into confusion and giving the enemy an importance that he lacked, exaggerating the number and quality of his forces, and supposing Houston in command of hundreds of formidable and warlike veterans who really did not exist. In order to act, General Filisola should have thought not of the number of his opponents but of his own duties, not of the dimensions of his difficulties but of the obligation to overcome them, not of the consequences of going after the enemy but of the importance of destroying him.

According to one author, a wise and orderly retreat demands the most penetrating military genius and is more glorious to the vanquished than victory itself. Nothing had been prepared or provided for our retreat, because we never believed, we could scarcely even imagine, that we would have to do it: there was no foresight, but once retreat was undertaken it was carried out in the greatest disorder, the worst of it being that the enemy was a witness to it. He did not pursue us, because he was still as weak as he had been before the victory, but General Filisola nevertheless wished to move fast. The enemy's safety depended upon our retreat, and he harassed and ridiculed our prisoners because of it; Filisola, on the other hand, wanted to abandon our artillery to him during the days when our march was slowed by the weather and the entire road was a muddy lagoon that seemed eager to swallow up everything that touched its surface. In the oft-quoted communication, it was said: "The army had already been stricken with dysentery, and we found ourselves without any means of cure and without physicians (indisputable truth), so there was no choice left but to perish by starvation or to abandon all (false, very false), saving only the men." A few lines further he states: "If, under those critical circumstances, the enemy had blocked our only avenue of escape, there would have been no other choice but to die or to surrender unconditionally, be-

155

cause not a single gun was in condition to be fired and most of the munitions were wet." What a different situation, he exclaims, from that of ten days ago. I beg you to overlook the fact that I express such surprise that a man of little courage and of much less natural ability could have reached the summit of a military career.

If General Filisola through either weakness or error has plunged us into a sea of misfortunes, believing in good faith that he was saving us, he is far from deserving the epithet of traitor that some have chosen to give him, particularly one commander, not a Mexican, who flattered the general while he was in command and consented to everything, but who, after he was separated from him, became the most outstanding flatterer of the new army chief. General Filisola, I repeat, made mistakes and committed many acts of weakness, but he did not retreat from Texas in order to make the lands he possessed in that territory increase in value, as some have said.

I should not proceed further without stating that the only act of weakness noted in the army after the news of the catastrophe at San Jacinto was received occurred at Matagorda. Colonel Alcérrica, who, with the Tres Villas Battalion, defended this post, received a communication on the 2nd of May from Colonel Garay informing him of the unfortunate event of the 21st. This, and the fact that on the 3rd the sapper officer Holsinger told him that one of the prisoners working on a fortification being built there had assured him that the previous night an enemy spy had surprised him and urged him to leave because in two days the post was to be attacked by superior forces, overwhelmed him with panic. On the 4th Colonel Alcérrica left Matagorda with two companies, leaving the command entrusted to Holsinger and ordering that the remaining corps follow within three hours and that the treasury chest be opened and the money distributed among the officers. Since Señor Alcérrica had taken with him the mules for a twelve-pounder there at the post, and since Holsinger was unwilling to abandon it, it was agreed not to march within the extremely short period as ordered and to request the mules from the commander in order to move the artillery piece. But the commander, instead of sending them, re-affirmed his previous order for the march and for the money from the chest to be distributed as instructed, and ordered the artillery piece and the ammunition to be thrown in the water. Consequently it was agreed that Holsinger should embark on two barges with the cannon and the chest, that the ammunition should be distributed among the soldiers, and that a sergeant, four artillerymen, a soldier from the Tres Villas, and fourteen to sixteen prisoners should go with him. Thus it happened, and I would be the last one to know if it was a wise move, for one thing is certain: Holsinger later showed up with the enemy, and it is still a mystery whether he surrendered traitorously or was taken prisoner.

Captain Lorenzo Calderón marched with the rest of his battalion along the Colorado River in the direction of Cazey [sic] Pass. On the road he met a company of grenadiers that Alcérrica had left under the command of their first sergeant, Miguel Alvarado, with orders to wait for him there, but as the march continued toward that pass, it was discovered that Alcérrica had left, leaving no instructions. Later he turned up demented, and it is not known whether he really was, or whether he assumed this role to cover up his culpability in abandoning without orders a point entrusted to his honor and the disorder in which he did so, with no enemy in sight. This is recorded because of the indictment against him, and it pains me to relate it because of the friendship Señor Alcérrica has professed for me; however, a historian should not hide the truth on account of personal consideration. Señor Filisola, in one of his many distortions, tried to burden General Urrea with this offense, for which the commander who committed it was solely responsible.

# ⤙§13§⤚

ONCE decided upon, the retreat was carried out in the greatest disorder. General Filisola certainly proved himself unworthy of his reputation as a good soldier which he held among my countrymen, but he did prove that one can be a good squadron leader without necessarily being a good general. We seemed doomed to take no step in Texas that was not a mistake; we had invaded the territory with no definite center of operations, and we retreated in a single column. Had the enemy been strong instead of weak, and in condition to attack us as General Filisola thought, how could that general possibly have committed the stupidity of retreating in single column to the rear? What did he think he could save of his army, which he thought he was saving, with such a disorderly and shameful reverse maneuver? If one could not justify the retreat in itself, much less can one do so by the way it was done. Nothing had been planned in advance, because, as stated before, we never even imagined that we would find ourselves having to retreat, executing it in great haste and so with ever-increasing disorder, and making such dreadful progress. An adverse change in weather, which started the very day that we left Madam Powell's, added greatly to our misfortunes. Many of these could have been avoided had we simply taken the road to San Felipe de Austin, which is higher and over which we had advanced without obstacles even in the midst of heavy rains. It was necessary to have seen and experienced it to understand the army's sufferings and the obstacles it had to overcome when it was already completely exhausted after so many prolonged marches. During the days of the storm, particularly the 29th and 30th of April and the 1st, 2nd, and 3rd of May, we went along roads hardly passable. The corps marching in the vanguard scarcely passed over a road before it became impassable; those who followed, divided into platoons, passed wherever they could; no one paid them any mind, since their officers and commanders hardly worried about details. The cannon and the loaded pack mules sank in the mud when least expected, and much time was lost and great effort expended to pull them out of these formidable mudholes. No one altered the others to the danger; it seemed that each corps marched on its own initiative, and each individual alone, as if their fate did not depend on that of the others. It appeared as if no general orders had been given and no common bond existed among them.

No enemy pursued us, because their forces were just as insignificant as they had been before the battle of San Jacinto; nevertheless, our general seemed to wish to move faster. The enemy depended for his safety on our retreat, and he ridiculed and humiliated our prisoners because of it, but Señor Filisola, as has been said, considered abandoning the artillery to them during the days when we had to march with the privations mentioned before.[56] The commander and officers of this branch worked with admirable perseverance to pull their artillery pieces out of the mud, for which they deserved the gratitude of the army. Should they be entitled to any praise for having complied with their duty, a part of it will be mine also, for I worked along with them, participating in all their hardships.

In this tragic retreat fatigue was as great as privations were excessive. So it was, after recrossing the Colorado, when the army had already lost its morale and destroyed all its matériel and was in no position to take the offensive against the enemy as General Filisola had proposed on the 10th of May, and even less so on the 12th of June, that General Andrade received orders to that effect from the new commander of the army. This was one of the days when we suffered most from thirst. Our situation was really desperate, for we could find no drop of water to quench our burning thirst in the midst of a scorching sun. On such days soldiers fainted beneath the weight of their arms, their gesticulations indicating the horror of their situation; yet some commanding officers passed by with the greatest indifference, appearing to be much more interested in their own situation than in that of any others. Nothing was said to the army to

---

[56] De la Peña repeats himself verbatim here, probably inadvertently inserting the same note twice.—*Ed.*

encourage it or to help it bear its sufferings, and after the deceitful proclamation of the 24th of April, not another word was addressed to it.

So the reader may judge for himself and be convinced that I am not speaking from memory as General Filisola has done, I will continue quoting from my diary, as it was written at the time.

April 28th. On the 26th we left Madame Powell's dwellings and our rear guard had not yet begun its march when columns of smoke were seen to rise, forerunners of the flames that were soon to consume those houses. Truly the sight of a fire is a beautiful and imposing spectacle for one who can put aside the feelings of great loss it produces. After traveling a short distance we crossed one of the three Bernardos, a narrow but deep creek, which took three hours and was not without some difficulty. Between eleven and twelve in the morning, rain began to pour, continuing heavily until nightfall, when we made a halt. The rear guard, protected by General Urrea with a reserve brigade, had not yet arrived when the rain began again, to continue through the night without interruption and consequently without any rest for us.

The 27th dawned with a persistent rain. Nevertheless, the march continued much later in the day, but we had traveled no more than five miles when we had to camp, it being impossible to cross the second Bernardo, which was greatly swollen. On this day we made our way through the mud, so the march was as laborious as it had been the day before, when we had traveled no more than eight or ten miles. It must have been around five in the afternoon when I noticed commanders and officers, soldiers and women crowding around the tent of the new commander in chief; I too drew near to listen to a messenger talking, who had just arrived with a communication from General Santa Anna, which reported that he had been made a prisoner and gave orders for the army to retreat to Béjar and to Guadalupe Victoria, stating that he had agreed on an armistice with Houston, during which negotiations would take place with a view of ending the war forever.[57]

---

[57] Santa Anna to Filisola, San Jacinto, April 22, 1836. The letter also advises Filisola to assume command of the armies (see *La Rebelión de Texas*, appendix 27).—*Ed.*

Mr. Smith,[58] who calls himself colonel, brought the aforesaid message but, angered at seeing Madame Powell's dwellings burned by us, told the courier that he was returning to his camp to demand General Ramírez y Sesma's head, saying that he believed him to be an evil-hearted man. He did return, exchanging that document for another one that the courier was carrying from the government to General Santa Anna. Smith made the remark in the very presence of General Ramírez y Sesma, whom he did not know, a mistake that excited laughter in some and gave rise to many comments. Referring to the captives, Smith reported that there were twenty or so commanders and officers among them.

Before going any further, one should note here that though General Ramírez y Sesma was one of the advisers most listened to, he had no special command and was therefore not directly responsible for the needless acts of vandalism that were committed.

The reader should also be aware that those men who had submitted to General Santa Anna's whims, those who had most applauded or who had acquiesced to all his acts (among whom General Filisola is not counted), were the first to raise the cry of disapproval once he had fallen into disgrace. Supposing him dead, they showered him with criticism, censuring even the little good he had done; they extended their criticism to bitter fault-finding involving even those events they themselves had initiated, approved, or helped to bring about. Some went even further, tactlessly rejoicing in his misfortune. So when these men found out that the hero they had cursed so much was still alive, fearing that someone might reveal their shameful conduct, they became greatly confused and appeared as if they had been struck by the thunderbolt of vengeance. Their fears could be read in their faces, and those who observed as closely as I will serve as witnesses.

It has already been mentioned that General Filisola, always hesitant, always walking in the dark, unable to find plausible pre-

---

[58] De la Peña does not identify Smith here, though he speaks of Benjamin F. Smith later. According to Joseph Milton Nance, *Attack and Counterattack* (Austin: University of Texas Press, 1964), p. 310, " 'Deaf' Smith reached Filisola's camp with dispatches from President Santa Anna" on April 27.—*Ed.*

texts with which to excuse his errors, seizes upon the first one that presents itself. He had said at first, on the 25th of April, that he was retreating to the Colorado in order to establish a needed base of operations,[59] and once this was accomplished that it was done to save the lives of General Santa Anna and the other prisoners, but, as one now sees, he actually retreated before he knew that the general was still living, in the belief that they had all perished. Later he maintained that his purpose had always been to retreat, but that he had made it appear that he was doing it in compliance with the orders of the prisoner general in order to make his retreat more easily; the truth, however, is that all these have been shifts and pretexts with which he has tried to excuse his grave error.

In General Filisola's presumptuous attempt to ridicule General Urrea and to censure all his operations, even those to which he had lent his own approval, he said that this general always chose the site of greatest safety in the case of any military action.

By general order of April 25th a new organization was given to the army. The First Brigade, made up of the permanent battalion of Morelos, the active from Guadalajara, and the auxiliary from Guanajuato, with two six-pounders and a howitzer, was placed under General Gaona's command. The Second, made up of the Sapper Battalion, the Querétaro active, and the first from Mexico City, with two eight-pounders and a howitzer, was placed under General Tolsa. The Reserve Brigade, made up of the Jiménez and San Luis battalions, all the cavalry pickets, and two four-pounders, was assigned to General Urrea. The same order stated: "Since the army must initiate its march tomorrow, its order shall be as follows: at the vanguard two companies from the Second Brigade; following it the wagons and the loads of ammunition, equipment, and provisions; following this, the Second Brigade, which the First in turn will follow, the rear guard being covered by the Reserve Brigade." The general order of the 26th outlined the march in the following fashion: "At the vanguard, the Sapper Battalion; following this, the

---

[59] Filisola to the secretary of war and navy, Madam Powell's, April 25, 1836, advising him of the defeat at San Jacinto and of the retreat he has initiated (see *La Rebelión de Texas*, appendix 28).—*Ed.*

Second Brigade, the wagons, equipment, provisions, commissary, and ammunition; this followed by the First Brigade; the rear guard covered by the Reserve," which continued to cover it until my commander was ordered to march with it to assure a crossing at the Colorado.

There was nothing to fear, because our general made efforts to keep us far from danger, but in the rather remote case that the enemy had tried to attack us, the Reserve Brigade would have been the first to engage in combat, unless the enemy had placed himself at our vanguard as General Filisola feared, but this was far from likely. It must be mentioned that the Reserve Brigade, in the inverse order in which we were marching, would have been the first to engage in combat had it become necessary. Our system of campaign in a single line did not put General Urrea in the place of greatest safety, as General Filisola has stated, unless it was certain that the enemy would appear at precisely the opposite end from where this general was situated. It is certain, very certain, that there was no enemy to fear, because the further we withdrew, the more freely he could breathe; moreover, the falsity of the assertion that General Urrea would have chosen the least exposed places for himself has been amply demonstrated.

In order not to be repetitious, which is always annoying, and to spare the reader as much as possible, I will not enlarge here upon the objections that were noted in my diary, and shall continue the insertion of it, reserving that for later.

Yesterday (written on the 28th) some commanders and officers offered to go to the enemy camp to clarify things, and the first to offer was General Urrea. They were not allowed to do so, and today General Woll was sent, whose selection was not well received, since he is not a Mexican.[60] Today we countermarched in search of another

---

[60] This officer carried out his mission with diligence, though without success. Various documents attest to the replies he had from the chief of the dissidents and the dignity with which he conducted himself. [Several letters were exchanged between Adrián Woll, Thomas J. Rusk, David Burnet, and Santa Anna. See *Mercurio del Puerto de Matamoros*, suppl. no. 86, June 24, 1836.—*Ed.*]

road and another crossing on the Colorado. Passing by the place where we had camped on the 26th, we made a 45 degree turn to the left and continued our march, crossing an immense lagoon, for the whole march has been through a swamp, in which we camped between four and five in the afternoon after going about ten miles.

## ≈§ 14 §≈

APRIL 30th. Yesterday our misfortunes reached their limit. The wagons had been delayed since the previous day, and some of our sick who were in them died for lack of the medicine and nourishment their condition required. One felt great indignation at seeing those poor unfortunates being ill-treated by even the generals, especially Gaona, as if the men were made out of bronze and not subject to illness, despite so much misery and hardship. The vanguard began to leave at eight in the morning, but by ten-thirty the rear guard still had not been able to march. Before the march began, armaments, munitions, nails, quick matches of rope, and other appurtenances of the artillery had been thrown into the creek to lighten the load on the wagons. The canvas bags were distributed among the corps, three to each man, and those of rope were cast aside, since the cost of transportation was five times the value of the articles. When this happens, some officers make use of three or four mules and the commanders, four times as many as they are entitled to. If they are hoping to load booty, I shall not be the one to affirm it.

Today I had to dismount, sinking up to my knees in the mud, falling and getting up, finally taking off my boots and continuing thus. We walked no more than thirty or forty paces before the soldiers had to help pull out the artillery pieces, an extremely exhausting chore, since they were poorly nourished, and much time was lost in this way. Between five and six in the afternoon, when we had traveled five or six miles at most, each corps camped as best it could, and likewise the commanders and officers, for conditions were beyond discipline. All around one could see groups at a distance one from the other. The artillery remained stuck up to the axles two or three miles away from the point of departure. The loads of ammunition, provisions, and equipment were left scattered along the road and the individual who at great sacrifice was able to bring up his corresponding equipment found it useless. Many loads were lost, many mules were ruined, and the troops could not have mess because it never reached them, nor was there any wood to prepare any if it had. It is difficult to describe our march on this day; it was a complete disaster. Exasperation among the officers and the troops. Grumblings because the roads had not been reconnoitered before we were buried in the deep mud and were made to suffer hunger and other privations. The road to Austin was solid and on high ground and we had been able to travel on it during heavy rain. General Urrea received orders to secure a pass on the Colorado, so he advanced, leaving his artillery.

Today (April 30th) the infantry continued its march, each corps leaving behind a picket to help pull out the artillery and the loads. For these had been moving forward as best they could, and it is impossible to see without regret more than 1,500 pack animals scattered in all directions, for no sooner are some extricated than others bog down, the chain of disorders continuing without intermission. Everything is misfortune, work, and hardship. Among the loads that were abandoned yesterday were found unlocked trunks, broken packs, and destroyed ammunition boxes, among which the shrapnel containers could hardly be seen in the midst of the mud. It looks as if the enemy had fallen upon these objects to destroy them.[61]

May 5th, on the Colorado River at the Moctezuma Pass, also known as that of the Atascocito. The 29th and 30th of April, the 1st, 2nd, and 3rd, of May have been for me the most painful days of the campaign. The last three I could scarcely travel more than twenty or twenty-one miles, on foot, in the mud, and without anything warm to eat, there being no means of building a fire. After I had helped the artillery commandant with his laborious chores, I advanced with

---

[61] In the pamphlet that former General Urrea published in Durango in 1838 [*Diario de las operaciones militares* . . .], I have found this and another part of my diary, but with some variations. However, they are of little importance. In one of these the tense was changed from present to past, perhaps because it was not copied from the original or because the author thought this change more appropriate, something I am frequently tempted to do but refrain from, preferring accuracy to concordance.

the cargo of my own corps, for I had salvaged everything, since it was the first to arrive here. On the 3rd, which was the day I crossed from the left to the right bank, I found a letter from Mexico that has caused me greater pain than everything I have so far suffered. It seems that fate takes pleasure in bringing together its deadly blows in order to immolate its chosen victim in the shortest time possible.

The letter mentioned is from a young lady whom I have adored for ten years—as beautiful, as seductive, and as endowed with many attractive gifts as she is also deceitful, fickle, and inconstant. When I faced adversity, she turned her back, just when she should have linked her heart closer to mine, if only because of compassion, that tender affection which enobles the beholder and which makes man equal to God. But this cruel one has demonstrated that constancy is just a fancy, and not part of human nature. Base persons, false friends, all conspired against me in my adversity, and this treacherous creature, more cruel than my enemies, let herself be seduced. She enlisted under the flag of my persecutors to add affliction to the afflicted, and even hoped to see me shed blood, all because of the cruel faction that has submerged our country in an abyss of misfortunes. In its fury and intolerance it has failed to respect the barriers surrounding love and has even persecuted those lovers it does not like. Sorrow and ingratitude wrest from me painful laments and blind me, so that I have publicly displayed my feelings. Why at my age, young as I am, should I feel shame because I am sensitive? Nature was generous with me, although I blush in not having helped her. I was gifted with extreme sensitivity, a passionate soul, and a vivid imagination, unfortunate gifts that bring only misfortune to him who possesses them if sane reason does not guide them in due time. The perjurer of whom I complain is the only woman who has been able to chain my heart and fill it to overflowing. I have loved her with all my strength, I solemnly swear it, and since I have lost her, I feel completely alone in the universe. Should the sobs my heart emits grate upon her ears, she could not help but feel painful remorse for having condemned me to such pain when she could have made me the most fortunate of mortals. But let it be known that although I am deeply offended, and despite my painful conviction that I cannot be happy with her or without her, I weep

167

for her and I pardon her, for I fervently wish her contentment. I shall not take the bitter revenge which is in order because of her horrible conduct toward me, in the hope that time or death will cure my deep wounds still oozing blood.

The stoics, men who have reached the winter of their lives, whose hearts have frozen, will say—What a fool! He wants to tell us about his affairs, which can be of interest only to him. But had they witnessed my vigils, my bitter anguish and anxiety; had they seen the bitter tears I shed without a friendly hand to wipe them; had they witnessed the constant torment that was piercing my soul, pricked by the infernal passion of jealousy; if these men, indifferent to their own sorrows as well as to those of others, could take hold of my sad reflections, my bitter recollections, and the terrible nightmares that at all hours, at all times, are pounding my imagination, depriving me of rest, they would then be indulgent. I ask no more of the reader than his indulgence and assure him that I am not ashamed to present myself as I am, rather than as I should be or would like to be.

Reason is of no use when an extremely sensitive soul finds itself deeply moved. A harsh destiny chained my life to an unfaithful woman, who could not appreciate my love for what it was worth.

The greater part of the foodstuffs was wasted during these days because the pack mules were not proceeding as a group and one purveyor could not keep track of them all, and the muledrivers leading them would steal and would let many be lost. Officers marching with only fragments of their troops and leading the cargos belonging to their corps would ask for more than they needed, because in fact many absurd orders had been given. During these days it had become necessary to send wood and meat from this place for those troops and the ones conducting the artillery, but in all this there were abuses. The general order of the day provides that from now on commanders and officers will not have more mules than those assigned by the rules, one for every eighty members of the troop. The proviso is just and had it been observed before it would have saved the nation much money. However, some have loudly protested against it because without rations they do need means to transport foodstuffs that might be allotted them; however, all this might have been solved with some common sense and prudence, which has been lacking even in the smallest details.[62] In time, I shall speak of the disorder regarding the mules, how some of their owners had made use of them, loading them with the corn they would gather and sell to us at exorbitant prices, though these animals had been contracted for army service.

May 7th at the same river. Yesterday Don Alejandro Alsbury arrived at the camp, a man from the enemy army, who confirms that our troops were defeated by surprise about forty-five miles (fifteen leagues) from the Brazos River on the western bank of the San Jacinto. Up to the day he left his camp, he says, there were 39 commanders and officers and between 550 and 600 troops held prisoner, and our dead still remained on the field without burial. He says that the action lasted twenty-two minutes and that some officers, such as Don Francisco Aguado, had died, not wishing to surrender their swords; that General Santa Anna was asleep and part of the troops at mess when the enemy appeared; that this general had been found the day after the action on a plain about one o'clock in the afternoon by a young enemy soldier. When asked where Santa Anna was, he answered that the general had gone away, and that he was one of his aides. Alsbury says that he was disguised when found and was made to appear thus before Houston, to whose tent he had asked to be brought, and that to this he owed his safety, for there was much animosity against him from the relatives and friends of those he had executed. It is said that an order from the commander of the enemy cavalry stipulated the safety of Santa Anna, and because of this, they called out to him from the woods. Alsbury also said that on the 23rd the enemy's ammunition and that captured from us was on the point of catching fire because of the ignition material in a cartridge pouch; that this set off some rifles and pistols, causing great alarm, for which reason the sentinels surrounding Santa Anna held him at gunpoint.[63]

Alsbury has agreed with me that we should not have marched

---

[62] Manuel Villalba, who was in charge of this branch, assured me that at the Brazos we had food supplies for more than a month, especially beans, but as a consequence of the aforementioned disorder, we were soon compelled to feed ourselves with meat only.

[63] This is one of the episodes referred to in my diary that has not been confirmed but it does not lack probability.

the way we did, but should have gone by Goliad. He is a reasonable person but impassioned regarding his own. He is presumptuous and arrogant, as they all are who believe that they are worth more than we are, when in fact they are worthless as soldiers. Last night and today I have had several arguments with him to demonstrate that they have been able to conquer only Santa Anna. I have agreed with him regarding the justice of their position in disposing of the lands that legitimately belong to them in Texas, but I have emphasized a thousand times that it is necessary to maintain at all cost the integrity of our territory, or else cease to exist as a nation. Santa Anna's weakness in accepting the agreement. My opinion regarding this unfortunate general in his present situation, who might have neutralized his weakness by offering himself as a mediator. Alsbury relates that on the 26th Santa Anna had a conference with Lorenzo de Zavala and that, when he asked Zavala why he had not waited for him at Harrisburg, Zavala answered with considerable bitterness that he was not such a———[sic] to do it, for, not satisfied with having persecuted him in Mexico, he was still doing it in Texas. The question was unwise, but it is certainly an ignoble action to insult a man in his misfortune because of resentments held against him. The artillery, thanks to the strong arms of the soldiers, began to arrive yesterday and finished between one and two o'clock in the morning. The activity and labors of the commandant of this branch of the service had been on this occasion as diligent and painful as they were at the crossings of rivers, in which his officers and I participated. On the 2nd and 3rd, Señor Ampudia had some disputes with Mr. Henry Karnes and with Don Juan Nepomuceno Seguín regarding claims they made about the delay of a Texas courier in our camp, as well as about some Negroes and other properties. They were commanding a small force and promised not to interfere with us.

The 9th. The day of the 8th was taken up in moving across all the appurtenances of the army, and today, when this operation was completed, we left the wooded area and camped on the right bank. The previous day General Urrea and his brigade marched toward Guadalupe Victoria. General Ramírez y Sesma had done so on the 3rd, and some of those present have assured me that he carried with him sixty-seven loaded mules.[64] The eleven wagons belonging to Don José Lombardero that were accompanying the army have been abandoned and in them some of our sick, for although Señor Ampudia had ordered most of the wagons to be drawn by mule, the first active of Mexico City alone was lacking eight, a fact confirmed by the commanders of this corps. Twenty-six cases of ammunition were also abandoned, in addition to the quantities that already had been wasted. With these wagons there also remained a blacksmith's forge, a gun carriage with spare parts, and a large transport wagon; and from the 1st to the 7th a wagon and a covered wagon, all belonging to the artillery train, as well as gun and rifle cases and lance handles, were burned for firewood. Today a courier arrived from the capital, from whom we have learned that the legion of honor has been approved, when we have already lost it. We have seen newspapers from March in which the events are adulterated, but which will soon change their language; there will be many reflections about the way things are exaggerated at the capital. We were in the tent of the commander in chief passing the time with talk about the legion of honor when a message arrived from the advance force that had been left at the river, in which its commander reported the arrival of an enemy force that asked to be given free passage to Béjar. Señor Ampudia, who was present, was commissioned to parley with the commander of that force. He told them, as on other occasions, that the arrogance of the enemy was suffered in order to spare the life of General Santa Anna. National honor is above his life. Irresoluteness and lack of energy among those who command. The armistice has been agreed upon by a general who is a prisoner, without any freedom of action, and the terms of it are not known; whatever they are, the enemy should be prevented from going any further, especially from going to Béjar. Suffering such humiliation is not possible for him who upholds the honor and love of his country. This incident has produced great excitement among some in the army.

---

[64] This I did not witness, nor have I been able to confirm it, but the person referred to is well known, as are his activities during the second expedition.

The 10th. Today we left the vicinity of the river and camped at San Diego Creek after we had walked about thirty miles. For several days the troops had eaten nothing but meat and beans because the corn rations had been issued for only a few days, and when they were received there was no recourse left the soldiers but to eat it roasted. The soldiers grumble because they are required to make long marches when they are so ill-nourished; today they have had no reason to complain, because it was essential to walk as far as we did, for there has been no water along the way, although certainly they might have at least had some rest. A communication has been received from General Andrade in answer to the one advising him about the misfortune on the 21st. He states that he has under his command 1,001 men of all divisions of the army, moved by the most ardent desire to avenge their comrades and ready to march to wherever it may be deemed advisable, notwithstanding the deficient condition of his cavalry, some of it on foot; and that of the total force, 201 men are either wounded or ill.

The 11th. Today we left the aforementioned place and have camped at Navidad Creek where, after traveling eighteen or twenty miles, we have found a unit of eight dwellings, as well as thirty-three barrels of crackers and four of lard from Goliad, the supplies so many times promised and so many times wished for; however, this has been merely a crumb to the hungry multitude, only whetting their appetites. The crackers have been distributed among the commanders and corps that arrived first, leaving those less prompt without any, from which have followed the rivalries and dissatisfactions to be expected from such lack of fairness. The commander in chief summoned the generals and commanders to inform them of the necessity of hushing the gossip that was circulating concerning the retreat, for which, he said, the rigor of the military code should be applied. After a lengthy speech in which he tried to justify his decision and established the basic principle that an army is not a congress in which what is best should be discussed, he said that if any individual within it would present him with a plan that would convince him that the fate of the army would be a brilliant one, he would submit to it; but Señor Gaona objected that such a proposal could be made only in strong positions, an objection very much in accord with the current code. It is necessary to reflect, whenever this can be amplified, that my censure is not so much for the retreat, to a certain point necessary once it had begun, as it is for the way in which it was done. The wisest and best combined plan would hardly have any effect eighteen days after the first backward step had been taken. What can one do with soldiers who even now keenly feel the deprivations they have so recently suffered? What can be done, I repeat, after they have lost their moral will, after so much suffering and the conduct observed toward them? It is quite noticeable that none of the corps commanders were consulted when the retreat was agreed upon, who now are called and instructed to quiet the criticisms that are generally made against it.

Guadalupe Victoria, May 15th. On the 12th we left Navidad Creek between eight and nine in the morning, camping at Garcitas Creek at sundown after we had walked between thirty-four and thirty-five miles without giving the troops any rest. We had made the three previous journeys through an oak forest, except for one-half of the last one, which was over a plain where many aromatic plants and a great abundance of laurel were observed.

Between eleven and twelve on the morning of the 13th, we arrived at this colony of Mexicans, where General Urrea had arrived on the 10th. Among them are some Irish and American families, and some of the inhabitants have also been participants in the revolution, among others, Don Plácido Benavides, whom General Urrea had believed to have been killed during his defeat of the force led by Dr. Grant. Likewise the de León family lives here, whose father was empresario of the colony, which is situated on the left bank of the Guadalupe. All their dwellings are of lumber, and one in particular has greatly attracted my attention because of its unique design; but what really beautifies this small town are the clusters of lilac, a picturesque tree, which one sees around many houses and along its short streets. According to some of the officers, there are some beautiful women. Here, after four months, we have been able to eat bread and a meat turnover of scarcely a pound in weight; we have deemed it expensive at ten or twelve reales, likewise, a pound of flour at four reales. On the 14th General Urrea marched toward Goliad, whence he will continue to march with his brigade as far as Matamoros in compliance with orders received to that effect. Today General Gaona has marched with the First Brigade.

The 16th. General headquarters and the Second Brigade left Victoria today; in a short time we forded the Guadalupe and after a mile of forest we emerged at a plain beautified by clusters of trees to be seen to the right and left of the road. After dark we camped at the ranch of El Coleto, where the Gaona brigade was. On seeing the campfires, the soldiers became excited and in their imaginations began comparing them with the lights that one sees around the plazas of our towns. The sappers particularly had such fanciful ideas. A few families had accompanied us, but most had remained at Victoria or in dwellings along the banks of the river.

The 17th. After eighteen or nineteen miles of travel we arrived between one and two o'clock in the afternoon at the ruins of Goliad, theater of ignominious and bloody scenes, the details of which are even more horrifying than the deed itself. About seven o'clock in the morning we left the ranch of El Coleto and in nine or ten minutes we passed the Perdido camp, where the greater part of the prisoners who were executed had fallen and where there were still remains of those killed in action.[65]

---

[65] Nothing is recorded in the diary from the 17th to the 22nd. His record of May 22 is out of chronological order, found in chapter 7, p. 87. —Ed.

# ✒15✒

MAY 23. A month ago today, while on the Brazos River, I should have briefly described the virgin woods that are found along the banks of the rivers and creeks. The trees that grow there seem to take great pride in reaching immense heights, interlacing their robust branches to form domes impenetrable to the sun's ray, and passing beneath them is a delightful experience for the traveler. One can say that these woods are inexhaustible paradises and storehouses of treasures for maritime construction. Those at a distance from the rivers are made up mostly of green cottonwoods, ashes, elms, cedars, alders,[66] pecan trees, *ayagil,* soapberry trees, *anacuas, malaguíes,* yaupon, sassafras, loquats, cypress, and mulberry, and other varieties of beautiful trees, the names of which no one could identify. The green cottonwood is well known; the height of its topmost branches, the pattern of its leaf, its dimensions, and its clear green color make it different from the ones known to our promenades. The ash is thick and rather abundant in these woods. The elm is a picturesque tree, standing out among others because of its dark green color and the shape of its leaves, as well as the distribution of its branches, its top appearing in the shape of a sphere. The cedar, of the pine family, is as high or higher than the elm, but scarce along the rivers that we have crossed; it is found in the vicinity of Béjar, on the road from this city to Matamoros, and along the Medina and Nueces rivers. The alders resemble the orange tree by the shape and the color of the leaves, although paler and the branches more spread out. The *ayagil* and soapberry resemble each other and bear some resemblance to the ash. I find no terms of comparison for the *anacua* and the *malagui;* their trunks are short, not as noticeable even when they

---

[66] Alders do not grow in the region; the trees were probably river birches, which are very similar in appearance.—*Ed.*

175

have heavy foliage. The yaupon holly is also a low tree and its leaf is very similar to that of the laurel. The sassafras is aromatic and its bark is boiled to make tea. The cypress is scarce along the Guadalupe and Brazos rivers but found in abundance along the Sabinas, mention of which has already been made in this diary. The mulberry trees found in these woods are also tall; the soldiers pulled them down to take the half-ripe fruit. They are found in such abundance and multiply with such ease that they really invite the cultivation of the silkworm, which would yield abundantly; however, the colonists preferred the cultivation of cotton, from which the produce is soon gathered, and therefore not a single attempt was made to cultivate it. The trunks and branches of many of these trees are completely covered with blooming vines all twined together, but what makes these woods even more delightful is the variety of birds inhabiting them, which with their trills and warblings give greater animation to a nature already overflowing with life. Among others, there is an abundance of the goldfinch, the mockingbird, the cardinal, the hummingbird, and the woodpecker, a bird that makes himself noticeable by the continuous effort with which he drills the tree trunks, choosing the harder ones in particular. There are three classes of these, but one of ashen color with a golden neck and a red tuft called the *pito real* is the most beautiful, though it differs from the bird of the same name found in the mountains. A sensitive soul will be transported beyond himself within these woods, where he will find such seductive delights; absorbed by the present, he will care little for the future. Under this somber and melancholic foliage those things which are dear to the heart vividly appear, ornamented with their enchantment and magic. Here the heart is moved by a supernatural force to love, and to love with enthusiasm, the enchanting person one has left at an immense distance, and who, perhaps, has cast her admirer into oblivion while he is subjected to danger, while he suffers all types of privations because of duty and loyalty to his country. In these woods, in the solitude of nature, man could live protected from calumny, intrigue, and the curse of others.

If the woods of Texas are so grand and produce such sensations, I find myself at a loss to find words that would express the beauty of its meadows, carpeted with a great variety of exquisite flowers that seduce the eye and intoxicate the soul. The sense of smell delights in the fragrance they exhale, and this balmy atmosphere seems to bring with it thoughts of heaven.[67] All is picturesque and enchanting.

Yesterday (I refer to the 23rd) at five o'clock in the afternoon, Henry Karnes and William Redd, aide-de-camp to Rusk, the present commander of the Texas troops, arrived at the camp. The interpreter who accompanies them says that there are over eight hundred officers held prisoner and over six hundred troops, and that they come for the purpose of arranging an exchange, but the few of theirs still with us had left for Matamoros two days ago. The commander in chief, accompanied by General Tolsa, Colonels Amat, Montoya, and García, and other officers, went to meet these representatives at the point where the advance guard had called a halt, an action much criticized by those who wish that the commander of the Mexican Army would show greater dignity.

Goliad, May 26th. The 25th was a day rich in episodes to relate. The previous night the commander in chief had received news that the Americans were at Victoria. Since Redd and his companions, who returned on the afternoon of the 24th, had assured us that there were no troops there, some fearful souls believed that they had not told the truth and that they possibly intended an ambush. It was also said that when one of them entered the town to visit one of their prisoners in the hospital, it had been to observe the situation prevailing in the fort, and it was even said that they were seen reconnoitering. Nothing had been said regarding the march in the order of the previous day, but at dawn on the 25th the first signal was given, followed quickly by others. We arrived at these ruins on the 17th during which night and the day following it poured excessively, but it had not done so again until today, when it dawned

---

[67] Texas, in fact, is a vast fertile garden where all of the earth's beautiful things flourish. There are two crops harvested each year; a soil of which it might be said that man has only to gather the harvest, without effort. Its climate is healthy, except for the coastal region. The fields form beautiful meadows, difficult to describe. The multitude of aromatic and medicinal plants one finds there and in the woods would give great joy to the botanists, who could aquaint us with the virtues of each plant. Unfortunately, I am not one, nor is there one among us. Among the well-known and common plants is the honeysuckle, in great abundance. Also the laurel, anise, wild garlic, and the *epazote*, of which there are thick woods. Today I have visited one of the sites of the bloody episode.

with a strong north wind blowing and an abundant rain lasting three hours. We had been here eight days waiting for Señor Andrade to join us with his Béjar forces, as we have said; but the precipitance of the march, in spite of the bad weather and the precautions taken the night before, gave way to unfavorable thoughts and speculations. It was still raining and the last signal had been given when two soldiers and three other persons appeared, whose presence excited enthusiasm and caused some to believe that the enemy was advancing, and they repaired to await him. In fact, these were Benjamin F. Smith, McIntire, and Henry Teal, who called themselves colonel, major, and captain of the Texas Army, and who brought the agreement entered into between the one who still calls himself the commander in chief of the Mexican Army, and the president of what is titled the government of Texas. The two orderlies with them are the only two uniformed soldiers we have seen up to now, which has caused some amazement among our men. The substance of the articles of that agreement was immediately obvious, in spite of the mystery with which they had tried to conceal it, so the just indignation expressed among those receiving the news proves that there are still Mexicans in the army who wish to preserve its name with honor. The agreement brought about by the promoters of Texas separation could not be more ignominious for us, but it is still more so for the Mexican who signed it. Never has General Santa Anna performed a more contemptible deed among the many that he has committed during his political career than in selling out his country by relinquishing Texas' delightful territory, as if he were the sole arbiter of the Republic; this is what the agreement amounts to. Anyone else in his position and circumstances would have blown out his brains before signing his own disgrace, for there is no greater degradation. He should have submitted to the fortunes of a war that the cruelty of his heart had made so bloody and savage, and he should have given no orders; for this, he had the best excuse for those who compelled him to sign it: that it should not, could not be obeyed, as in fact it ought not to have been obeyed. General Filisola, who had already said amen to all that the prisoner had ordered, said it again after he had examined this infamous treaty, and answered that it would be complied with; if he used the language of condescension toward the enemy it is, in my estimation, because it is advantageous for the decision he has taken, and not to please the captive general. Nevertheless, this author ardently wished that at the moment when he was addressing the Texas commissioners, he had chosen a language more worthy of the position he holds and the army he commands. I wished to breathe my desires and sentiments to him. Including the forces of Generals Andrade and Urrea, Filisola has over 4,000 men under his orders, whereas the enemy could hardly have more than 1,500, for he himself assures us that he has 2,000, and it is well known that he always has a tendency to exaggerate, although there are established facts to support only the first figure.[68]

It is true that because of the scarcity of supplies, the rainy season which is upon us, and other causes of which I shall speak later, it is impossible for us to take the offensive, but we can adopt an energetic and honorable attitude toward an enemy who has believed himself victorious on account of having surprised one division of the vanguard.

Since one of the articles of the agreement permits the delivery to the colonists of all their properties, and another one compensation to them for the things that we will have to take during the retreat, General Filisola started complying with that agreement by returning a Negro he had taken when we crossed the Colorado, who was serving him as a coachman,[69] offering the return of everything that they could identify, for which purpose two of the commissioners

---

[68] Before the events at San Jacinto, all the men under arms in Texas did not amount to 1,200, as has been stated before; victory did increase their number, but they never reached this total.

[69] I was still at Goliad waiting for General Andrade when the commissioners arrived with the aforementioned Negro. When we were left alone for a moment, this poor wretch explained to me his anguished situation and the cruel tortures that awaited him. I would have committed a crime against humanity, as General Filisola did, had I not protected his freedom and delivered him from the punishment in store for him. I sent him, disguised as a soldier, to where the army was, and in this manner he reached Matamoros. My reward has been the pleasure I took in seeing him so full of gratitude, the last time when he was serving under Major Benito Zenea. Other unfortunates were liberated the same way by other army officers. [De la Peña refers to the incident of the slave again in his notes on the weakness of Filisola, included as appendix 31 in *La Rebelión de Texas.—Ed.*]

(Smith and Teal) marched with him, for this purpose and to arrange other matters; but as to cash payments, he had said that he had no available cash and that this would be paid by the government.

Since nothing of what we lost at San Jacinto will be returned to us and since the only indemnity the nation will receive for the costs of the war is the loss of the territory that we had come to defend, no commissioners have been selected to represent us. General Filisola, I repeat, is unusually kind and honorable, and if the measures he has taken are worthy of reproach, most of the time he is worthy of pity. Perhaps he wishes to do what is best, but he lacks the capacity and he has no one to help him. He would gladly relinquish the bonus to whoever would take over his command to be free of his crushing burden. We have read the agreement superficially and it is our belief that he was not bound to carry it out until it was agreed to by the government. If the government should be weak enough to approve it, which is hard to believe, its shame would be greater than that of the one who signed it, its downfall would be inevitable, and out of its ruins would come forth a national government that would avenge the insults to our country. I wrote to Mexico on the 4th and 12th of this month, admonishing them not to dismay nor to give in to whatever weak men write, and warning that it is a lesser evil to die than to relinquish this beautiful territory. Neither the government nor the nation yet knows its worth, but even if it were worth nothing, its honor is above all. Let it be sold or given away as a gift, but after we have learned how to preserve it. The army marched yesterday, but I have remained with a section of cavalry guarding the supplies assigned to General Andrade and the surplus.

Today, the 26th, I went over the sites where the ashes of the executed prisoners are to be found. What a vast field for a philosopher—a town devoured by flames brought on by the fury of war, in the ruins of which have been burned the very ones whose inhumanity brought this misfortune upon so many families! When the unfortunate Fannin gave orders to burn Goliad,[70] how far were he and his subordinates from imagining that the same live coals that turned that place into ashes would do likewise to them and would

---

[70] Later I have been convinced that there was no such order. Goliad was set on fire by some adventurers without any orders from Fannin.

mix those ashes so soon. This fire stirred up the vengeance so cruel to them. The reunion with friends, the army in motion, and the noise of military equipment made these ruins appear less frightful. Yesterday one family still remained, but today there are no inhabitants other than the cats and dogs, whose howls for their masters' absence give this mansion of the dead a most dreadful aspect. Goliad, located on a hill on the right bank of the San Antonio River, although not as advantageously situated as Béjar is, would not be unpleasant; but today the searching soul seeks in vain for a place in which to expand itself, for in whatever direction the eye is cast, it meets only desolation and death, in whatever direction one might wander, he could only stumble over the remains of those so barbarously murdered. There is one added circumstance that makes this place even more frightening, and that is the smoky atmosphere and the ground constantly covered with flies.

# 16

San Patricio, Sunday, May 29th. In this Irish colony, in which there are seven or eight Mexican families, I continue my notes. On the night of the 26th, the commissioners who had followed the army returned to Goliad, taking with them the ratification of the agreement signed by General Eugenio Tolsa and Colonel Agustín Amat, acting as commissioners for the commander in chief, whose signature was also affixed to it. They arrived just as I was starting to set fire to the great pyre composed of barrels of supplies that had been left there, which caused them no little surprise, since the commander in chief had offered them those supplies in case General Andrade had not disposed of them. They appealed to this offer made by the commander in chief, as well as to humanity, and so dissuaded me from carrying out my intent.

In a long conference held with Smith and Teal, I displayed my personal indignation at this agreement, an indignation that prevails among the members of the army with whom I have spoken about its conditions. I made them aware of the patriotic sentiments of the army and told them as much as any man with any enthusiasm for the honor of his country could. They recognized the bravery of the Mexican soldier and the advantages our cavalry had over theirs; likewise I conceded to them the superiority of their firearms and their gunpowder, and I made them see how easy it would be for us to obtain both these things of the same quality that they were using. I made them aware that two essential branches had not participated adequately in this campaign, the artillery and the cavalry. General Santa Anna had not known how to make use of the former and had rendered the latter useless; but I added that for the next campaign, which I foresaw as inevitable, we could bring a thousand horses, with two in reserve for each rider, so that they could withstand long distances and thus be in good condition for the day of the engagement. We spoke a long time about the battle at San Jacinto, and I did not have to speak very long to persuade them that only the element of surprise could have defeated the force commanded by General Santa Anna, and the confidence and disdain with which this commander viewed his enemy. They related several incidents to me in detail, verifying some of those I have already noted in this diary, one of them being the commanding general's disguise. Everyone with whom I have talked, among either the enemy or our own stragglers, is in accord regarding the surprise, although some of the former, in order to make themselves appear courageous, say that our troops fought back well. When asked whether I, had I been in position of command, would have marched against them after our misfortune, I answered in the affirmative, for this had been my wish as well as that of the greater part of the army. I further explained to them how, out of sheer respect for discipline, we were acting against our sentiments. They blamed Fannin for having delayed ten days in complying with an order received to retreat, and they stated that the cold-blooded execution of him and his companions had excited great fury, increasing their strength and giving them resources they had not had until then. Since Béjar, every one of those not blinded like General Santa Anna had predicted this. Smith and Teal assured me that since some among the revolutionaries had holdings, their families had placed these at the disposal of the military leaders in order that the war might continue, and that there had been some ladies who would have ordered arms to be cast at their own expense to avenge the blood of their dead.[71] They said that for each man executed, ten more had appeared, and, since they believed that the killing of our men would yield similar results, their commanders made great efforts to save as many as possible, and especially our commander. They well knew that he was solely responsible for the murders committed against them, and they insisted that this be made public in order to vindicate the good name of Mexico, so seriously compromised in the exterior because of this incident.

In spite of the blame they placed on Fannin, they nevertheless praised him greatly, but more so Travis, who they never thought

---

[71] The reader will determine to what degree one should give credence to the enemy during moments of intimate conversation.

would find himself in a tight spot, because, as I have said repeatedly, they never imagined we would march by way of Béjar.

During the course of our informal conversation, they said that if we did not yield to the Río Bravo, next year we would be forced to yield as far as Saltillo.[72] This boast provoked laughter and I laughed, although not very willingly. We spoke at length about a future campaign in which a nation would be victorious against a handful of men, regardless of distances and deserts. Many times did I insist that, were we to be vanquished, the nation should cease to exist. My conversations with these gentlemen and others who have come to the camp have had as their main object the investigation of the truth, though my diary has given some fools occasion to say that I am yielding to the enemy. This is the phrase they have used, which even today was repeated to me by one who calls himself my friend and who has seen that my opinions against the retreat have invited many controversies and disagreements. There are offenses one cannot forgive, even though one might be willing, and this is one of them.

When I told the commissioners that General Santa Anna should have submitted to execution before signing the agreement, they answered that they never thought that he would sign it.

On the 27th Smith and Teal left for Victoria and I left to join the army, having received an order from the commander in chief to leave Goliad if I had not received positive news concerning the direction in which General Andrade was going. I made a short stop at Mujerero Creek, where I caught up with the rear guard, and continued to Aransaso Creek, where we camped that day, which must be about thirty miles from Goliad; there is another creek, named the Blanco, before these two. On our arrival at Goliad we had found rice, lard, and biscuits. Part of this, which had come from Cópano, was spoiled. The eight days we remained among these ruins the troops had only meat to eat, for since the march had been unexpected, nothing had been made ready. Three hundred mules had

---

[72] During this conversation one could clearly detect the designs the Texans had even then, designs which now are about to be put into action through the blindness and obstinacy of our rulers.

been sent to Señor Andrade and two hundred loads to Cópano to be shipped; nevertheless, there were not enough mules to pick up the existing supplies, in spite of the fact that those that went to Cópano had returned on time. Since this lack was not noted until the very hour of the march, the soldiers had to carry eight days' rations on the march. There was such disorder and such confusion that only the biscuits were distributed to them, but no rice, which was more abundant, because the lard could not be distributed. The next day the general sent me thirty mules to transport part of the supplies, but we were able to haul only thirty mulepacks of rice, twenty-two barrels of lard, twenty of biscuit, and some flour and salt. There was much surplus, especially of the first two mentioned articles, in addition to rations destined for General Andrade should he pass by Goliad. Those loaded on the thirty mules were also ruined at Mujerero Creek, since they were already loaded and could not be overloaded. Why were more supplies taken than those actually needed at this place? Why such lack of preparation and such confusion?

On the 28th at seven in the morning we began the march, and after traveling twenty-five miles we arrived at this colony between four and five in the afternoon, with the troops having had no rest, except for a short one taken by the head of the column a mile from the town. This system of marching with a blazing May sun and without any water to quench their thirst can cause much distress to the soldiers. The Irish residents here and all the families from Victoria and Goliad who had been compelled to abandon their holdings to follow the army showed great surprise on seeing our soldiers and on learning that we were retreating. The residents of Goliad, who had suffered much, became quite angry with us and insulted us, saying that we were fleeing as cowards from a handful of adventurers. We were obliged to offer explanations without denying their charges, lest we appear ashamed of something of which we are guilty. Today a special messenger arrived from Mexico City, commanding that Santa Anna's life be saved at all costs and that the honor of the army be preserved untarnished. The former has taken place; the latter has been looked upon with criminal indifference. We have been assured that the legion of honor has been approved for distinguished service. I wonder what those will say who felt so sure that they would have a badge that would say, "He went to Texas"?

May 31st, on the right bank of the Nueces River. The colony is situated one mile from the left bank. On the 29th, the First Brigade and the artillery crossed the river. On the 30th, the Second Brigade and general headquarters, together with all the baggage, crossed. I was quartered in the house of John Stefferman, a man who had unfortunately been murdered by the Indians last April, together with his brother, the brother's wife, five nephews, and a cousin. Mistress Margaret was left with four orphaned children, among whom one's attention is drawn to Miss Mary, whose amiability and misfortune had touched my sensibility. This last day of May, Karnes, Teal, and others from the enemy returned to the camp for the purpose of continuing toward Matamoros to scrutinize the army, for which they were given authorization, much to our shame.[73]

I renewed my conversation with Teal, repeating in the presence of sapper officers Ricoy and Almazán what I had told him on the night of the 26th; I told him nothing was greater proof that General Santa Anna had been taken by surprise than the few wounded and fewer deaths the enemy had suffered. They told me that all their artillery had been lost at the Alamo and at Perdido, and that the two four-pounders they had at San Jacinto had just been sent by two young ladies from Cincinnati. I, being duly piqued, answered that our fair sex would give up the jewels that enhance their beauty to meet the needs of the next campaign. But who will be the beauties to do it? If the heroines in our country were less rare, if, as in ancient Sparta, there were mothers sending their sons to war, and if our lovely ladies would reward with their love only those who went forth to defend their country, what a great number of volunteers there would be and what heroic action we would see! "What great

---

[73] When these commissioners arrived at Matamoros, General Urrea imprisoned them. It is questionable whether he should have complied with what had been agreed to with the enemy, what had been so illegally conceded to him, but since he had no authorization for doing what he did, I disapprove.

things would be done," exclaimed Rousseau, "with the desire to be esteemed by women, if this force could only be mobilized . . . !"

June 2nd, Corpus Christi. The last day of last month the enemy prisoners who had been sent to Matamoros returned, and the first of this month they traveled to San Patricio, from there to continue at liberty to join their troops; but when, according to the agreement, shall we see some of our prisoners? Yesterday an order was given for the First Brigade to march toward Matamoros and for the Second to move its encampment to Lipantitlán. There had been complaints, because it was thought that one brigade would rest while the other remained to suffer, but such an idea is unfounded. The march has not taken place, and it is not unlikely that it was cancelled to prevent further complaints, for we are at the stage of having to temporize with an army that daily loses more discipline as a result of its hardships. The same order provided for the presentation of claims regarding campaign bonuses due the commanders and officers since April, especially since some of these had requested payments on the bonuses.[74] Since it is the law, it is only fair that payment should be made, the more so when the regular pay is not sufficient to cover all necessities, but the soldier has had nothing but meat as food since March and has been given only one real per capita, from sergeant on down the line. Equitable action was necessary to avoid criticisms from the weak, but this equality, for which so much blood had been shed, is neglected and of no value among Mexicans. The soldier undergoes the greatest suffering but receives the least attention.

This morning two natives appeared, saying that those families who could not follow the army and those who had found it expedient not to do so and remained in the neighboring ranches are being forced by the enemy to go toward Victoria, after being deprived of their oxen, beasts of burden, carriages, and arms. This last is credible, because in Texas everyone carries arms and these people have arrived without any; one of them was riding bareback, unmistakable proof that he had scarcely had time to flee. I urged them to complain

---

[74] Payments were made only to the staff of General Gaona's brigade and to all of General Urrea's brigade.

to the commander in chief with the greatest possible force about their experiences, but I have purposely chosen to ignore the outcome, for the ill-fated agreement provides no guarantees for Mexicans.

The troops that had not heard Mass since Béjar heard it today, the second time from Mr. Kelly, an Irish priest we found in the colony, but truly this was what was least needed.

Some *piloncillo* received by the quartermaster was distributed equitably, with strong admonition by a special order that it would be confiscated from anyone selling it for more than four reales. This is the first measure we have seen taken regarding such matters; had it been taken two months before, it would have brought much respect and a good name to the commanders instead of the criticisms and curses for permitting the infamous trading we have repeatedly mentioned and will have further occasion to repeat again.

On the 3rd, the First Brigade, the greater part of the baggage, all the sick, and the enemy commissioners left for Matamoros, the latter going toward this place, where they would continue humiliating us.

Today, the 4th, General Andrade arrived with the force that had remained at Béjar; they had camped on the 1st within cannon shot of Goliad, already occupied by the enemy, who was holding funeral services for the souls of their comrades sacrificed there. After the departure of the commander in chief, this general had remained in command at Béjar where the matériel of all the corps and all the army supply train had been left. To comply with the order issued to abandon this post, he has had to surmount many difficulties in order to dismantle the hospitals and to save some of the army equipment. One could say that these difficulties have been as great as the number of victims and as useless as the blood that has been shed. During his stay in that city, he had labored to put the Alamo in the best possible condition for defense; this had already been improved when it became necessary to raze it; and few do not know the pain such an operation causes a soldier, a pain even greater to one who knows the duties of his profession well. When he was drawn up before Goliad, the order from the commander in chief was delivered, commanding him to yield to the enemy all that he designated as belonging to him. Andrade replied in a way worthy of a Mexican soldier and refused any investigation in his camp. Everything that Señor Andrade could not bring with him he ordered to be destroyed, as had been provided in the retreat order given to him.[75]

On the 7th we had to strike camp along the Nueces, and after we had marched as far as we could, given the hot weather, the scarcity of water, and the cumbersomeness of our movements, we again camped at the plain of Las Pintas. Seeing our wounded by the flank of the column, dragging themselves or walking on crutches; seeing others in carriages that were sure to fall apart at the least roughness or hole hit along the road; seeing some of these unfortunates roll from the wagons, to their greater discomfort, when such accidents occurred; one could do no less than protest, and protest violently, against those responsible for such misery, against their cold indifference and the disdain with which they looked upon the soldiers' heroic sacrifices sealed in blood. We had to turn our eyes away from these painful scenes, which were not within our capacity to remedy. Everything became still more miserable when it rained and the wounded were compelled to protect themselves against it, bunching up on top of each other. The fate of the officers was not much better, except when they were carried on the shoulders of soldiers belonging to their respective corps. However, all the wounded equally lacked the resources of the healing art and food or nourishment adequate for their situation. The generals never foresaw this when they agreed on a retreat. They should have considered the obstacles that impeded its execution just as they had considered the lesser ones in favor of advance.

On the 8th, after having traveled sixteen to eighteen miles, we camped at Santa Gertrudis Creek, where we arrived striking up the march because we met a detachment there with fifty thousand pesos for the army. At night a meeting protesting the retreat was held after communications were received from General Urrea. The meeting was more political than military; each one of those present seemed to believe that he could guess the intentions of Señores Urrea and Vital Fernández. Who knows who is right; only time will clarify the truth.

---

[75] Filisola to Andrade, Goliad, May 18, 1836, giving instructions for the evacuation of Béjar (see *La Rebelión de Texas*, appendix 30).—*Ed.*

On the 9th, after traveling between twelve and fourteen miles, we camped at the Motas de Doña Clara, where we found a few pools of water and scarcely any wood. On this day Almazán [Almaras?], a sapper officer, got lost, and I repeatedly heard the report that when we left Goliad, it was to have been with the object of charging the enemy in combination with General Andrade, but that this plan had changed with the arrival of the agreement. But as the plan was worthy of the army and the honor of its commanders, the more reason there was not to have accepted this cursed agreement.

On the 10th we camped at a place called Santa Rosa after we had marched between fifteen and sixteen miles; our thirst was excessive that day, for we had only muddy water. An artillery sergeant, Jacinto Hernández, mortally wounded his wife for some slight provocation. To attack a weak being such as a woman is a reprehensible act in any man, but especially so in a soldier. The women who followed the army merited all consideration, as they did all they could to help the soldier. Some carried knapsacks, and they would leave the road for a mile or two in the hot sun seeking water; they prepared their food and even attempted to build huts that would protect them from the elements; obviously they did not deserve stabs as a reward.

On the 11th we spent the night at Las Mujeres Creek where there were, as on the previous day, numerous mesquite trees; nevertheless the soldier was made to carry wood. We might have traveled about fourteen or fifteen miles, but in spite of a rather moderate journey, the heat was so excessive and the water so scarce that the troops were in great despair and very fatigued. Some of the vanguard cried out, "Water, water," as they located a lake on the right and saw that no halt was ordered. To avoid a mutiny, one of the officers had to investigate the outcry. So a halt was ordered, the water was tested, and it turned out to be salty. Along the fields we found only small pools with muddy and foul-smelling water.

Today some confirmed the rumors that had been heard before, that Almonte was responsible for the catastrophe at San Jacinto. Someone has spoken of him as a traitor.

Mexicans, there are the facts. Judge for yourselves, and let your terrible verdict fall upon those who may deserve it. That to which

190

I have been an eyewitness I have narrated faithfully, and that which I have not witnessed I have verified through the most circumspect and trustworthy men. If my sentiments do not please, my frankness will testify to the fact that at least I am honest, for I say what I feel and I judge without prejudice and without fear of the hatred of those in power.

I have concluded this narrative during the most pressing moments, a few hours before resuming the march, as I have already been informed about San Luis.[76]

José Enrique de la Peña
Matamoros, Tamaulipas
15 September 1836

---

[76] No exact details have been found regarding the cause of Lieutenant Colonel de la Peña's sudden departure from Matamoros to San Luis Potosí in September of 1836. It might have been due to the suppression of a popular outbreak against the implementation of the new system of government, that is, centralism.—*J. S. G.*

# Index

Aguado, Francisco, 169
Aguirre, Marcial Peralta, 124, 132
Aguirre, Miguel, 123, 124
Alamo, 188; description of, 45, 48; Texans at, 33, 35, 36. *See also* Alamo, battle of
Alamo, battle of, 37–57; artillery at, 38, 39, 42–43, 47; Bowie at, 38–39, 39 n; casualties at, 39, 47–48, 49, 52, 54 and n, 59, 61; Cos at, 14, 43, 44, 45, 48, 51; Crockett at, 53; effects of, 43, 58, 131; final assault at, 44–53; lack of medical care at, 55, 61; plan of attack at, 43, 45–46, 55, 56–57; reconnaissance at, 44; Santa Anna at, 49, 53, 56, 58, 67; strength of Mexican forces at, 37; of Texan forces, 54 and n; survivors of, 44, 53, 54 n; Texas reinforcements at, 41, 43; Travis at, 39 n, 41–42, 44, 47, 50; troop deployment at, 45–46; uselessness of, 54, 55, 56–57
Alazán Hill, 38
Alcérrica, Agustín, 156–157
Aldama, 23
Aldama Battalion, 13, 37, 62, 111; at the Alamo, 45, 53; with Cos, 111, 113; fires at steamboat, 108; with Ramírez y Sesma, 65; at San Jacinto, 123; sappers of, 33, 39, 40, 109
Almazán (sapper officer), 186, 190
Almonte, Juan Nepomuceno: at Alamo war council, 43, 44; at San Jacinto, 124, 190; and Texans, 114
Alsbury, Alejandro, 169–170
Alvarado, Miguel, 157
Alvarez, Secundino, 39
Amat, Agustín, 96, 116, 117, 118 n; at the Alamo, 43, 46, 49; meets with enemy, 177; as signator to armistice, 182
ammunition: allotments of, 15–16, 157; care of, 6–7; with Cos, 109; of 1st Brigade, 15; for Goliad, 66, 96; loss of, 33; in retreat, 156, 157, 162–163, 165, 169, 171; of 2nd Brigade, 16; transportation of, 29, 100; waste of, 156, 165, 169, 171. *See also* weapons
Ampudia, Pedro, 100, 148, 149; commands artillery, 13, 128; and enemy commissioners, 170, 171; and retreat, 145
Ampudia, General, 141
Andrade, Juan, 12, 13, 20; at Béjar, 58, 135; condition of forces of, 172; leaves Béjar, 188–189; ordered on offensive, 159; praised, 27, 66, 80
Arago, Juan, 12–14 *passim*, 21, 33, 94
Aransaso Creek, 184
Arenal, Ignacio, 124
Arenoso Creek, 105
Armadillo, prominence of, 32
armistice agreement: commissioners and, 170, 184; objections to, 178; ratification of, 182; Santa Anna and, 83, 160, 171, 178, 184; terms of, 179, 187, 188, 190
Arredondo, Joaquín de, 36, 44
Arroyo, Dr., 61
Arroyo del Molino (a farm), 107
artillery
—Mexican: and Alamo, 33, 38–39, 42; with Cos, 109; cost of, 42–43; for Goliad, 66; under Ramírez y Sesma, 79; in retreat, 159, 165, 186; to San

193

121, 160, 190. *See also* individual battalions; provisions; transport

Mexicans: attitude of, toward war, 6; as colonists of Guadalupe Victoria, 76; as soldiers, 115; world image of, 83

Mexican-Texan relations: declaration of Texas independence, 4, 6, 36, 84; de la Peña and Texas commissioners, 182–184; Mexican army as viewed by Texans, 40; Mexicans impose war to death, 82, 92; result of conflict, 125; Santa Anna and prisoners, 84–85; sources of conflict, 3–5, 15; treatment of Texas, 81–83; United States aid to Texas, 4, 16, 18, 40, 85 n. *See also* Texas campaign; Texas colonists

Mexico: civil war in, 5, 7, 8; government of, 10, 23, 180

Mexico City Battalion, 13, 116; in retreat, 162; at San Jacinto, 124; at Thompson's Pass, 136; with Tolsa, 66

Mier, 67

Military Code, 135

military theory, 136; at Alamo, 54–57; concerning insubordination, 147; concerning speed, 65; concerning troop conditions, 70; of Napoleon on retreats, 146; on restricting battles, 130; of Solís, 10 n, 16; Texan, 73

Miñón, Colonel, 38; at Alamo, 44; at Goliad, 86

Missión Concepción, 38

Moctezuma Pass, 166

Monclova, 20, 23; de la Peña at, 26; march toward, 15, 19; Santa Anna at, 24

Montoya, Cayetano, 66, 177

Montoya y Salas, Colonel, 148

Mora, Esteban, 62; at San Jacinto, 124, 132

Morales, Colonel, 78; at Béjar, 38, 39, 44, 46; at Goliad, 65, 73, 75, 76; and retreat, 148; and Urrea, 65, 77

Moreau, Jean Victor, 16

Morelos, Colonel, 50

Morelos Battalion, 13; with Gaona, 135; in retreat, 162

Moro, Dr. José F.: 60–61

Morris, Major, 69

Motas de Doña Clara, 190

Mujerero Creek, 184, 185

muledrivers, 22; desertion of, 33; escape of, 26; profiteering of, 115; at San Jacinto, 132; steal mules, 168

mules, 23; with Andrade, 184–185; in 1st Brigade, 31; losses of, 27, 28, 113, 134–135, 159, 166, 168–169, 185; move slowly, 29; muledrivers and, 26, 168; in retreat, 159, 166; shortage of, 170–171, 184–185; theft of, 134–135, 168; uses of, 7, 33, 103, 156, 165. *See also* transport

Murat, Joachim, 79

Múzquiz, Don Ramón, 30

Nacogdoches, 103, 121

Napoleon, 12, 16, 136, 142; Santa Anna compared with, 52, 79

Nava, 32

Navarro, Antonio, 4

Navidad Bayou, 78

Navidad Creek, 102; de la Peña at, 172–173

Negroes, 104, 170; at the Alamo, 44; Filisola and, 179

New Washington, 114

Nueces River: area of, 34–35, 175; de la Peña at, 34, 186–187, 189; enemy at, 35; Filisola at, 154; *Watchman* at, 142

Nuevo León, department of, 20

Old Fort, 107; de la Peña at, 116. *See also* Thompson's Pass

Orazimbo, 104

oxen: difficulties with, 28, 31–32, 33

Peña Creek, 33

Perdido, 186; prisoners from, 86; Urrea's victory at, 72–76, 81

Pesquería, 23

*piloncillo*, 59, 188

Portilla, Manuel de la, 98, 125

Tejocote Creek, 101

Texan army: at the Alamo, 38–57 *passim*; artillery of, 38; avenge the Alamo and Goliad, 131; casualties of, at San Jacinto, 131; financed by private citizens, 183; initial troop deployment of, 35–36; lack of discipline of, 125, 132–133; losses of, 7–8; marksmanship of, 63, 72; at Perdido, 72–73, 75; in retreat, 129, 130; at San Jacinto, 128, 131, 133; strength of, at Alamo, 54 and n; strength of, after San Jacinto, 136, 179; in uniform, 178; and war to the death, 82, 92, 131

Texas: agriculture in, 96, 101, 106, 111, 118, 141, 184; birds of, 107, 112–113, 176; dwellings in, 100–101, 108, 118–119; hospital in, 108; industry of, 108, 111–112, 114, 119; livestock of, 96, 97, 99, 101, 105–108 *passim*, 118, 119, 141; pecans in, 36, 62; potential of, 82, 101; topography of, 35, 81–82, 102, 173, 174; trees of, 36, 62, 175–176, 190; vegetation of, 34, 35, 72, 101–104, 105, 106, 173, 174, 176; wildlife of, 32, 33, 36, 97, 113

—descriptions of: at Brazos R., 13; at Guadalupe R., 98, 99; at Nueces R., 34–35; at Peña Creek, 32; at San Felipe, 107

Texas campaign: compared with other campaigns, 6; cost of, 5, 7–8, 42–43, 153; failure of, 125, 180; importance of, to Mexico, 20; inhumanity during, 90, 120; Mexican government and, 5, 7–8; preparations for, 5–13; reasons for, 3, 4–5; reconnaissance for, 18, 44; role of politics in, 5, 6, 82–83; strategy of, 16, 18, 35–36; support for, 6, 20, 23. *See also* Mexican-Texan relations

Texas colonists: among Alamo forces, 51; executed at Goliad, 90; flee from Mexican army, 114, 119–120, 129, 130; industriousness of, 101, 106; losses of, 7–8, 112; as Mexican citizens, 85; during Mexican

retreat, 182, 185; as rebels during Spanish regime, 36–37; weapons of, 187. *See also* Mexican-Texan relations

Thompson's Pass, 107, 126, 129, 134–142 *passim. See also* Old Fort

Tinaja de Arroyo Hondo, 36

Tola, Luis, 13

Tolomé, 130

Tolsa, Eugenio, 12, 149; as commander in 2nd Division, 13; and enemy representatives, 177; marches through Gonzales, 100; at new headquarters; 109; plunder of, 108; with Ramírez y Sesma, 66, 80; and retreat, 145, 162; as signator to armistice, 182; at war council, 128; weapons of, 66

Toluca Battalion, 13, 36, 62, 64; chasseurs of, 47; marches to San Felipe, 65; to rejoin Santa Anna, 113; at San Jacinto, 123; sappers of, 33, 39, 40; and steamboat, 108

Tornel, José María, 5, 84; criticism of, 60; and legion of honor, 21

Torres, ———, 49

transport: of ammunition, 100; barges used for, 100, 127; of cattle, 104; cost of, 153, 165; difficulties of, 7, 29, 32, 96, 98–99, 113, 125, 126, 153, 160; on march to San Felipe, 100; needed planning, 6; preferred methods of, 9–10; in retreat, 153, 160; wagons used for, 100; of wounded, 171, 189. *See also* mules; oxen

Travis, William B.: at Alamo, 39 n, 41–42, 44, 47; death of, 50; and Fannin, 36; message of, from Alamo, 37, 41–42; praise of, 46, 50, 183–184

treasury, Mexican, 5, 7

Tres Villas Battalion, 136; at Goliad, 89; at Matagorda, 156; at Santa Anna village, 78; Urrea and, 66

Tres Villas Regiment, 13, 89; de la Peña with, 29

Turena, Eugenio, 16

Turenne, Henri, 56, 130

201

United States, 82, 108; and aid to Texas, 4, 16, 18, 40, 85 n

Urrea, José, 126, 189; advances to Colorado R., 166; to Guadalupe Victoria, 170; booty of troops of, 126; at Brazoria, 138; criticism of, 70; and Fannin, 84–87 *passim*, 92; Filisola's attack of, 68, 143, 151–152, 157, 162; generosity of, 142; at Goliad, 44, 65, 71–76, 90, 173; at Mier, 67; and Morales, 65, 77; ordered to rejoin Filisola, 144; at Perdido, 72–75; praise of, 82, 84, 90, 95, 125, 143, 152, 163; at Refugio, 70–71; and retreat, 128, 134, 136, 138, 145, 147, 149, 160, 162; at San Patricio, 42, 68–71; and Santa Anna, 80, 82; size of forces of, 20; victories of, 37, 67, 81; weapons of, 66, 72, 77, 99, 109, 116

Vaca Creek, 102
Valera, Mariano, 107, 135
Vattel, 86
Velasco, 109, 136, 144
Vences, ———, 47
Ventura Mora, General, 38
Victoria. *See* Guadalupe Victoria
Villalba, Manuel, 169
Villa de Dolores, 34

Villasana, Lieutenant, 62
Volney, Constantine, 146

War, Ministry of, 5, 114 n
Ward, William: execution of, 86, 90, 91; surrender of, 77
*Watchman*, 142
weapons
—Mexican, 65, 79, 105–106; at the Alamo, 33, 38, 39, 42–43, 45–51; care and transportation of, 6–7, 103; in retreat, 155–159 *passim*, 162, 165, 171; at San Jacinto, 124; with Urrea, 66, 72, 77, 99, 109, 116
—Texan: at Alamo, 38, 47, 48; of Fannin, 75; at San Jacinto, 127, 186
Woll, Adrián, 109, 149; appointed quartermaster, 13; at Colorado R., 103; at enemy camp, 163; with Filisola, 141; under Ramírez y Sesma, 80; and retreat, 128, 145

*Yellow Stone*, 105–109 *passim*
Yucatán: troops from, 68, 89, 136

Zacatecas, 23
*Zapadores. See* Sapper Battalion
Zavala, Don Lorenzo de, 4, 114, 170

202

PEÑA, José Enrique de la.  With Santa Anna in Texas; a personal nar-
rative of the revolution, tr. and ed. by Carmen Perry.  Texas A & M
University Press, Drawer C, College Station, Tex. 77843, 1975.
202p il 75-16269. 10.00. ISBN 0-89096-001-1. C.I.P.
The diary of a participant in the Mexican campaign into Texas during
1836 under the command of General Santa Anna.  It is a valuable addition in the field of Texan and Mexican history, supplementing the
standard works of Barker and Justin H. Smith.  Highly personal, the
narrative gives a fresh viewpoint regarding the siege of the Alamo, the
battle of San Jacinto, and other key events.  The English translation is
clear and well done.  Photocopies of the original manuscript give the
reader an opportunity to compare the translation with the original
text.  Suited primarily for advanced undergraduate and graduate history courses, this volume offers the student of the Texas question a
valuable source from the Mexican point of view.  The index is adequate,
and the editor supplies helpful footnotes on many obscure names and
events.

CHOICE          FEB. '76
History, Geography &
Travel

North America

WA
F
390
P39
EP

589